D1555645

AROUND THE HEART IN ELEVEN YEARS

A TRAVEL MEMOIR

EPP PETRONE

Around the Heart in Eleven Years

A TRAVEL MEMOIR
PART 1

PETRONE PRINT

Text copyright: Epp Petrone and Petrone Print, 2010
Illustrations copyright: Kudrun Vungi and Petrone Print, 2010

Cover design: Anna Lauk
Layout: Anna Lauk, Aive Maasalu
Cover photo and the photo on page 8: Epp Petrone's archives

Thanks for helping with the book: Tiia Falk, Mele Pesti, Justin Petrone, Penelope Piip, Kaja Pino, Silver Sikk.

ISBN 978–9949–9043–8–9 (full trilogy)
ISBN 978–9949–9043–7–2 (part 1)

PETRONE PRINT

www.petroneprint.ee

For Marta,
who wants to become an astronaut
and fly to the moon.

Contents

Dear reader,

In the beginning, my plan was simple and straightforward: to publish the book of travel features I had written for newspapers and magazines. I had worked as a journalist for over ten years and gathered quite a large catalogue of articles about different places around the world where I had been. All these pieces were just gathering dust in the library archives, and I felt that they deserved a fate better than that.

There were a lot of these articles. They weren't "the whole truth about me", but it was still *a* truth, bits and pieces brought together from exotic lands. My employers back then were either not really interested in the confusing stories about how I happened to end up in one country or another, or they were too polite to ask and just gossiped about it behind my back. As far as I know, they just thought I was someone who went on strange trips every now and then, but at least I always came back and was tremendously productive afterwards in writing new articles.

So I had enough material for a whole book, descriptions of cities, countries and people: moderately exciting, not too uncomfortable, just the way travel stories are supposed to be –

and it would have taken me about two days to put it all together. A neat and convenient solution.

But sitting there in the library and reading those published articles...

It tore it all wide open again and I decided to physically and literally stare my past in the face. Already flying back to one of those places I started to understand that the only way to make peace with this book and maybe my life as a whole was to be honest and tell the stories behind the articles. Why and how did I go on those trips? Maybe in the course of writing I could succeed in finding answers to the questions from my past that had remained unresolved? That was the hope.

I was already set to put the last finishing touches on the book, when life added another unexpected (yet long awaited, twenty years to be exact) act and another flight back to the past. So this book became not only the story of a young woman, passionate about travelling, gaining life experiences along the way, but also the story of a son whom one man lost somewhere in this great big world.

I have to apologise because my story is about to start jumping back and forth, here and there, east and west, but isn't it the same way in life? Stories melt and combine with an absolute disregard for time and all too soon ten years can feel like ten hours. What we left undone yesterday can remind us of its existence again tomorrow. In any case, it seems to me that there's a common thread that runs through these stories and fates, and that thread has nothing to do with time.

All the events described here are real, at least the way I remember them and as I wrote them. But the names? Even though the characters gave me permission to use their real names, in the end I felt it was better to choose new names for most people (and their families), because the stories about them can sometimes be painful.

Real names have been preserved for those closest to me: Justin, Marta and Anna, whom I would like to thank so much for being so good to me while this book was being finished.

Epp Petrone,

a writer from Estonia (a little country between Finland, Sweden, Latvia and Russia, in case you did not know).

How I lost an old friend

January 2009. Arguineguin, Gran Canaria

That house. I've seen it in my dreams. Sitting there in the bus, I wasn't sure I could find my way back, but as soon as the bus closed its doors behind us and I got a good look at the street winding down the mountainside, it all came back to me.

Supermercado – the sign can be seen from far away. It doesn't look like much has changed around here.

Stepping inside the store tosses me back in time. That old corner market is almost exactly the same as it was ten years ago, when I hopped in here with a goatee-sporting, Jesus Christ lookalike. Harri and I made an exotic-looking couple while we were travelling around and selling goods in the markets. Wait, a *couple*? The two of us were never a couple! I even lied to people and told them that Harri was my uncle, so that no one would suspect that there was anything sexual between us.

I stare at a man with bushy eyebrows who stands behind the counter. Ten years doesn't really change a middle-aged person that much. It's Jorge from Cuba, the same one who worked here a decade ago.

"Jorge, do you remember me? Epa! *La periodista del Estonia*, the journalist from Estonia?"

A puzzled shadow passes over his face before his mouth stretches into a wide smile. "Epa! How many years have passed?"

I've probably changed more than he has; the twenty-something slight girl has become a voluptuous thirty-something woman.

"Yes, I know, time flies! How... how is Marco doing?"

"Not bad! But he missed you; he was waiting for you to come back for years!" After all, Marco wasn't just Jorge's boss, but a friend as well.

"When is he coming?" I ask. "Is he coming today? We just arrived on the island yesterday and the first thing we did this morning was come here."

I don't want to allow any pauses in the conversation, let the air be filled with words instead. My two daughters are running around behind me, while their father, my husband Justin is watching over them. A week ago I sat him down and told him that it was time to jump on a last-minute offer to Gran Canaria, because I had been planning and postponing this return trip. Now we're here, ready to face the careless world traveller Epp from ten years ago. Ready to face my past. And somewhere here, in the possession of the shop- and hotelkeeper Marco, a bag is waiting with my clothes, books and travel journals documenting the most confusing time of my life.

"Marco isn't coming today; he's at the doctor's. His heart is not good, *los problemas**, Epa..."

Jorge doesn't ask me, "How come you never called?" I remember that Jorge was always very tactful. My travel companion Harri, the wild Christ-lookalike, liked to classify people, and he judged Jorge to be a specimen of high intelligence and alertness. Marco, on the other hand, was greedy and stupid, according to Harri. I'm sure that his opinion did count for me at the point when I had to choose whether to stay on the island or not, whether to return later or not... And Djellah, my best friend at this same hotel, she also kept telling me the same thing: "For Marco, you are just a girl passing through."

I spoke of many things with Djellah back then. It was right here in the hotel above the store, or on the beach in front of it where we spent time together and discovered each other. Twenty-four years older than me, born on the same date, she had grown up with the same itch in her

---

* "Problems" in Spanish.

soul, a fever burning under her skin – to move, to travel, to experience the new, to melt into it, take it along and move on. I filled up five cassette tapes with interviews with Djellah and wrote a long article for an Estonian magazine about her: "That strange woman still flashes through my thoughts, like a dream I saw or a thought I didn't get to finish. It's as if I've touched something at once plaintive, humorous and beautiful. Something intangible and incomprehensible that I can't ever completely forget..." That's a series of flowery words that I once stitched together to describe my experience. Unfortunately the article was rejected: "This person is nuts, why should we publish a story about her?" argued one editor. "The city trams are full of these half crazies pushing fifty. You probably haven't had any contact with real bohemians, but it's normal, you're still young!" Another magazine did end up accepting the story after severe editing: a piece about a woman without a homeland or mother tongue; a woman who still holds a place of honor for me as one of the most unique people I have ever met.

But I haven't had any more contact with Djellah. I accidentally left my journals, notebooks and the little phonebook with her contacts, as well as the contacts of so many others, in the bag that I left here, at Marco's hotel. Soon after that, I had to block out most of what happened here on this island and those whom I had met.

Sometimes, though, I listened to a CD Djellah gave me of her songs – she was a travelling musician. Weeks went by, then months, then years; new trips came along, new people, new crises, new searches and discoveries...

How did ten years manage to go by so fast?

"Have you heard anything from Djellah?" I ask Jorge after he's dealt with some tourists that wandered into his store.

"Djellah? But Djellah is dead! They discovered she had cancer, a few years ago. She left us in a matter of weeks. Before that she lived here for a couple of stretches. For a while she left, to go somewhere else, and then ended up, coming back, you know!"

Yes, that's right, Djellah had kind of adopted a girl in this village, the daughter of a prostitute that worked down at the port. Of course, she'd come back here, and repeatedly, unlike me.

I can't think any further than that.

But what did Jorge just say about her being dead? It had to be some kind of a sick joke.

Suddenly, I remember sharing another thing with Djellah. We were both just a bit over twenty when our mothers died of cancer. And just like me, Djellah also said that she still hadn't gotten over it (she was forty-eight when we met) and, just like me, she was afraid that it, *the disease,* could happen to her.

"Dead? But she was still so young!" My eyes tear up. My children are fighting at the other end of the store while loud German tourists are passing the supermarket's open front... Daily life and the past have mixed together. I'm crying. I've finally made it back here, but it's too late.

The tale of a woman without a homeland

Ten years earlier. May 1999
Arguineguin, Gran Canaria

I'm sitting in the market dust and writing. Today is one of those days when nobody seems to be interested in what I'm selling. I've completely run out of money and I have no idea where I'm spending the night if nobody buys anything from me today! Maybe one of the magazines will give me an advance if I write a story about Djellah's wondrous life and send it to them?

"She was walking around the local market: a tall gangly woman, with a strangely weathered stare, a pony tail bleached by the sun to all the different shades of blond, dropping phrases left and right in many different languages," I start putting down on paper the moment that happened close to here just a few weeks ago. "I asked her, "Where are you from?" like you're supposed to do when starting conversations with strangers you meet in touristy places. "I'm from everywhere and nowhere," she answered, with a crooked smile, as if she was joking.

Later on I understood that she really was telling the truth. She was born into a family of diplomats and they've always been on the move from one country to the next, so instead of having one native language, she has five, or maybe six.. Her mother and father are both of mixed blood, so Djellah ended up being a cocktail of the whole world: she's got some French, English, German, Dutch, Jewish, and Gypsy blood running through her veins. The first years of Djellah's life were spent in Pakistan. As a toddler, she was constantly getting lost somewhere and found again, for example, half a day later wondering in the woods a few miles away. Her parents were scared that a girl with curly blond hair and green eyes would fall prey to child abduction because of her exotic beauty..."

I lift up my head for a moment. Yes, that does remind me of something. The desire to run away. Specific images: the touch of the coat fabric in my hand, sticking my hands in the sleeves, searching for button holes with clumsy fingers, the crunching snow, the glow on the horizon, and then someone running after me, irritated and restraining me, "Come back, you can't leave!" Or a moment from springtime, my cheek pressed against the soil, the sound of the stream, the smell of the cherry tree, the green light that the low foliage of the tree cast around me. And the sweet knowledge that I had ran off. Why? For no compelling reason.

I continue writing, "Following a few years in a convent school in Italy, she returned to the safety of her parents' home – what a weird word for another ambassadorial residence! For a few years their temporary home was in Hong Kong. Receptions, mingling, small talk, and cocktail dresses, Djellah went along dutifully with her parents' life until she turned nineteen. That's when she announced to her father, "This life is too superficial and hypocritical for me. I need to go out into the *real* world!"

Djellah still gets well along with her father. She just mentions that from that day, his financial support ceased. With the same briefness she also talks about discontinuing her classical music studies in Germany – it was too constraining. She felt that she needed room for inspiration. Djellah says things like that with no pretence, only slight apprehensiveness: I'm different, she tells herself, and I'll have to manage with who I am."

Someone is coming. A shadow falls on my notebook and I set it down quickly next to my feet, to wait for the next opportunity.

Looks like a Spanish woman. "Look," I use what little Spanish I have on her and gesticulate as much as could possibly be appropriate. "Have you ever seen Tibetan mantra boxes before? And these little silver bottles, also from Tibet, you can wear them as a pendant and put perfume in them!" Djellah has taught me sentences about my products, word for word, and Harri has taught me to trust my intuition and offer each customer something based on that first immediate flash of recognition, because in these first moments people are absolutely infallible, according to Harri.

But no luck this time. The woman with a dark ponytail bares her white teeth for a moment in a weird smile, and walks off.

It's now noon and I still haven't sold anything!

I didn't know before how easily pride and self-respect could slip away. Their price is about as high as a bunch of bananas, a box of tampons, or a night at a hotel... If you can't get any of these – even in dire need – you get this disgusting feeling of humiliation, worthlessness.

I'm thinking that I need to ask Djellah how to manage these feelings that a lack of money creates. You can always suppress a stomach from growling by drinking water, but what are you supposed to do when it's your spirit making the same noise? Will I eventually be proud of not making money at some point? How does it work?

Or, am I going to learn to swallow my pride? Marco is rich, he's right here on this island and we have some kind of a "relationship" going on, but for some reason it would seem like the worst desecration of my pride if I admitted my money problems to him. I do realize that by behaving like this I am building walls between us. I also realize that Djellah has never learned how to quash her pride.

"Djellah hasn't asked a man for help with money in her whole life," I continue writing my story. "At times this independence has meant quite literally starving. Her rich boyfriend, a German named Rolf, is somewhere sailing around the world, because he has enough money to never work again... But at the same time our tough Djellah is looking for a job so that she can eat, taking odd jobs around the market. "Rolf has always been offended by this pride. He says that self-confidence also means having the courage to ask a man for help if needed. Unfortunately, I don't have that kind of confidence. When we lived on Rolf's boat, of course, I'd eat the food that he bought for us, but at the same time I also did a lot of work on the boat. If he'd only had a box for money on board and said, "We'll both put in what we have and take some whenever needed." But no, he was always waiting for me to turn to him and ask for help, he still is..."

I put the pencil down.

Yes, why is it so hard to ask for help? You can see this problem much more clearly in other people than in your own life. It's hard to say whether Djellah's skewed views are a sign of naivete or life experience, when she talks about her relationships. For the past thirty years she has been an incredibly beautiful woman who has never dropped anchor anywhere in the world: she has sailed on almost all the great world seas, living a life at sea with different men, but sooner or later she's always been the one to leave.

"I want to be with a man only if I'm a hundred percent sure of my love for him," she says.

Is it ever possible to find that someone whom you're a hundred percent sure about, Djellah?

Last year she apparently sailed with Rolf on the Caribbean for six months. Life on a yacht is testing, psychologically as well as for a relationship. I try to imagine that as I continue:

"I love and I hate life on the water," Djellah admits. "Those open seascapes, being able to breathe it all in with all you've got! And on the other hand, the boat itself, which really is an extremely constrained space. You're sleeping and eating with the other person right by your side all the time. Even in the toilet you feel that your companions are only a few metres away. I get these moments, when I need to just wave good bye and say *"Adieu*, I'm off on my own now, back in a few days...""

Oh, that's a cop's blue shirt in the crowd! It's a good thing my sixth sense made me look up.

I know already what I have to do. I stick my notebook under my arm, slip between the beach towels in the stand next to mine, and from there to the next aisle, but not before getting a nod from my neighbour: he'll keep an eye on my jewellery. The cops and I must not meet!

The geometry of relationships

A week later. May 1999
Arguineguin, Gran Canaria

Djellah and I have met five times for this coming feature and each time I have had more and more questions. Of course, five times less would have been sufficient for a story, but in my own way, I've completely fallen for her. She is *me* in the future! That's the life that waits for me: always on the go, just a touch melancholic and exciting at once, captivating. Except I'll be a new and improved version of Djellah, an evolutionary step, for not only will I experience all the rough edges of the rocky path through life, I'll write about them too. If she feels stressed just writing postcards about how she's doing, then I'm equally suffocated by not being able to write. This is the only major difference I've found between her and me.

Djellah wants to meet me too, time and again. She seems to have developed a maternal or older sister kind of sense of responsibility towards me. For me that is baffling, yet endearing.

"Epp, I don't think that Marco is serious about you," she keeps telling me. "Do you know what he calls you behind your back? *La rusa!* The

Russian girl! He can't even get your nationality right! Don't trust him. I've seen so many of his affairs..."

Djellah and Marco have known each other for a long time, their relationship goes back to when she was a hippie chick with long braids and he was a white-capped marine school cadet. It was back in the 1970s, that Djellah first arrived at the fishing village of Arguineguin. She was on a trip and just passing through, but Marco was actually from here, his roots on both sides of the family firmly planted in this island and in this village. From what I gathered, these two, who were the most important people in my life at that period, had also partied together back in the day, because Marco used to hang out with members of the local hippie community. Djellah stayed at the hotel that is owned and operated by Marco's father and mother. Later on, Marco sailed the world seas as the captain of a ship, but he still came back from time to time to visit his mother, meeting Djellah sometimes, too.

"By the way, have you seen what kind of a conservative witch his mother is? How can you even picture being in a serious relationship with a man who has *that* kind of a mother?" Djellah rhetorically asks. I don't know what to think of that. Somewhere on the top floor of that hotel, in an apartment with the best view of the sea is where Marco's mother Maria lives: an old woman wearing a head scarf, always dressed in black and walking along the very sides of the stairways. She always bares her teeth to me in a way that's left me puzzled as to whether she's smiling or growling a warning. I also have no idea how much she knows about the relationship between her son and me. But that doesn't matter to me – I smile at Maria and I'm happy that life has introduced me to this type of person.

"My mother has always said that Djellah is not right in the head," Marco tells me. "And the more time goes by, the more I see that my mother is right. My mother warned me about her a long time ago already! A long time ago... well, I kind of had a thing with Djellah."

When I ask her about this the following day, Djellah only laughs. "That was really nothing even worth mentioning! I've never been Marco's type and he's never been mine. Marco collects interesting, international, young specimens, who are never lacking on this island. Before you he had a Norwegian girl."

I guess that makes me Marco's type... but is he mine? He's of a medium build, with black, slightly curly, short hair, a dazzling smile and a strong, sharp manner of speaking. I don't know if I'd like him just from seeing his picture. But I like the scent this strong man gives off, because my own world right now is so dangerously feeble and insecure.

I have the hardest time choosing between Marco's or Djellah's company, they both have their friends on the island and their own events where they keep inviting me. These are two separate worlds: one day I'll go to Djellah's fake wedding that she's putting on to generate gossip among the villagers for her amusement, with the whole expat community in attendance. The next day I'll go dancing with Marco and his friend at a salsa club meant for middle-aged Canarian locals. Harri, the third most important person for me on this island, thinks that Marco is a "person of unfortunate genetic inheritance, with lacking intelligence". However, Djellah does get a break from Harri. What's more, he even gives Djellah work: she joins us walking around the markets in the morning, carrying around handfuls of fans, hats and necklaces. In the evenings, she plays the piano and sings in the restaurant of an expensive hotel: in her low, raspy voice she performs songs in an unbelievable style: a mix of Latin American rhythms, Indian melodies and French chansons, topped off with Djellah's own personal brand of jazz. I think she's divinely talented, but fate just hasn't given her the opportunity to become a world famous singer.

In the afternoon, we like to sit by the window in her hotel room.

Both of our eyes on the horizon, sitting on the windowsill, we've suddenly started talking about relationships. It's funny how Djellah seems to be the type of person who should appreciate the allure of unattainability, but in reality she's extremely straightforward in matters of the heart, sharing her words of wisdom with me as well. "It's so not true that men love women who are hard to get!" she says. "They love women who have enough courage to approach them and get to know them! It's also not true that distance makes the heart grow fonder! Most men forget. Very fast. Period."

"But... what's the problem then?" I'm searching for the right words, trying to figure out how to ask: why did the dozens of relationships that you've had all fall apart and why are you still alone?

"Look!" she starts to laugh. "I'm the one who needs unattainability!" The laughter then stops, sharply cut off. All of a sudden Djellah is sitting there like a broken doll, head sunk to her chest.

"What happened?"

"I'll tell you... There's this American guy. Michael... Wait!"

I'm waiting. Djellah has decided to spend the last of her money on a bottle of red wine and returns a few minutes later from the store downstairs – yes, Marco's store. The wine and Djellah's story start flowing... first to the 1960s.

Once upon a time there lived a romantic young man whose name was Michael. The propaganda worked and he volunteered for the war in Vietnam, where he tortured and killed Vietnamese people, and where his best friend was killed right in front of his eyes. For two decades, Michael succeeded in stuffing his nightmares far into the corners of his subconsciousness and lived a proper life, but then snapped. At the time when Djellah met the man, he'd lay in bed for days on end, without wanting to even move a muscle.

"Look at him!" The photos show melancholic eyes in a manly face and a slack pair of lips.

Djellah is squatting on the hotel floor, next to the mound of photos she's dug out of the chest of drawers and her long blond hair makes her look like a helpless child. "I still feel this incredible passion! See... there have been many times when I've severely fallen for severely difficult types, I want to help them in their severe turmoil and depression, but I usually end up in even greater turmoil and depression myself. When I realized just how deeply in love with Michael I was, I told myself, stop! Think about it! Do you really need this complicated relationship?"

"I think complicated relationships are interesting..."

"You don't have to tell me! I've lived with a writer going through the pain of birthing a novel, had to mother his fluctuating creative spirit, I've had to live with an unemployed alcoholic, hid his bottles from him..."

I'm looking at the photos, the wine and the stories still flowing. So Djellah ended up severing her budding, but complicated relationship and ran away from the US, from Michael. A year and a half have passed, but the passion that wasn't allowed to properly burn won't give her peace. "It's my masochistic nature, it yearns for adventure and pain! I suppose it comes from my childhood of moving around."

A succession of photos slips through our hands, full of memories and men, while Djellah runs her fingers through her hair and continues. "Talking to Michael makes me feel the weight of the world. I like dangerous and unstable characters... But when I'm with him, I can't laugh! That's one secret that I've discovered over the years: if you can freely laugh in a man's company, it means that you can be happy with him for some time. With Rolf I can laugh!"

I look at the pictures that have slipped to the floor: the dark-blooded, mystical Michael between beige sheets, and the light-skinned, smiling Rolf in a sailboat, with the blue sky as his background. "Rolf is this simple and fun type! It's just that... when I've looked into those sincere, light blue eyes for a couple of weeks already, I'm really sorry that those eyes are just *so* transparent."

Yes, I know, Djellah, I think while listening to her stories. I too have a man with transparent eyes, waiting for me at home, but unlike you I have not had the courage to be honest with my man. Yet. Maybe tomorrow!

Meanwhile, Djellah has arrived at a new topic, or rather circled back to an old one.

"What were you asking before? Why do my relationships break up? See, there are too many experiences and nationalities inside of me. Men can accept only the part of me that is closest to what they are. But I'm a mix of all of them! I can only suppress my other aspects for so long. With Rolf, I'm a proper, work loving, punctual German. The same way with others I've been a loud Spanish woman or a reserved English woman or a coquettish French lady... When I change languages, I even change my mode of thinking. Sometimes I try to figure out who I really am, but I can't, and that scares me."

I listen to her and realize that it is a *real* problem, even though at first it may sound a little boastful.

Another story and the accompanying stack of photos slip through our hands: in these pictures, Djellah's features have become almost Asian, her eyes slanted like a Chinese woman's. These photos are of a time when she lived in London among a Chinese community. "One time these English guys came to a party there. They all stopped and stared at me with gaping jaws: what is this tall, blond girl doing here among all these Asian people? Laughing and gesturing like they do, chirping their language, just a head taller than the rest?" And you know, the strangest thing was that I was staring back at them and I saw the Englishmen as strangers, white people, distant creatures. So who am I really, huh?"

"Hey, is Djellah alert?" I ask Harri once. I like the way my employer puts people in categories without hesitation. Sometimes, for example, we are taking the bus from one Gran Canarian market to another and chatting away loudly in Estonian: he's diagnosing his fellow passengers, determining how alert each of them is.

"Well, let's say that Djellah's intuition is stronger than average," Harri says, a bit flattered – of course, he likes it when I ask for his opinion on the ways of the world. "But your instincts are better than hers. And her rationality is very strong – but not as strong as yours. The only thing in which she is stronger than you, of course, is self-discipline! You're really weak in that. Well, just take a look at your life, see for yourself!"

I'm a little surprised that Harri launches into this comparison straight away, but as usual when it comes to his speeches, I don't argue and prefer to just listen.

"You see," he says, "a person has to have all three parts equally developed. Your problem is that your self-discipline can't compete with your intuition and rationality. Therefore, the goal of your life should be to learn to control yourself!"

"But Djellah?"

"Well, I mean, she's got everything more or less in place. She may have her problems, but she has them in a balance, her vitality is equally spread to the three whales: intuition, rationality and self-discipline. Besides, she's already been toughened up by her past. If there was another great war, Djellah would be among those who'd manage to stay alive."

Indeed, Harri knows how to measure people. I've watched him do it for sometime already.

"But me?" I want to know. "Would I survive a war?"

"Well... your years of toughening up are still ahead of you! You still have time."

Harri's still looking at me, squinting his eyes, and again it feels, like many times before, that he sees much more of the future than he's willing to tell me. But maybe I'm just imagining things. The next instant he's just another neurotic, raving, useless, long-haired old man, on whom

I've developed a dependence for some strange reason and whom I follow around from market to market, despite the fact that we don't seem to be earning a thing...

A new morning. I'm sitting by a dusty road and waiting for a bus to go to Puerto de Mogan, a sweet little tourist trap in a harbour town, where they have an outdoor market. Hopefully I'll find a good place for selling: out of sight from the cops, but right in the middle of the tourist beat... I can dream, can't I?

What was it that Harri said yesterday – "Just look at the mess in your life!" Yes! But I don't have enough energy to look at it right now. I dig out my notebook: let's rather escape into my magazine story about Djellah.

"Djellah can't have children. In her twenties she had an accident and an operation. It seems that just as with her mother's death two decades ago, Djellah has also not managed to come to terms with the idea of infertility. She loves children so much. In the fishing village of Arguineguin in the Canaries, the children of boat-dwellers follow her around, "Hey, let's go make sandcastles! Let's go play with your synthesizer for a little bit!"

But there's one special girl, who is almost always at Djellah's side, even if it's a salsa party that lasts until dawn. "She's better off with me than with her grandparents, they pay absolutely no attention to her," Djellah says. This girl is Salma, a thirteen-years old love child born to a local woman.

Djellah met the two-year-old girl when she was living in a boat at the port with her Portuguese boyfriend. "We noticed this little curly-haired girl running around the port and nobody was ever looking after her," Djellah recalls. She started feeding the girl, playing with her, taking her in their boat to sleep. By that time, Salma's mother had become a prostitute in the harbor and a junkie to boot, so she had nothing against having a babysitter.

A few years later, Djellah came back full circle to the same place and started living in a commune of musicians in the mountains near the village. Salma remembered her! Once again Djellah took the girl in almost as her own. Her travels found her coming back to Gran Canaria more and more often.

Salma's mother is dead now. The teenage girl looks like an angel, but she's prone to wild mood swings. "The things she's seen," Djellah sighs. "Her own mother having sex with different men. Junkies in stupors... She has a heavy burden on her heart. I try to help her as best as I can. We talk and discuss the ways of the world. Sometimes when I see her get downtrodden by it all, we go into the woods together and sing in Spanish at the top of our lungs, "*La bella vida!*"

Djellah smiles. There are times when she speaks with a maternal pride about Salma, like how she finally learned to use a knife and fork.

"Djellah, why don't you adopt this girl?"

Her face becomes somber. "Her grandparents have nothing against that. But I don't have a place to live. I live in hotels, one day at a time. Where would I go with her? Soon enough I'll roll my dresses up again, pack my synthesizer and head off... Where to, I don't know, but I'll be back and I'll see her then."

I listen to her explaining this to Salma as well. The girl pleads: "I'll come anywhere in the world, as long as I can be with you!" – "No, you have to go to school. Anyway, I'll write to you this time!" Djellah promises.

"Everything has its price," she says to me later in that dry way the British Djellah speaks. "My sister is jealous of me because I can travel and move around, go wherever I want. Many of my female acquaintances have said: "Oh, our Djellah's life is a never-ending vacation! She gets to sunbathe all day!" They don't think about the fact that all I have in this world amounts to about twenty kilos of clothes and books, and a musical instrument. I'd say that's not much for a middle-aged woman. What do you think?" She squints her eyes as if she's about to break out laughing. And then she adds, "But that's all you need to live. Some clothes, books, an instrument, air and freedom... Or maybe there is a little girl missing from that list, huh?"

I put the notebook aside and stare off into the distance. Children, that topic again. How much did my own "unborn children" push me into coming here? And where is Djellah pushing me now?

The bus is coming!

---

* "The beautiful life!" in Spanish.

On flying here and in space

Ten years later. January 2009
Between Tallinn and Las Palmas

I like sitting in a plane that has just taken off – even though I know that this is precisely the moment when this miracle machine is most liable to explode and even though I know that flying is environmentally the most harmful pastime that a single person can undertake.

There's nothing I can do about it: leaving the ground and heading for the skies is a kind of addiction. I think I know what Leonardo da Vinci felt while drawing people and machines in flight. He must have had an especially strong longing pulsating within him, something that jolts you up from sleep at times, something that must reside in each person. You wake up fully knowing that you could fly, but then the harsh truth of it comes back to you: you're not a bird, you're human. Leonardo could physically never feel what most people today have experienced: the force of the plane upon lift off, the energy in your body that tugs at you like a giant swing propelled towards the sky.

Each time I hope that once we get above the clouds, I'll see that same strange atmospheric phenomenon I saw with Harri one morning, when we were flying from Riga, Latvia to Warsaw, Poland to catch a flight to Tel Aviv, Israel. It was late winter, a humid and foggy time of the year. Clouds covered the surface of the earth, as they mostly do around that time along this latitude. The plane shot through the clouds and...

A pink field spread out below us, as far as the eye could see. For the first time in my life, I fully experienced what it really means when people say, "Above the clouds, it's always sunny."

I'm sure meteorologists have a name for that pink phenomenon and I'm sure they can calculate exactly the necessary humidity and temperature required for something like that to occur. But for me, those colourful rays reflecting off humidity in the air was a reward for not losing faith during the long, cold, dark February, a sign of better things to come. At that moment, I was glued to the window. I wasn't surprised, just full of joy: the bleakness under those clouds won't get me now, I thought, a pink desert surrounds me, I could open up the window and just go jump around in it if I only wanted to!

Through blind faith, urged on by a strange inner force, I had arrived at that seat in the plane. The bearded man next to me smelled so strongly that I'm sure everyone around us wondered why it smelled like an Indian temple or an exotic incense shop. And when further investigation lead them to the source, I'm sure they asked themselves: who is that odd couple, that bearded, long-haired old man and that wild-eyed, young, blond woman? Where are they going?

I stare out at the clouds behind my window today. They're just regular clouds, no pink. The energy of the ascent is starting to dissolve and wear off now bit by bit, at a height of ten kilometres. The familiar sounds ring out, the hollow dings, the clicking seat belts and a steadily humming motor in which we all have to trust. One of my children has fallen asleep and the other is dangling in the aisle, neck craned to see when the "plane lady" is coming to bring us food and drinks. Justin is sitting next to our daughter, his dark hair covering his eyes. I can't tell if he's asleep or just thinking. In any case, he doesn't look like he's up for a conversation. At the moment, I don't have anything to do. Nothing depends on me right at this moment. The main thing has been done – getting us on this plane, so that we could fly into the past and through it arrive at the future.

The past and the future are always connected, even though sometimes it would be nice to unravel them and think: what if...? What would my life have been like, if I had never met Harri? Is it possible that my first marriage wouldn't have broken up in that case? Is it possible that I wouldn't have become a vegetarian and an an environmentalist? Is it possible that I wouldn't have become the homeless cosmopolitan that I am in my soul at this moment? Would I see the world altogether differently?

Harri was "crazy", but he got inside my head and changed me.

The time when Harri came into my life – or rather when I stepped into his and demanded to be taken along – was in hindsight one of the most terrible times I've ever gone through. On the surface, everything was fine and that, in turn, made me feel even guiltier: why can't I be satisfied with my secure and nicely bolstered world? I had money, a husband, free time, a prestigious job, but... something was wrong and I felt it every morning when I woke up and looked around: is this it? Is it everything that life has in store for me? Is this how it's going to be for years and years? That winter a peculiar physical restlessness stirred inside of me. I wanted to jump up, literally tear off my skin and run away. I couldn't stand still, I had to move constantly, but usually even that didn't help – I did push-ups at home on the carpet to work off some of the stress. As soon as I sat back down again, it all came back.

That fateful morning started much in the usual way, except I was expecting something more than before. I had just returned from a ski trip to Slovakia, and I was physically and spiritually shaken. At the beginning of the trip, I had fallen and injured my back: it was nothing compared to what had been off for quite some time in my heart, but it still forced me to spend a day under medical care.

However, returning from the clinic, I greeted the New Year lying in the mountains, between two camping sites.

Alone.

There was a group of people somewhere below me and another group farther above. They were my colleagues, who all seemed to be satisfied with their lives and I had no idea how to tell them what was wrong with me. They weren't my friends, because we didn't talk about the things that mattered. I was trudging restlessly on through the snow, when I realized that the camp I was heading for was much farther than I had anticipated and I was thankful for it: just think, at this important moment I get to be all alone, by myself!

Alone.

My husband Tom couldn't make it to the ski trip, because he didn't want to leave his old and lonely mother all by herself. "I've spent every New Year's Eve with mother, except for the year that I was in the army." I, however, went on that ski trip with my colleagues to "air myself out," as I put it.

Alone.

I threw myself on my back. My internal clock told me that I'd been plodding through the snow for about an hour and it should be more or less the moment when the year changes. A new year was beginning. I laid there smelling the snow that was melting around my body.

It was one of those moments that I have longed to return to later on, but it has never quite happened again the same way. I was lying there, exhausted, watching the moonlight reflecting off the snowy peaks to form a halo around the moon while I breathed deeply, like sleeping. It was time for promises to be kept and prayers to be heard, I could feel it from the stars. But the question was: what am I supposed to promise, what should I pray for?

"I'll do it," I swore, eyes on the vast, expanding emptiness behind the stars. "I'll get somewhere, I'll get out of this dead end!"

The longer I stared at the moon, the more I was filled with a sense of levity. Outside of my body, flying among the stars, I looked back and saw the snowy mountain. Down there somewhere laid a young, confused woman, asking the universe for a change.

But for starters, the responsibilities I had in this world were waiting for me. My social life was expecting me nearby. It would be seriously unpleasant for all the rest of them if I slipped into an eternal slumber here in the mountain snow! I pushed myself up, fighting the urge to stay as I was, and resumed the climb. The trails my companions had made were clearly visible in the night lit by a full moon, so I kept suppressing the desire to just turn off the path, go somewhere else, stay a while longer just by myself in these mesmerizing mountains.

After another turn and a bend, a fire appeared in sight, surrounded by people, huddled up and enjoying a wintry picnic. "Where did you come from like this? Come here!"

Suddenly my eyes welled up and I joined the others in their shared warmth. I wasn't so alone after all, there was a spot waiting for me here by the fire.

You can lose yourself in a fire just as easily as in moongazing. I don't remember much else from that night, aside from the new resolution: it's time to change and to be changed.

However, back in Estonia, the same two offices were waiting for me, two jobs: one in television as an editor, the other with a magazine as a writer: in both places I was just another gear in the clockwork, whose wear and breakage went unnoticed.

Looking back at that pivotal morning, I remember that I was chatting with one of my colleagues in the smoking room. That was back in the days when we all were frantically addicted to nicotine. Maybe we all were worn and broken inside, but just couldn't see it in each other?

"I think I'm going through a midlife crisis at the age of twenty-four. I want to get out of here!" I knew how lame that sounded, but still I went on, "Spring is just so far away and I'm so tired of my life."

What are you supposed to say to that? I didn't know how to verbalize it in an appropriate way that would fit that mundane setting, didn't know how to put into words that obscure calling, the scent of expectation, the hint of something new on its way. Even if I had, I'm sure those words would have come out just as lame.

However, at that moment a young man from the neighbouring office sat down next to me and he had the answer I was supposed to receive.

"Ah, but did you know that Harri Hommik is here in Estonia right now and he's getting together a commune of Estonians for Hawaii! They sell jewellery and handicrafts."

He made it sound as if it was the most obvious thing in the world as to who Harri Hommik was, like "Didn't you know that Michael Jackson's tour arrived in Estonia this week?"

January 2009

Stumbling on that recollection makes me quietly laugh to myself, while looking out at those pale grey clouds covering Northern Europe this morning. For some reason, I've never told to that former colleague how he changed the course of my life with just a few imprudent sentences.

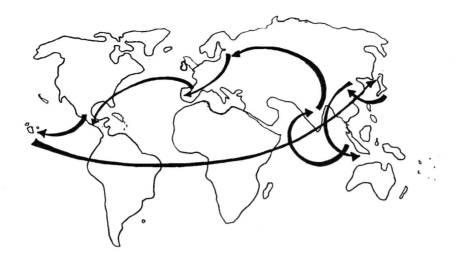

Please take me with you!

Ten years earlier. January 1999
Tallinn, Estonia

"Do you know anything about a guy named Harri Hommik? He's starting a commune of Estonians in Hawaii..."

My excited fingers almost randomly tap out the letters as I finish the email and send it to all the contacts on my address list.

A good acquaintance of mine Mari answers almost immediately. She's replied to everyone to whom I wrote as well. "That man is a dangerous psychopath! He's been in the nuthouse and he took his four children to Siberia and lost them there. People, whatever you do, stay away from him!"

Really?

I would like to believe Mari, but something inside of me has been set off and I'm already imagining myself by the Pacific Ocean, selling handmade trinkets on tropical islands, and I see Harri, this crazy, exciting man next to me, telling me his whole life's story, starting with the nuthouse and continuing right up to losing his kids – provided that all the gossip is true. After all, I'm not a child that you can lose, I tell myself. I'm a brave, skilled adult woman!

And the images in my mind are so vibrant. Why, it's like I'm on a paradise island already. What I don't yet know is that dreams do tend to come true, but usually with a small catch.

"You'll know who this guy is right away. He has long grey hair and a goatee, he looks a bit like Jesus Christ," my colleague from the smoking room tells me later that day. "If Harri is still in Estonia – and he was a two weeks ago – he'll be sitting at the Kloostri Ait* bar in the Old Town, telling young people about his adventures and theories, so don't be surprised if there's a crowd of people listening to him with their jaws hanging open."

After work I almost run to the bar.

And there he is, sitting in the middle of the room, looking exactly the way I pictured him: of an indistinguishable age (somewhere between forty and seventy), with grey, wavy hair half way down his back, grey beard, wearing a printed shirt and faded pants, holding a small woven backpack in his lap, leaning over a table and sipping tea. He is alone.

"Hi, are you Harri?" I start in as soon as I reach the table. "I'm Epp and I'd like to come and work for you!" My intuition tells me that I can be as free and as bold and intrusive as I like with this strange character.

His blue-eyed gaze stays on me just long enough for me to start feeling a bit uneasy. He's got the strangest eyes: at once penetrating and still distracted, as if he was somewhere else, and such a lovely shade of light blue, too, shining in his tanned face. He motions for me to sit and begins in a fitful, high-pitched voice. "It's a long story, but to put it bluntly, I'm not taking anyone along to work with me anymore. One week ago my business visa to the US was revoked and I got a five-year entry ban for some bloody bicycle bullshit one of my employees got into over there because he didn't pay his fine!"

Without giving me a chance to say a word, he launches into his long tale. A Greek tragedy is unfolded before me, about how everyone meant for the best to happen, but what happened in the end was a total mess. How a whole house full of Estonians lived on the island of Oahu, in the city of Honolulu, all with working visas and how everything

---

*   "Monastery Barn" in Estonian.

snowballed when a guy named Leo left a tiny little fine unpaid, which caused a conflict with the officials, that in turn ended up with everyone's visas being revoked and Harri being blocked from entering the US and flown back before he could even set foot there again. "I told Leo before I left to pay that fine! It was a small amount, just a hundred bucks, just for riding his bike on the sidewalk, but he didn't pay it! The moment I met him at the airport in Tallinn – he had to leave the US as well –, I gave him a right hook for that, sent him flying to the floor and that's the last I've seen of him!"

I'm listening to that peculiar man sitting in front of me and I already adore him – I've always felt unconditional affection towards people who like to tell stories. My emotion is intensified by the strange, pungent smell that emanates from him. It's a mix of body odor and Indian incense, the scent of faraway adventures and unexplored spaces.

"Oh, I have to show you what I sell – maybe you want to buy something?" In a flash, the storyteller becomes a peddler, and, like a true salesman, he grabs the bag that's lying in his lap and empties it out on the table to reveal a heap of beautiful silver items with precious stones and a handful of dark brown knobby things. "These here are bracelets from the Philippines, made of grass. They look really small, but when you put them in water, they swell up and you can wear them. Want to buy one?"

"But Harri, just because you can't get into the US it doesn't mean that you'll stay home now, does it?" I ask, feigning aloofness as I handle the various trinkets. The rest of what I'd like to say is simmering inside, "You're going to sell these things somewhere else now and you probably need someone to help you sell them, right? I don't need a set salary, I'm happy with just a part of the commission. And I have enough money in my account to buy plane tickets to wherever and get along fine there for some time – even if there's no real income to speak of at first."

He stops and stares at me.

"Young wolves do choose their leaders themselves," he then says. He doesn't say, "Yes," but that sentence sure sounds affirmative. My head is swimming, as I realize that something very special is about to begin in my life. How it will all play out and where in the world we will wind up, I don't know, but something is definitely about to happen.

"I have a husband," reality pulls me back in for a second. "Can he come too?"

"Come where?"

"Wherever you're going!"

"But I haven't even told you where I'm going."

"That doesn't matter."

I've made an impression on him. "All right, Epp, you seem like an alert person. I don't think I've met anyone this alert for a long time. Let's say, yeah, in Indonesia, about a tenth of the people there are alert and that's something already, most countries in the world have less of these kinds of people."

"Aren't Estonians alert?"

"Estonians are a very old and very important people in the history of the world. Russians, after all, are genetically also Estonians, or well, Finno-Ugric people, but they've just forgotten their language, having been violently forced to speak the Slavic language. Finno-Ugric tribes have affected Europe as well as Asia much more than all these little busybodies here realize." He looks me in the eye for a moment and then continues, seemingly on another random topic, "And can you imagine, in Tibet they have a volcanic mountain and can you guess what it's called, huh?"

"No, I can't."

"Tulekeel*! The name of that mountain is Tulekeel!" With a high-pitched shout, he jumps up and assumes a half-squatting position, as if he was expecting an explosion, eyes fixed on mine to make sure I understood the full implications of what he was saying.

"Tulekeel?"

"The name of that mountain of fire is Tulekeel!" He's almost shouting with a passionate expressiveness that has also roused the attention of those around us. "I've been researching this, the Estonian people have an ancient legend, according to which our ancestors were gods who came down the mountains high above. I'm sure it was the Himalayas! There are also myths in India about light-eyed gods who came down to earth – we came through there, then across the Ural Mountains and on until the Baltic Sea. And Estonian was a great international language back then, like English is now, all kinds of black and yellow people

---

* "The tongue of fire" in Estonian.

were learning to speak it. Because after the Estonian gods came down from the mountains and reached men, they taught everyone some of their language. Don't you agree...?"

"Yes, well, maybe so; it's an interesting hypothesis," I quickly answer.

"Do you agree to research these things and spread the word? Because, you see, the lead wolf has his interests as well. The leader of the pack can't choose his followers, but he sure can run away if those followers don't suit him!"

Huh? His way of speaking is a bit muddled, but in a way it's pretty intelligent, full of metaphors and parallels, certainly a lot more inspirational than what I have been dealing with during these last years as a journalist.

"Spread the word? I'm actually a journalist and I'd like to become a writer," I admit. So far he's asked nothing about me.

"Oh really?" he responds in a dry tone, a little suspicious.

"My husband is a journalist too. If you want, we can definitely spread the word about your theories... But if you don't we'll keep quiet about them."

"You know what," he tosses a hand in the air. "Come back at the same time tomorrow and bring your husband with you. I'm going to do some thinking until then."

That night a classic clash of values plays itself out in one Estonian household.

"How can you imagine just picking up and leaving our life here to follow some old man – and you don't even know where?"

"Everything is possible. We can put the house up for rent..."

"We have a mortgage, this house belongs to the bank; we're not even allowed to put it up for rent."

"I already looked at the mortgage contract, there's nothing in there that would forbid it."

"And who do you think is going to rent a place like this in the middle of winter? This isn't an apartment for some student; it's a house after all."

"It's a house in a private place with a view of the sea. You remember how happy and lucky you felt when we found this place? I'm sure someone would love to live here! Just have a little faith and we'll find someone."

"I wouldn't be surprised if you wanted to sell it altogether on this little whim!"

"Yes... wait, so if you'd rather sell it..." We had bought our little house by the sea about six months earlier, after another confusing and crisis riddled period.

"And where would you put the dog? Put him up for rent too?"

"He'd go back to the countryside to live with my dad. He was just fine there last year."

"No! He's our dog, so he's our responsibility. Why should he go live somewhere else again?"

"It wouldn't be just anywhere. He's spent half of his life there!"

"You can't do things like this just on a whim. You just went on that ski trip and now another thing pops in your head, you want to push everything aside and leave again... I can't believe we're even discussing this! It's just so absurd; it's not even worth talking about it. I have a job, you have a job..."

"But jobs are something that you can leave! Or, let's say, you can go on leave. Just think what an opportunity for the two of us to go see the world and grow as people."

"No."

"I haven't travelled almost at all. Okay, so there was that one trip to Slovakia!"

"How about Tunisia? And Hungary?"

"Yes, and that's all there is! I've been to three different countries, everywhere for just a week, enough for a little taste, that's it. But look at how big the world is! And you know what, this guy has some interesting theories about the world! I'm sure being around him would also help us develop in a way. At the same time, with you it would be safer than if I just went alone."

"That man is insane!"

"No, he's actually quite the businessman in his own right. He told me how he buys handcrafts from poor countries and sells them in rich ones, making a profit of up to thousand percent sometimes! What he's saying actually makes perfect sense."

"And you can really see me selling seashells to tourists in some market?"

"Well, it's not seashells, it's beautiful jewellery and things. I can see it, really. Would you at least be willing to meet him?"

"No, I see no reason for that."

"Please!"

"We have our own life here. All right, we can go away somewhere for a week sometime soon, we'll find someone to house sit and feed the dog. I'm sure I can get off work for that much..."

"How are you not getting this? I don't want to go on a phony week-long tourist trap of a trip! I need to see the other side of the world, something *real*, something *new*, something *honest*! I'm wasting away in this sterile journalist's life. You are too, even if you don't realize it yet!"

"This is all just in your head. If you want to, you can develop just the same anywhere. You can read books and..."

"I want to *write* books!"

"Yes, I know. So go ahead and write. Quit your job and start writing, I'll take care of you. We don't have kids – yet – and right now you have all the opportunity you'll ever need."

This is a painful subject for me: having kids and becoming a writer are two things that I have been desperately expecting to happen in my life, but yet they always seem to slip away into the future.

"Don't you see," I shout. "I'm not moving ahead! I can't get rid of this journalist's life! I keep getting hired for new articles, new TV shows. The whole road until my natural end has been paved. The eulogy is already complete. I'm going to waste away to nothing, if I don't break out of this myself and see the other side of the world. Besides, I feel that somewhere else another reality is *waiting* for us!" Tom wants to cut in, but I won't let him, "Remember, you were the one who said how you were wasting away in the army and losing your creative edge? And you wanted to leave, but couldn't?"

"That's hardly comparable! You have no idea what my life was like in the Soviet military. Are you seriously comparing your life right now to that! You have the freedom to give your employers notice tomorrow if you wanted to and just start writing your novels."

"But I'm not ready to write them yet! And the fact that we haven't had kids – yet – well that's just our luck, our chance to go out into the world, travel, mature, get ready to move up to the next level. Then we'll have something to tell our grandchildren that they can be proud of: see, what our grandparents were brave enough to do. They'll see how everything is possible in this world!"

"I don't really need my grandchildren to be proud of me going to wander the earth with some deranged hippie to who knows where. I'm happy enough building another floor on this house and redoing all the plumbing. Why do you even think that all this travelling is something you can afford?"

"Everything is possible, if you have faith!"

That's how we argue, round and round. Dog-job-mortgage-house versus need-to-discover-world-and-self, all this witnessed by our unborn children, for whom we are ready to walk through fire, at least for the sake of the argument.

"Just think what kind of an impression it would leave on your children, leaving like this? What kind of complexes would it give them, knowing that once upon a time, their mother left her home behind and ran away?"

"Maybe it's genetic, maybe they'll want to go travelling around someday too? I'd understand them."

"Phhh!"

The next night I'm back at the bar, alone and waiting. A gust of cold air brings in with it the smell of Indian incense and Harri, noshing on a wrinkled apple, his long black coat swinging around him, wearing a hand-knitted elf's hat with silvery locks of hair hanging out from under the rim. I suppose it wouldn't matter where in the world I was, if he passed by, my eyes would follow him for a while. With his extravagant appearance it must not be that hard to sell jewellery. But what about me, how well could I sell?

"My husband is not sure if he's coming," I say for starters, fully feeling how awkward it sounds. "All the same, I'm still definitely interested in everything you have planned – and I promise that I'll never tell anyone. Just him. I hope he'll come with us, but if not, it's possible that I'll be coming alone."

Harri looks at me for a second and then mumbles something to the effect of, "Well all right, but I'd still like to see this guy, because if you're coming with me, then I'll be the one responsible for you as an Estonian woman. But we'll see," and with that he spreads out a paper on the table.

He's drawn the two hemispheres on this piece of paper.

"So. Our trip would start..." – almost imperceptibly his "I" has become "we" and I'm so glad noticing this change – "...see about here, in Spain. As I told you, my business is based on workshops and, well, good acquaintances in villages in different parts of the world, where the labor is cheap and the people are talented. India, Indonesia, the Philippines... And I've sold these things in expensive places like Japan and Korea. For the last two years, I was working on setting up the business in the US, more specifically in Hawaii, and I was doing really well there, until this bloody bike thing went down!"

"And now you want to test the European markets, in Spain?"

"Exactly. Since it's just a test of the sales potential and local interest, I don't exactly know where we'll be doing this – it's definitely going to be a tourist destination, because these places are full of people who want to spend money, and my jewellery is beautiful and unique, it sticks out among all the others! In any case, it's pretty cheap to fly from Spain to Mexico."

"Mexico?"

"Yes, we'll need a visa to get there, but I've always gotten visas everywhere. I have my old passports too, I show them in the embassies and they understand that I'm not the guy to settle down somewhere, I'm someone who's just going back and forth all the time." Harri's face dons a proud smile as he adds: "I can show you my passports later."

"But how easy would it be for me to get visas?"

"Since you mentioned that there's a house in Estonia in your name and since you're married and you've had a steady job, then I'd say it would be really easy!"

"I don't know anything about Mexico."

"Well, I'll be going to Mexico for the first time myself. I've gotten to know all the Asian cities and regions, and that's quite a lot, but now it's time for me to move on: my target for the next decade is to get to know Latin America."

"By the way, I heard a rumour about you losing your kids in Siberia," I suddenly mention, startling myself with the bluntness of the question. Harri shoots me a look.

"Telling that story takes a couple of days," he says. "I'll tell you someday, promise. It wasn't my fault and they weren't left there alone, but with their stepmother. And it wasn't Siberia, it was Tajikistan. I didn't have money to come back and... Basically, it's a long story."

"All right then, I'd love to hear that story." The promise of a good story is something very tempting for me, even if he really did end up losing those kids. I ask on, "Where were we... what are we going to do in Mexico?"

"I've heard there are some very good and authentic craftsmen there and their work is not expensive. Our goal is to find them, sign contracts with them and buy their stuff cheap. Maybe in the future I'll ask them to make something using my designs – we'll see. You see, all decisions have to be made with intuition and rational thinking working together. Making decisions requires a certain meditative state, but there's no point in forcing yourself into this state until you have the right context, meaning, until you have all the necessary facts."

"That's understandable," I reply, feeling as I did the day before that this man has a few things to teach me.

"So. In any case, last night I was busy making my decisions and I understood how you could be useful to me. If you agree to what I'm offering."

"Yes?"

"The thing is, see, I have my goods in Hawaii and I can't get there anymore, because my business visa to the US was revoked and I have a five-year entry ban. So here's my plan: you'd fly alone from Mexico to Hawaii and take care of things for me. I can draw all the maps for you and give you all the addresses of shops where I have things on sale. You'd go collect all the money that's coming to me and also take all the things that haven't been sold yet. For example, I have some really beautiful batik beach skirts, bikinis and hats. You'd send them to me using marine cargo to wherever I tell you – right now I don't know where exactly this would be. Maybe to Spain? But maybe to Japan instead."

"I don't have a visa to the US."

"You'll get that for sure!"

"All right, I can do that, all that is not that difficult," I tell him, already imagining myself doing business in those shops. It's all very interesting, refreshing, and besides that it's useful for someone. For Harri.

"There's one more thing," he adds, nodding his head. "In addition to having goods on sale in different shops, I also have a small warehouse there."

"Really? Well, I guess that's where all the Estonians worked who lost their visas over that bike thing?"

"Precisely! When all my employees left there in a panic, they gave all the goods to Frank, a real estate agent who took care of the building. He's a local guy there. I don't have contact with him right now and it's getting me worried. What's going on there? He's not picking up his phone. Has he put these things on sale somewhere? Could he maybe ship all those things to me?"

I listen, sympathising. It seems that Harri's special way of life gets him into strange situations. What could it feel like, owning a heap of goods on the other side of the world and trusting your fate to someone who, albeit, has a name like "Honest" Frank, but who won't answer your calls after your visa is revoked?

"I don't want to worry over nothing," Harri continues calmly, intensely focused, running his fingers through his beard. "It could all turn out just fine, but my alarm bells have gone off a bit. Just yesterday I still thought that Frank is my representative there and he could collect all my money for me, transfer it to me, even finish selling all the goods, or send them back to me. But when I couldn't get a hold of him last night either, I started to suspect that he's ignoring my phone calls and maybe he's just planning to rip me off! I don't really have anything at the moment to influence him with."

"Just me, once I arrive?"

"Precisely! You'll arrive there as my representative and sort things out with Frank."

I nod, feeling a mix of pride and excitement.

"He won't be any trouble for you," Harri continues, sensing my apprehension. He's set aside his cup of tea and turned his whole body towards me. Something in him scares, but still charms me. "You see. Frank is a comfortable person. Right now he may be thinking that it would be so easy for him to rip me off. However, if a confident person shows up and is up to date on everything that's going on, he'll work with you. The fact that you're a journalist could also work in our favour."

"I'm not going to have to start blackmailing him or anything, am I?"

"Oh, not at all. You'll just mention that you're a journalist. Maybe you should even apply for a journalist's visa at the US embassy, it would leave quite an impression."

I don't understand how Harri knows anything at all about visas for journalists and I can't imagine how I'm going to start waving around my passport somewhere in Honolulu... But I am willing to do it, especially considering the alternative – a boring, infinitely predictable horizon in Estonia.

"And when would I go to Hawaii?"

"Well, for starters we'd spend a few weeks, maybe a month in Spain and then a few weeks or a month in Mexico. From there you'd fly to Hawaii – I'll pay for that leg of your trip, as well as the US visa, as well as your hotel in Hawaii. And from there you should fly to Japan."

"What? To Japan?"

"Yes, by that time it will be early summer there and that's a really good time for sales. By the way, I have my own corners where I have permits to sell in Japan as well as in Korea, because the owners of the stores nearby are my good friends. The locals love me. I have my clients there too, who are always coming to buy something from me. Things like amber, for example, that goes over really well there – I take the shipments of Baltic amber over to Indonesia myself, have them make the jewellery according to my designs, and then I sell them to Korean and Japanese clients."

"But what am I going to do in Japan?"

"I know a couple of really good street vending sites and we'll just split up there, sell in different places. Oh yeah, I haven't even mentioned it yet: your salary will be a ten percent commission of all the sales."

"All right, ten percent is fine with me," I answer lightly, but it seems that Harri was waiting for something more. He flinches: "Hey! You have to learn how to haggle!"

"I see, I will. But what happens after Japan?"

"After that I'm planning on flying to Korea real fast and you can come with me. Sales are so easy in those places for me, those countries are the smoothest part of the whole trip! I've sold in Korea a few times already and I know a bit of the language too..."

"But I don't!"

"You'll learn, it's a simple language and you only need a couple of basic expressions for sales." Harri stops for a moment, tilts his head and then starts talking in Russian instead: *"Harasho? Harasho!"*

"What?"

"See, you know some Korean already. In their language that means 'did you understand?' and 'I understand.'"

"But wasn't that Russian?"

"No! The Koreans brought that word to Russia. Genghis Khan's army was mainly made up of Koreans, without them he wouldn't have been able to do anything. By the way, did you know that Genghis Khan had blue eyes! That's saved in historical documents, along with the fact that he came to Mongolia from the west and I wouldn't be a bit surprised if he was Estonian. In any case, our tribesman!" Harri gives me a victorious look. My head is spinning, I'm trying to stay on the topic of the future, let the Tatars in Mongolia be for now.

"And... and then what happens after our Korean leg of the trip? Do we have...?"

"See that's something that is open at the moment," my companion quickly adds. "Would we buy one-way or round-trip tickets for the trips? Because, you see, the price of round-trip tickets is often the same as a one way trip, so it would actually be more economical to plan two trips! Everything should be timed in a way that we could get back to Estonia and then do the whole trip again in reverse, do some more business and use our return tickets."

"Huh? So we'd go around the world once, come back to Estonia for a bit and then do it all again in reverse?" I'm getting a slight case of vertigo already, looking at the paper with the drawing of the two hemispheres. But it keeps getting more complicated.

"Actually, it would also be possible not to go straight to Spain from Korea, but stop by Indonesia and maybe India too, get more goods from there – all this, of course, if the Spanish market proves to be suitable for me... So there are so many open ends here, everything depends on

---

* "Good? Good!" in Russian.

circumstances and, to a certain extent, also the tickets that are available, whatever is being offered for a low price. One thing is sure: we'll be back in Estonia sometime at the end of June and right now I'm planning to take off at least in the beginning of March. So you have four weeks to decide whether you're coming or not. I can't give you any plans more certain than this, everything is open ended and many things will stay that way."

"Well all right then," I say. "You cannot measure and cut this kind of life with the ruler and scissors, I see!"

"Of course! There are people who think I'm a bohemian and a nutcase, but in reality, everything in my life is planned out. The difference is that my plans have a flexibility in them from the start, but I'm not going to bother explaining all the different options and variables to a random person."

I'm glad that I'm not a random person for him. Questions are swirling around my head and I know that I'll soon have time enough to ask them, in the coming weeks and months, while travelling together.

We shake on it. On the other side of this paper filled up with our planet, I start listing the countries and embassies I have to contact for visas: Mexico, USA, Japan, Korea. According to what Harri said, I can apply for Indian and Indonesian visas as needed on the spot in Japan or Korea.

"So by summer solstice we'll be back in Estonia!" And just like that, Harri tells me about his new, young wife Anne and their toddler son, who are always expecting him back – I'm glad to hear that, because it affirms my feeling that Harri agreeing to take me along has nothing to do with him wanting to... well, seduce me or anything.

But what about Tom? Will he come along? We don't talk about him that day anymore. In the end, I just mention to Harri that I'll "work on my husband" and Harri says with a distant look, "Of course, everything we talked about you can do together, the two of you!"

"Let's go! Let's put up the house for rent and let's go!" I'm greasing my husband again. We haven't reached the phase where we don't talk about it anymore. First thing every morning and last thing every night, we bump into that elephant in the room – "Epp wants to go on a round-the-world trip" – and we just have to talk about it.

"You're out of your mind!" is a phrase that repeatedly comes out of his mouth. "Out of your mind! You're not really serious about this? This is not how things are done!"

I've had contact with Harri almost every day and I see that it is, in fact, how things are done. Harri's reality does exist and it's right here, running parallel to Tom's reality. I've been to an incense shop with him in the Old Town, one of the many where he sells things he's brought back from his trips. And I've seen for myself how he simply fishes out a piece of paper from his woven backpack, shows the store manager some numbers and signatures – and then the manager pays him a few thousand crowns right there for jewellery that they've sold since his last visit.

"This business model works. I'm not saying that we'll get rich like this, but at least we'll see the world! Come on, let's go, please!"

"You can go by yourself, if you want! Leave me alone with all that!"

I see obstinance in his eyes. And I see surprise, when more days go by and he realizes that I'm actually going. A walkman for learning Spanish appears next to my pillow, my passport slowly fills up with all the necessary visas, among those the journalist's visa for working in the US – Harri was right, I really did get this fancy permit, and he paid for everything. Those two facts fill me with confidence in Harri, as well as the turn of fate he represents. At work it's smooth sailing too: I get out of my television editing work with no problems, but as a magazine writer, I don't even need to take unpaid leave, because I can write the articles needed for the four months ahead of time and also get a four month advance on my salary. It seems that my proper "housewife" of a boss at the magazine publishing house is living vicariously through me, with all the things she didn't have the chance to do and all the craziness she never let out. Whatever the case, she listens to my round-the-world plans, her mouth wide open from astonishment and excitement, nodding her head all the while.

"Yes, I'll support you, if you get your stories done before leaving," she finally says.

Doing four months' work in four weeks may seem impossible, but working in a women's magazine it's doable, especially if the author has been overcome with a maniacal need to write. I sit in the office, night after night, and just work. I want to push myself through this phase of life as fast as possible, so the next one could begin.

One night I reach that dead point, something that I've heard people swimming across the river go through. The moment when you're ready to give up and just quietly sink to the bottom.

Tallinn is hit with a snowstorm and the power goes out. I'm staying at the office overnight and I just know that if I stop working tonight, I'll never finish on time. Pressing my forehead against the icy windowpane, I look into my own eyes reflecting off the glass. I'm not giving up! I find a candle and keep writing, on paper. Outside the white storm rages on and shadows shimmer in the corners of the office.

A new moment of weakness comes and I call my husband. We start arguing again. What else could it be but that elephant again who has moved in with us.

The storm hasn't ceased by the morning. It's Sunday and the city looks abandoned, there's just the wind swirling snow around. The trams aren't running, the sidewalks don't exist anymore, nor do the streets.

I'm all alone.

I wade through the dunes of snow, sleepy and exhausted, towards the bus stop that should get me home. Surely that major artery has been cleared of snow? I'll get home somehow, right? My feet are wet, my eyelashes and any hairs sticking out from under my hat have frosted over. New snow is coming down, the wind is blowing it all around and I feel like this is my Calvary Road: I just have to get through the suffering, one step at a time, just looking for the next spot to make it to, not thinking about how far my final salvation is...

Five days are left. Then we fly to Spain.

Harri still hasn't decided to which city we're flying. "We have the date more or less set, so now I'm waiting for the cheapest last minute offers," he explains and so far it's been good enough for me.

Harri doesn't have a phone. He considers it to be a waste of time and energy. We meet regularly, each time setting a time and place for the next meeting.

This time he's at the bar before me and he's looking a bit anxious.

"There's a slight change in our travel plans," he announces. "We're flying to Israel!"

I quickly grab a seat, thinking to myself, "What if Tom's right? What if this guy really is a complete lunatic?"

"I know I hit you with this out of nowhere, but listen. I noticed an offer for cheap flights from Riga to Tel Aviv. I think there's probably also a market in Israel for my goods, because it's a wealthy country and people there have good taste. I'm talking about Jews, of course."

"Haven't you always been interested in Judaism?" I remember that among all those exciting stories Harri's always pouring out, he's mentioned the World Zionist Congress, where he participated once.

"But of course! I may be the biggest Zionist living in the former Soviet republics. All the other ones have moved to Israel..." he cackles a short little laugh. "It's really a sin that I haven't made it there so far myself. It's a very special country with very special people. It will most definitely be good for you to go see it for yourself. I have some ideas of my own that I want to feel out in Israel: what to do with the Gaza sector? And the west bank of the river Jordan? When I find the solution, I'll be able to spread it all over the world."

I've understood already that Harri thinks everyone, especially himself, has the power to change the world: you just have to talk to everyone you see and enlighten them to your views. It may seem far-fetched, but if you look at it another way, why shouldn't I trust him? I listen to his theories with great interest and I can really see him standing behind his sales counter and explaining things, people all around him, listening with their mouths open, like he's a modern day prophet. After all, this is a picture I've actually seen a few times when I've arrived at the bar here in Old Town, all the people gathered around him just like that.

"Well, all right," I sigh. "Let's go to Israel then. But what about Spain? I already went through a Spanish textbook!"

"Umm, well, we'll go there too, straight from Israel!"

"It can't be true! Do you realize that you can get killed there?"

"Right here on the other side of Tallinn there are people who went shopping and the ceiling of the mall came down on them instantly ending their lives. You can get killed anywhere!" I shoot back. "There's an armistice between Israel and Palestine, there's no bombing right now!"

Tom and I are sitting in the car, heading home from the city centre and I'm genuinely sorry that this upstanding young man happened to marry a madwoman like me. Our union was made official quickly and at a young age and it's not until now that I'm beginning to grasp the reasons. My mother was dying in a hospital and my father's house, our home, had burned down, so I dived headlong into the first real relationship of my life: the warmth of Tom's mother's home, security, with a good man, full of mutual affection and respect, everything seemed to be in place at that moment. But now what? Where does his tolerance end?

Knowing that his young wife is going on a trip around the world for four months, starting in Spain, but the rest of the itinerary is wide open, just like the actual duration of the whole thing – the only sure thing is the first stop: Spain. And then five days before takeoff, it turns out that, no, wait, excuse me, we're going to Israel instead?

But there's no turning back for me now. I bought the ticket a few hours ago, because that's supposed to help you get the visa. And by this time next week I'll be in Jerusalem, of all places! That's where Harri wants to go first when we get to the Holy Land.

Seeing my husband's reaction, I haven't had the guts to tell our friends and acquaintances about the details of my trip. They don't need to know all that. I'll just send them an email about how I'm travelling for four months with a "group of jewellery sellers" (because technically two people do already constitute a group, right?). Tom knows more or less the whole truth, but refuses to meet Harri and refuses to believe that I'm really going.

My most "tuned in" friend is Jane; in her case, I've often suspected that she might be clairvoyant. She replies to my message in a very serious tone (most of those who got it are either literally speechless, or sending short messages about how they're speechless and "Boy, you're so lucky!").

"I don't have a good feeling about you leaving," Jane writes. "My intuition is telling me that you'll get in trouble along the way. Do you really have to go?"

I stare at the computer screen before starting to type. The answer is forcing its way out, even though I can't fully explain what it's all about.

"Yes. I have to go."

There's another thing that occurs to me as I get on that early morning Tallinn-Riga bus with Harri and wave at my husband who's staying behind.

I realize the reason why I've invited him along: I'm not happy with him, just as I'm not happy with myself. I kept hoping that we'd fly through this adventure together and reach the next level, to a place I may have touched with my fingertips at some point, and maybe him, too. I hoped that this trip would bring us together, because there are so many factors pulling us apart in life. Some of them can be verbalized, and others just haunt us, unnoticed.

But he's staying behind. The tall, hunched figure waves in the misty morning, until the bus turns around the bend.

I fall asleep as we get closer to Riga, and have a dream. I'm in a flying car, sprawled out on the back seat, looking out the window, happy and free, admiring the clouds we're driving through. Suddenly I notice that I'm the only one in the car. There's nobody in the front seat. I have to climb up front and start driving myself, except... I don't have a license and I don't know how to drive!

At that moment, panic seizes me.

Of fish and men

One week later. March 1999
Haifa, Israel

Harri and I are walking down a street by the sea. Little by little I'm getting used to my new reality, even though at times I still feel the need to bellow, "Unbelievable! How great is all this!" Everything has been going well since we arrived in Israel. We've been taking buses across desert landscapes and storming enthusiastically down streets lined with blossoming trees, eating sun-warmed fruits. Harri's been telling me about ancient Sumerians and Etruscans, mixing and whipping it all up with Israel and Palestine: the torrents of facts are running over and across each other in my head, all combining in one exciting current of information. We've been visiting the places from the Holy Scripture: the famous olive grove, Bethlehem, Nazareth, the Dead Sea, Calvary Road. These places really exist! All of a sudden the world is immediately around me, spatial, savoury, tactile, and perceivable in a different way than ever before. The busy worker ants of three monotheistic religions have hauled the energy of their faiths to Jerusalem. Christian bells are ringing, some Jews pass you by, mumbling prayers to themselves, and then all of a sudden the sweltering midday is pierced by loudspeakers atop of minarets blaring, "*Allahu-akbar...*" What is it that I'm experiencing in this Babel? I can't fathom it, but I'm still covered with goose bumps and the knowledge: I *experienced* it.

My life in the magazine publishing house seems like a surreal dream from this vantage point. Could it really be that I've only been gone for six days? So much has happened. It's like I've been away for an eternity, or at least two months. So that's how I came up with a motto for the first page of my travel journal: "The feeling when you've slept so hard you wake up and can't tell if it's a dream or the reality... I've decided to start living so hard that I could ask the same question each waking moment!"

Yesterday we arrived in the city of Haifa by the Mediterranean Sea, where as luck would have it, we found a Christian youth hostel. Here we've talked to young people coming from Australia and England about God and faith. Harri has introduced his theories on Estonians to all the inhabitants of the hostel in his uniquely fitful English. I've been enthusiastically getting into the bunk-bed-lifestyle, playing with the hostel keeper's kids and learning real English from them, moreover, managed to lose my bag with my money and documents somewhere out in the town and got them back thanks to an honest finder. And now, of course, Harri and I have made it to the beachfront of Haifa to start peddling our wares.

We've decided to work together at the beginning. Harri wants to train me so that I'll know everything about the jewellery, and I can tell the whole story and the right story that goes along with each item. In the future, I will start selling things all alone at some other location, but *where* and *when* is something we don't know yet, nor do we know *how long* we're staying. To me, that knowledge – or rather absence of knowledge – seems incredibly and liberatingly awesome. Where am I going to be in a week? In two weeks? I have no idea!

We walk along the beach until we reach a corner where a wide street meets the promenade. This is a corner that gets Harri's approval. "The best place to sell is one where people are walking slowly, but where they're also getting a little bored," he teaches in his high-pitched voice, while laying out the goods from his bag onto a cardboard box. "You know, all kinds of beach promenades are ideal places to sell, as a rule, but the only problem is, damn it, the wind!" Indeed, every so often it does come in gusts and whips around us, but it can't blow away our goods: everything has been affixed to plastic binders that Harri has bought in some office supply store sale. From what I gather, he's had a lot of money in his life, "You can't even imagine how much!" But right now he's just going through a "temporary low point."

"So how much money did you have?" I ask, expecting a good story, after we've smiled at yet another promenading couple, told them about our things and even sold two amber pendants – looks like people around here think Baltic amber is exotic enough to merit a purchase.

"Ah, money..." Harri says slowly and starts searching for the beginning of his story with obvious pleasure. "Well now, could you imagine a big sports bag, filled with money, and that's your day's wages? You haul this one home to dump its contents into the huge pile of money you have stacked up in your closet already! I made most of this money from selling fish, of course!"

A tiny, peculiar fire has ignited in his eyes and I don't think it's because of the money, but rather the fish. Fish are this man's greatest passion, as I found out in an aquarium store in Tel Aviv, where we popped in and where he launched into a lecture on the species-diseases-behavior of all the fish. Right away I learned that sick fish get dull in colour and usually swim closer to the surface, but that it's also possible to recognize the "alert specimens" according to how they move, just as you can with humans.

"All right, but tell me – how did you turn into this fish aficionado?" If there's one thing I don't understand at the moment is why Harri doesn't breed fish anymore if he loves them so much and if they provided him with such wealth. Maybe the story that's about to begin will hold the answer.

"See, since I was little, I've had fish. As long as I can remember. Already at about three or four years of age I caught little babies from the sea and raised them in a big glass jar." Harri settles into the story by sitting down in the sun, turning his chin up towards the source of light and waving to a passing Jewish family.

"But didn't they run out of oxygen in that jar?" I've learned from Harri's lessons that fish need an air compressor, space and plants to survive in an aquarium, I had never thought about that before in my life. Aquarium fish, for me, existed in a strange parallel universe that was now charmingly unwinding and unfolding itself before me.

"No, I mean, why should they run out of oxygen?" Harri cries out his answer. "Well, how could it possibly run out? I mean, I wasn't stupid enough to stuff the whole jar full of fish! I put four babies in a ten-litre jar, I had a few water plants and that was enough for those little ones! After that I got a pretty good aquarium and started breeding fish, selling them to the other kids."

Our conversation is interrupted by an older couple out for a walk, who have stepped closer to look at our jewellery. It's obvious that with his extravagant appearance, Harri is quite liked by the Jewish locals and they in turn by him. "I've had good friends who are Jewish all over the Soviet Union, they're really trustworthy," he sings their praise when we have another moment to talk.

"Umm... and what about that huge pile of money?" I say, trying to get back on that topic after a pause for making the sale.

"Oh, my God, you couldn't imagine it!" Harri shouts so loud that the older couple who's now at some distance from us turns to look back in alarm. "The money I made in Russia off of fish in the Soviet times, I couldn't spend it all! You could buy a car for a day's worth of work and have plenty left over!"

"So did you?"

"No, I don't have a driver's license, I'm not interested in that. But I did buy a huge apartment for a bagful of money. And then twelve wagon loads of timber for building a castle for myself, but then, well, times got complicated... That's another story, for next time, all right?" He gazes into the distance.

"But why did you get so much money for fish?"

"Because fish are beautiful!" Harri perks up again. "If you'd only seen my little fish, you'd have paid just the same. They are like from another planet, and picture a hundred of these colourful fish in one tank – see that's a luxury and a pleasure that people all over Siberia were dreaming about! After all, water is calming, fish make people happy, it's literally psychotherapy. Three rubles a pop, a thousand fish every day, that's what I sold!" And he tells me about how he made three thousand rubles a day, while regular people made two hundred rubles each month and how he flew all over the Siberian towns with his aquarium-suitcases, sold fish on the markets and was a famous man all over. People knew the days he was selling by heart and came looking for newer, even more exotic fish: "There were constantly about ten people in line, I was busting my ass with a plastic bag and a ladle! The whole of Russia was in an aquarium fever: huge houses went without windows, airport expansions went up with no glass; they'd have to bring new glass for windows five times in a row, because it kept getting cut to shreds, people were building aquariums for themselves! And fish tanks are expensive, compressors are expensive – so what are you going to put in there, some junk or a proper, beautiful creature? A proper one! Anyone with any self-respect wanted to own some expensive fish!"

"Did you infect Russia with aquarium fever?"

"No, they had that infection before me already, but I sure did develop and spread that disease!" Harry cackles. "Like, for example, a kid comes up to me and complains about not having any money, tells me that he wants to breed complains – so I give the kid two free guppies, one plant too. Soon enough the kid sees that the neighbour's kids have prettier fish, he goes begging his daddy for the same, getting all hysterical, right! Then the daddy comes to me himself, with his wallet in hand, he and I pick one out together – and soon enough the daddy is a fan himself!"

We laugh together and I'm picturing the fish mania still swimming around Russia after being spread by this guy sitting in front of me.

"In some cities, for example, the politburo secretary comes to me," Harri continues his story with excitement. "The guy says, 'You know what, I'll pay you more than you're asking for, but give me a fish that you won't sell to anyone else in the city!' 'No problem', I say – 'Pay up and you'll get your unique fish and nobody else in this city will get one of the same species.' Another hot shot will come, I promise him the same, just sell him another species. I have enough of them! Then the two bosses get together and can't decide which fish is fancier – but I haven't let either one of them down! "

Strange how Harri tells these old stories in the present tense, as if they were happening right now.

"So what happened to your fish business?" I ask.

"Oh, that... I gave it away, because I couldn't get back to them anymore... It's a long story," Harri says and then gets worked up again, "But you know what, I had the largest fish collection in the Soviet Union. Other breeders didn't have the fish I did and I crossed breeds all the time. There were thousands of them just multiplying away in the back room of my home!"

Things have been packed up for the day, we've sold a handful of jewellery and now we're walking along the city's streets – "taking a little stroll," as Harri said, but by now this little stroll has probably turned into a ten-kilometre sojourn at least, but that's all right. Harri says that a person with a healthy lifestyle should walk at least ten kilometres a day. I notice we're walking past some kind of temple, my eyes register its existence, ears listening to Harri talking all the while – all interesting enough, but does not require much effort on my part, as he does not expect me to interrupt anyway. Now he's going into more detail about breeding aquarium fish.

"Like the labyrinth fish: first foam will come out of the male fish's mouth for two days and he'll make a nest. Then he'll go and nip at the female, nip, nip!" he speaks loudly in Estonian, walking down the street at a fast pace. "Hang on, let me show you!"

Boom, his bag hits the ground and he launches into a show on the darkening street that makes a few people stop and stare with its liveliness. "So, this hand is the female, she's just hanging out and then she comes closer. If the male nibbles at the female and she doesn't leave, the male will wrap himself around her like this, see..." Harri starts pressing one hand with the other, "And, see... shivers a little from the effort of pressing the eggs out of her, getting sperm on them at the same time... When the female's eggs are all pressed out, she's all cramped up for a moment and then swims off to hide in the plants, while the male carefully assembles all the eggs in the nest. Twenty-four hours later the little ones come out!" He bends to lift his bag again. 'All right, let's keep going!'

"So what's so hard about breeding fish then?" I shout towards Harri, who's taken off walking against the wind. I don't get it: why was Harri the only serious fish breeder in Russia, at least according to himself, why didn't anyone else raise beautiful fish and carry duffel bags full of cash?

"Well, sure it's hard!" he shouts back. "Of course, you can put together some random fish and sell the offspring for a certain price, but that's not really breeding."

"So... the choice of which fish to put together is really important?"

"Of course, and it's the same thing for humans. You can spoil your genetic inheritance if you have kids with the wrong man! I focus, meditate and calculate, before putting fish together. I have to consider their colour, shape, I have to know what their parents and grandparents were like and so on. When I buy new fish, I try to get their pedigree too. I decide which fish should have offspring!"

"So you have just one male and one female put together in one tank for reproducing? Poor fish, don't they get to choose their own partners?" I ask, quickening my pace, but Harri ignores my question and keeps going, excitedly speaking and speed walking: "It's better to put three similar females and one male together. In that situation you have competition between females and that is good! Who gets to spawn, right? When there's competition, they're not as picky, each one would like to couple with the male. And when the male wraps around them, they don't try to get away. If you have just one picky female, then what can happen is that the male will be foaming for days and building a nest, but then the female will be playing hard to get – and in the end the male just gets fed up and kills the female!"

"That happens with humans too," I chuckle.

"Right! But if you have several females, everything is fine. They let the male take turns pressing the eggs out of them and in the end I get several new sets of offspring. For example, if the male is a blue fish and the females are red, I get interesting combinations, a few thousand little ones to choose from... "

"What do the offspring look like when you put a blue and a red fish together?"

"Well! Some are going to be, of course, blue and some red, but some of them are multicoloured. I'm interested in the multicoloured ones for breeding! Some can be really beautiful, for example, a red fish will have blue fins. Ah-ha, I decide, that's a type of species I want to breed. So now I have to make a strict selection. The ugliest ones will go on sale first, then the less ugly ones, and in the end I'll have ten fish who I'll keep and who I'll use for breeding."

"I get it. But still, I don't understand: what's so difficult about breeding?" I dare say. "All that you said sounded simple and logical."

"You know what's complicated? Most people have no imagination! I look my clients in the eyes and for the most part, they're completely useless lumps. Did you notice, they cannot figure out how to use a double-knotted twine on the necklaces, so they come back the next day and complain!" Harri shakes his head in disgust. "And, see, that's why most people will never breed fish, because they just don't have an imagination. Only a minute part of all humanity does!"

We walk in silence for some time, while I think to myself, and I have to admit that I still don't get what's so hard about breeding fish.

"See, for example, I have this plan for the future, once I get myself into a better situation financially," Harri continues, "I want to breed a blue-black-and-white guppy, just like the Estonian tricolour: blue dorsal fin, black body, white pelvic fins. That would take about ten generations of guppies or two years, and for the breed to get official recognition, it will take five years. They would sell for a very high price, I could sell them to the President of Estonia: here you go, some fish with the national colours for the state's most important aquarium!"

"Ah!" I'm beginning to see what a sense of imagination means in breeding fish. "So you could breed all the different tricolours of the world, huh?"

Harri gives me a look. "Hey, you could become a fish breeder, you're thinking in the right direction! And those fish could be really expensive indeed!"

"Why?"

"Because you can't get them from anywhere else, I don't sell the females! You can only get that species from me, only males at that. It's usually fine with people, because the males are more beautiful anyway." I'm almost running, as I hurry after Harri, who's walking ahead way too fast again. "See," he shouts at the same time. "The males are always more beautiful, no matter the species, in humans too! Well, just look at you and me. Who's flashier? I have a beard, and I have a hairy chest. I'm like a rooster! Or like a goat, with magnificent horns!"

"But I have breasts!" I laugh, surprising myself with the spontaneous response.

"Those don't count! That's a reproductive organ, not decoration."

We walk on in silence, till a new question pops into my head: "Listen, but brother and sister fish, can they have offspring, doesn't that make them weak?"

"Yes indeed, yes indeed," Harri nods his head, like a professor in front of an audience of students. "They can. It does make them less vivacious, but at the same time it reinforces certain traits that I need to not lose. But every so often, you do need to bring in new blood, to keep them healthy. For example, every five generations you have to take a distant relative with recessive traits – so these traits won't dominate, but the genetics are stronger afterwards."

All this captivates me. For the first time in my life I have started thinking of humans as a species that needs reproduction and breeding. Harri seems to be reading my thoughts. "It's the same thing with humans, for example, if they live in a mountain village, in a small tribe – every five generations or so, they need to bring in someone from farther away. That's why the genetics of mountain people is getting weaker, because who's going to happen to pass through and bring new blood, huh? Sea countries have had this all along, because there are new people constantly coming by: pirates, merchants, wars come through and blood gets improved."

"So wars are good? Genetically speaking?"

"Yes, genetically speaking, wars are pretty good!" Harri adjusts his bag to the rhythm of his pace and continues, "I look at random people sometimes and cross breed them in my head, try to find the right partner for them, who'd make their offspring better than they are. See, interesting things can happen when you put together two unrelated specimens with completely different appearances – you can end up with a really poor result, but it can be really outstanding too, there's quite a bit of risk in it, it's an experiment! At the same time, if you have two relatives with good traits, the good result is a sure shot."

"So that means... relatives should marry?" I ask, startled.

"Well, yes! But the best result is when the male and female are unrelated, but they have very similar characteristics in their appearance! Or if they've been related like a hundred generations ago, a long, long time ago, but they look alike. That's an infallible formula, when it comes to offspring!"

"Are you talking about fish or people now?"

"It's all the same! Dogs, cats, rats, it's all the same!"

I think on this some more. "But listen, if fish can reproduce by sisters and brothers or by fathers and children, could that actually be the case for people too?"

"Of course! For example, the Hawaiian royal line had this tradition until not too long ago: the best new king is born from the current king and his daughter. Hawaii was a kingdom until just recently, a hundred years ago, you knew that, right?"

"Wait, what?... So you're saying that if I had a child with my father, it would be the best possible specimen? That's perverted!"

"But it may be completely true, if both the father and daughter have good genes! If they want certain traits to remain – then they're sure to dominate and not disappear. If you want the new king to be the old one's clone, the most practical way is for that king to have a child with his daughter. But yeah, after the fifth generation, an exception should be made and new blood brought in, right?"

Again he speeds off at such a pace that I literally have to run after him. At the moment, I have no idea how far we've ventured in the dark, warm night in the Haifa suburb, but what's the difference – it is interesting, that's the main thing.

Warped mirror of the future

Three months later. June 1999
Arguineguin, Gran Canaria

It's the month of June, off season on the Canary Islands. The Northern European tourists are not coming, because they're happy enough with their weather, and the midsummer vacation period of the Spanish tourists from the mainland hasn't started yet. Harri and I go from town to town, since there's a market here on the island in a different town every day. We ride along the winding mountain roads, dragging our bags of goods along with us, but clients are miserably few and far between. Sometimes I regret ever leaving Israel, but then I do realize that I'm the one who promised to trust a trip with an open schedule and I'm the one who wanted to see the world. And I've gotten to do that!

I do understand why Harri and I are still here: he's out of money and stubbornly waiting for that mysterious Frank from Hawaii to fulfil his promises and send us the goods. Harri complains that he has spent hundreds of dollars on phone calls already, but each time Frank seems to have either just left the office or is just not answering his cell phone... The possibility of me going to the US has been out of the question for some time now, simply because neither of us has the money to buy the ticket. I'm jealous when I hear Harri calling in a phonebooth to shops that sell his wares in Estonia and tell them to send all the money to his spouse Anne in Estonia... "But what about sending me to Hawaii?!" I want to interrupt him. "You promised to buy me a ticket to go there!" I still hope that everything will work itself out soon enough. Sometimes Harri tells me stories about Indonesia and India, where life is supposedly much cheaper even in luxury bungalows, compared to the small, dirty, budget hotels in the Canaries, and there are other stories about Japan and Korea, where money is waiting for him in shops, it's just a matter of getting there... But until Frank saves us, we're miserably stuck on this island, carefully counting the remaining pesetas.

"How come you're not leaving, there's not much money to be made here right now?" I ask Djellah. Even though she could very well manage to get work in almost any tourist destination thanks to her throaty voice, wide repertoire and instrument playing skills, she keeps putting off leaving the island. I have a feeling I know why. Little by little part of my heart has sprouted a root in this island and I can already tell that this connection will never be broken, no matter what the rest of my life will bring.

Sometimes I suspect that the volcanic soil of this island is like an energy-emitting magnet that draws people here. In Arguineguin, for example, there's a host of old hippies from Denmark, Sweden and Norway, who lead the so-called bohemian life here with their communities. Mostly this means wearing interesting clothes and letting hair grow wild, but there are also cosy afternoon gatherings that start in cafés and end on the beach at night. Then there are the "boat people", mainly from Spain, who have docked at the harbor and don't plan on going anywhere, at least not for longer than a short trip. I've heard whispered rumours about them smuggling in narcotics, however, their official business is bringing up salt from the bottom of the ocean and selling it on the markets. When I go with Djellah to the marina to visit her friends who live aboard boats, I admire their small, functional living spaces: with the smell of salt in the air, on bobbing yachts beside the dock, you can see that only a few square metres can provide a comfortable existence.

The places I stay on the island here fall into three categories.

First, there's the hotel that belongs to Marco's family, where I stay if I have enough money. I don't want Marco to give me a free room and he's not offering me one either. A room with two windows that look out to the sea. At night I close the shutters, but the sounds of the ocean still pierce its slats. In the morning, I hear the clangs and clamour of the street waking up: a shop door is being pulled open. These thick shutters won't let the sun's rays enter, but the muffled conversations of tourists and the smell of burning corn waft in through them and wake me each morning.

My second home is Marco's villa, in the mountains near the village, where I sometimes come with him for the night and end up staying for long days afterward. Yes, *a villa* sounds grand, but in reality, it's just the excessively big and messy home of a bohemian bachelor, where half of the rooms are devoid of furniture and where the wind from the mountains only blows in more new sand if you open the windows. The property is surrounded by tall white walls and unusual trees blossom in the space they enclose. "In a few months, you'll see what kinds of fruits you can pick here," Marco dodges my question, like he's so sure that I'll even be here in a few months. Mountains sprawl around us as far as the eye can see. I'm happy that chance has brought me here, away from the tourist beat, to lands that have belonged to Marco's ancestors for centuries.

The third possibility for me is to spend the night with my employer in the mountains, in the open air. Ever since he ran away from the looney bin, Harri's got some basic principles for spending the night outdoors: it has to be a remote place, outside of town, where there's an overview of the surroundings, and it has to be off the main road, so that you wouldn't catch the attention of random hooligans. That's how we've come to sleep underneath bushes in a suburb or in the mountains, at a hike's distance, between cacti and bushes that looked like huge horsetails. Apparently there are no snakes on this island, but there are plenty of spiders and other critters.

"And why do you think a spider would climb on a sleeping human? Do you really believe that? Are you that sheltered?" Harri ridicules my fear before it has time to bloom.

Early one morning I wake up to see a huge spider with hairy legs climbing on my sleeping bag. Strangely enough, it doesn't send me into a panic and I just flick the spider aside lightly. I guess that was a pretty good compromise: it got to live and I got to keep sleeping. Later on I'm bursting with pride, as I tell Harri about the incident, but he's not as enthused, "If something is on your body, don't move, don't hit it! One time I was sleeping outdoors in the desert of KaraKum in Turkmenistan when I woke up to a tickling sensation. I found the most poisonous spider of those parts walking around on me. So I calmly just waited until he walked off. Had I touched him, I'd have been dead in a few minutes!"

I can see that Harri likes inviting me to the mountains for the night. Even though he calls himself a lone wolf, he does actually like discussing the ways of the world. "I knew since the seventies that the Russian Empire would soon fall," is one of his stories. "I went around and told everyone about it. I didn't know when it was going to happen, but the indicators were everywhere. I was sensing and analysing them and making my contribution to getting those processes going faster. And it all came true!"

The same enthusiasm emerges when he's talking about the start of World War III now and the cleansing of the world, as a result. "I don't know yet where it will all begin, but I've been to so many different countries and seen the psychology of people... this is going to be a huge chain reaction! All peoples hate someone else and when the opportunity presents itself, they want to conquer them. Besides, there are too many people as it is, there is too much useless mass out there and the only way to remain in existence on this planet is to go through a cleansing."

"Where is it safe then... in case something should happen?"

"Usually it's safest in the mountains: you need caves for cover and a mountain lake, where you could get fresh water. Do you know what to do in case a war breaks out?"

I think about that, reclining, my sleeping bag pulled up to my chin, with the lights of two villages shining in the valley below. "I guess I would isolate myself somewhere, farther away from everyone else. To survive."

"Precisely! All the alert people, those who can think for themselves, know how to save their genes and head out of civilization's way immediately. If you find caves with a spring that gives you water to drink, you have a good possibility of survival – and the farther you are from big cities, the better. It's also good to be far from the seaside, because the sea will most likely begin to rise..."

He goes on talking about this for a long time. He recommends that if need should present itself, I should flee to, for example, the southern part of Argentina, because they will be farthest away from the biggest collapses. But if there isn't enough time to leave Estonia, I should go to the caves by the ancient Lehola castle ruins in the middle of the country.

"Why there?"

"You know, I can't explain that very well. Let's just say that there isn't any big industry there, I don't think anyone would bomb the area or bring any ground forces near there, it's far away from all big centres and roads, so it can very well just be overlooked. But the main thing is that my grandmother, who was clairvoyant, told me so. I sensed that by myself later on and I understood that she is right. This is a place where it's possible to survive."

His eccentric grandmother is a topic that comes up every now and then, mostly in the dark of night. Harri's childhood, from what I gather while listening to these dark mountain night stories, was mostly spent in the care of this old woman who saw the future. "Grandma used to say: the Soviet Union will collapse and you – then she'd point to my mother and me – will be able to see it, but you – then she'd point to my father – are going to die before then. And then she said: after that, there will be a time when everything is going well, houses are going up, cities are growing... and then I see total chaos..."

Harri squints his eyes, as if he was trying to imitate his grandmother. He's speaking with a wheeze, looking down towards the valley: "I see ruins and people escaping in a panic, all going east!"

"Towards Russia?" I interject, as if there were any other possibilities from Estonia.

"Yes!"

"They're escaping from war? But why should we flee... east?"

"See, that's something I don't know, but it's what my grandmother saw." Harry seems satisfied at being able to get me worked up again. But in a way I'm satisfied as well, laying there in the sleeping bag, feeling the energy of those mountains at night. When I finally fall asleep, of course, I dream about a nuclear war. But I'm not sorry that Harri's reactivating these childhood fears in me. Who knows, maybe his words of wisdom will someday prove to be useful.

One night, when I knock on Djellah's door and slip into her hotel room, I find her in tears. She turns away.

"I'm still so broken up about losing my mother. It doesn't matter that soon it will be 30 years since then. Tomorrow would have been her birthday."

That day we talk for a long time. The midday sun becomes the fleeting evening light, which becomes a warm southern night. Djellah and I are drinking wine, hanging out on her windowsill, looking out to the sea, where ships are taking tourists to their destinations. She's wearing a short dress made of Indian wrinkle fabric, as usual, and I'm wearing short ripped jeans, like always. We see the passersby glance at us, as we dissect all that's important to us there between the sky, sea and land. I also see Marco passing below us and staring up at me. Djellah laughs, "Epa is here tonight, she's got things to do!" and waves, as do I, looking down the street. I hope Harri won't be around in Arguineguin tonight, I really wouldn't like him to see me drinking wine and then have to listen to the lecture that will follow.

I adore what Djellah's like when she's had a little bit to drink. Her reserved British demeanor disappears and she becomes this bizarre being, just like a stupid, little kid, and the classical *femme fatale* all at once. A beautiful bird with a broken wing.

Who knows what Djellah and I would have been like, if we'd had a mother's love for a while longer and if we had children? At the age of twenty-three, a year earlier, I also found out that having children could be problematic for me. Oddly enough, Djellah was just the same age, when she found out.

"By the way, I can tell your future: you will *never* get over your mother dying," she tells me. "How did she die? Cancer? I'm not surprised, my mother as well..." We're already used to these strange coincidences in our lives.

"And you'll never be whole, unless you have children," she says. "You'll probably learn to live without them and your life will be special – because a woman without children has to have a life that is special, strange, unique!"

"And you know what happened. I let the world go free," she tells me over the next glass of wine. "I started twirling the globe in front of me and putting my finger on a random place, because I knew that much I was given. Because I wasn't given any children."

"By the way, do you ever feel that you'll end up in the nuthouse?" she asks.

"Do you know what it feels like, when the world does not fit inside of you anymore!" she shouts out of the open window towards the sea and waves at tourists passing below.

That's how we reflect our worries and fury off of each other and of wine until night becomes early morning and I stumble through the dark hotel to the other wing to sleep in my room.

The next night one of Djellah's friends, Paul from England, invites us along to a party for local Brits. The three of us are sitting in a car, speeding down a dark mountain road.

"Oh God, I can't stand the full moon…" Paul moans, hunching his shoulders and pointing up towards the sky. "My favourite time is the first days of a new moon, that awesome feeling of growth that doesn't make me insane yet!"

Djellah and I look at each other. We don't need proof that the moon pushes and pulls and influences not only the oceans, but people as well. We've discussed this a long time ago.

"Paul, what's your sign?" I ask.

"Cancer."

"Ah, you're from our club, so that's why I've always liked you so much!" Djellah shouts. "What's your year sign?"

"Tiger."

"What? When is your birthday?"

"July 20th."

"No!"

Those kinds of moments happen when you travel. You're speeding down the road of a tiny island off the coast of Africa, there are people in the car of whom one is born in Estonia, one in England, and one in Pakistan. They've all got exactly the same birthday, and they're all born in the Year of the Tiger! Exactly twelve years after Djellah came into this world, Paul was born, and I came exactly twelve years later.

What does fate want to prove for us that she's put us all in this car tonight?

If that same car took off into the air and carried us out of orbit; I wouldn't be a bit surprised. That night I drink more wine than I should, to quiet the jitters I have inside.

But in reality, nothing happens. I never meet Paul again after that night. He was this bony, maladroit, kindhearted Englishman, who definitely had a lot going on inside of him, but who kept it secret from others most of the time, at least that's the impression he managed to leave behind that one magical evening and night.

I meet Djellah a few more times during the last two weeks there and then I fly away, leaving my bag at the hotel, complete with the little phonebook that contained her email address.

It's very easy to lose a person in this world, I had to admit later, when I returned to Estonia. From time to time, I searched for Djellah on the Internet, but I must have forgotten the correct spelling somehow. In any case, she wasn't there.

"You know what," I confessed to Djellah once. "I never want to leave this island. There's something that keeps me here."

That's when she smiled and said, "You may be one of those people, who feel like they need to leave wherever they go. Maybe you won't even need to come back."

What she said wounded me, especially since it was *her* saying it. I did need to go back! I was now back in my so-called homeland, tired and weary, and needed to go back to Djellah's room every single day. Everything else that happened on that trip had been too painful, but Djellah was still the one person I could recall every now and then.

And so I sat in the light of the Nordic summer night and tried to continue writing the article that I had begun hundred years ago on the faraway island and which, I felt should have become a novel instead with Djellah as one of the main characters. I thought back on how much Djellah loved books. "I need to escape into illusions," she'd say, and I escaped back into that illusion as well, the way I remembered her.

"Djellah has thought a lot about how everything that surrounds us is a collection of illusions," I set off to write again. "She has lived in too many different countries to believe in one single truth. People usually live in one place, in their own secure world and believe it to be the only truth there is. But if you take three steps aside, cross the border to another country, you'll see other people and their illusions... This book here, it's nothing but a grand illusion!" Djellah grabs a historic novel from her nightstand, her companion this week. "Look at this world, it's just paper and ink and it becomes the image of something else in your mind!"

As I listen to her, I understand why dozens of men have loved her. She thinks so intensely and uniquely that it creates an attraction from which you don't want to be far away. And in the end it's still hard to grasp: what is she really like? She's sitting at a table having lunch with friends and philosophising, when she suddenly jumps up and starts digging around in her bag, pulls out a cell phone and starts talking... Halfway into her discussion, she starts laughing like crazy and asks, "So, did you all really believe that I could have a real cell phone?"

A moment later she's staring at the sea and her companions have a hard time catching her eye... Every one of Djellah's words and steps contains the cheekiness, so characteristic to her, but also a hidden melancholy, a longing for something that has passed and at the same time, a restless rush towards some new world.

This is something that people with homelands will probably never fully understand. Djellah admits that she has always been fascinated by refugees and unrecognized nationalities and their identity crises. But her crisis is especially complicated. While refugees do have a country somewhere that they long to see again, then Djellah is in a real minority, destined for eternal suffering. "Sometimes I miss having a homeland so bad I could almost cry," she admits. "But I don't have one. There's an empty space where one should be. Nothing."

I'm fighting back tears myself while writing these words. So there, Djellah, you can't say that I didn't care! I did go back to my homeland and I did sit in my own comfortable armchair, but I escaped again, and wherever I went, I never forgot you.

I always remembered, for example, how you fought against getting down, how you could orchestrate these silly situations and then laugh in your hoarse voice... How you got the whole village in a tizzy, when you invented a whole new story. "You want to hear the joke of the century!" Terje with his white beard and beer belly came running up to me one day to announce the news. "The wedding is going to be next Saturday and the groom is that young kid who runs the Internet cafe. He's twenty years younger than our Djellah! Wow!"

I never understood whether Terje really did believe the story or whether he was just playing along. In any case, I did decide to play that game and spread the rumour just out of the pure fun of it. For no other reason than to just forget everything else that was so bleak in my life.

The wedding really did happen and before that you just had to spend the last of your money to buy this fake pregnancy pouch meant for mannequins from Las Palmas* and walk around the village with it on. "What do you think? Will they buy it?" To me it seemed that the locals would believe anything they heard about you anyway.

---

* The capital of Gran Canaria.

Where did the bag go?

Ten years later. February 2009
Maspalomas, Gran Canaria

It's been a day since we met Jorge at the supermarket, and that wasn't all... That day went on to bring other meetings and emotions that truly shook me: most of all, feeling guilty about why I didn't come back sooner... Yes, why did not I?

Should I be sharing all that I went through ten years ago – *all that* – with Justin, my dear safe companion, my husband and my best friend? He and I are from two different continents, one a North American, the other a North-Eastern European. I'm five years older and more experienced in life than him. I'm a blondie with blue eyes and he's a dark giant with green eyes, thirty centimetres taller and thirty kilos heavier than I am. We're not similar at all. But we've read all the same books and we think in amazingly similar ways and we believe that in previous lives, we've done some important things together, letting our lives intertwine in a symbiosis, at least once before.

Can a soul mate of a husband play the part of a psychologist in the process of a marital symbiosis?

Or should I let this storm inside of me just rage on and go see a professional therapist once I'm back in Estonia, if those questions keep on rising to the surface?

"Why didn't I come back to the island sooner?" is what I'd ask the doctor in charge of healing my soul.

For starters, I'm just sitting here on a playground in front of our bungalow, my two children and some of our neighbours' children running around me. I look at this question scratched down on paper and think: Why didn't I come? This is something I haven't wanted to think about for a long time. Looking back ten years into the past, I see a time full of pain and secrets. Back then I lied to almost everyone, lied about all kinds of different things and even started to believe some of those lies. Maybe it's the volcano pulsating underneath this island that's to blame?

Is this a door I should close again? Or should I bring everything out into the open, let it go with the passing wind, and send it out there for the entire world to see, in order to get rid of it myself?

Today has passed as if in a dream. I've been moving along two parallels: one of them is reality, communicating with my two small children, the people in the neighbouring bungalows, and the friendly waiter of the hotel restaurant. The other is the door ajar to my past, with long-forgotten confidential files jumping out of it.

Do you remember how sailors tried to rape you, because you were so gullible? Do you remember what it felt like when you had one man here on the island and another one at home, to whom you were afraid to admit the truth? And how taken aback you were when he found out about it?

How do you live with those memories?

Or do you remember how you told everyone at home that you were travelling with "a group of hippies", because you were too ashamed of hanging around with some old man, and remember how you had to watch every word in every letter thereafter, in order to keep the lie from coming out? Or do you remember how you told everyone in all the markets that Harri is your uncle, how you lied about it even to Marco and Djellah? And do you remember how Harri wanted to put an end to the lies one day – when he found out that you had spent the night with Marco at his villa in the mountains? He ran straight to Marco's store after the market closed and announced, "I'm not Epp's uncle! I don't want anyone to believe that this traitor of our people is my relative!" Remember how you explained it to both Marco and Djellah, "Harri is a crazy, eccentric old man, in a panic about saving Estonian genes, that's why he reacted that way, he is he black sheep of the family. Most of us don't communicate with him and he can disappear for years. But be that as it may, he still is my uncle!" You couldn't let go of a lie once you had started it...

By the time evening rolls around, Justin and I have opened a bottle of Canarian wine. It's been a long time since I've had alcohol: a long time ago I've purposely eliminated meat and intoxicating substances from my life, as many of Harri's ideals have carried over into my life. But today I'm making an exception for wine – I want a sip of something that will connect me to the soil here and, at the same time, give me the courage to talk to my husband.

Here in January, the nights are chilly, I need to wear a jacket while sitting outside under the palm trees. The kids are asleep, so there we are, sitting in silence for a little while. The wine's bitter taste from the volcanic soil of this island stings my tongue. I keep it in my mouth, fighting the urge to spit it out, but then I swallow. And begin.

"I have to tell you something. Marco, the one with whom I left my bag, well, he wasn't just the hotel owner..."

"I know."

"What? What do you know?"

"You've been so distracted lately. I know there are things you want to talk about."

So that's what I do. I talk. About everything I can remember and what seems important. How an unhappy young wife – or a young writer, with the fear of the blank page – went south to sell jewellery and find herself, but in the process may have lost that altogether, and most definitely trampled on her heart as well as the hearts of others...

"You know, the only thing I don't regret from this trip is that Harri taught me how to sleep in the wild and told me all kinds of interesting stories – and I wrote them all down in the journals that I left here. Now it looks like God has punished me for the sins I committed here and has taken my journals."

"Uh-huh, but that means you've atoned for your sins!" When my sorrowful confession ended, Justin's tone was full of laughter. "Why are you sweating over all this? Do you think, for example, that Ernest Hemingway travelled all around the world and remained true to his wife at home? During that time in your life, you were just like a young female Hemingway!"

Female Hemingway! Laughter bubbles out from inside and engulfs us. Laughter is liberating and redeeming, even if it is frivolous. Yeah, I've been a female Hemingway, all right! Just as Ernest paid for his sins and at the same time was recognized for who he was, I'm ready to answer to the world.

"Female Hemingway!" he says again and we writhe around, laughing hysterically. Just as it sometimes happens in flashes, I get a visit from a memory of Djellah. How did she put it? "A man with whom you can laugh freely is fit to live with," she would say. "At least for some time," she would add, since she was Djellah-who-didn't-trust-men after all.

In my heart, I know that I really am together with Justin now, deeply, touching the real depth of togetherness. I have no more secrets to keep from him.

And if he believes that this bumpy road, where I ran a few hearts over, was what taught me how to love in the end, why should I doubt it?

"You should write a book about all this," Justin tells me the following morning, as we're peeling tiny local bananas in the hotel dining room.

I won't even ask why he thinks so. Suddenly, I realize that my fingers are itching and I've come to the same conclusion as well. A storyteller recognizes if the story flowing out of him or her is a little story, or a Big Story. Oddly enough, ten years of settling has made my story a big one. I saw the reflection of it in my husband's eyes last night.

Funny, how I've distanced myself from that girl of ten years ago. Now I'm ready to write about that insane four-month long trip exactly as it was, because there's nothing really to be ashamed of.

But in order to really properly recall everything, I need – now more than ever – to get back my journals from those times! That was the only place where I completely and honestly saved traces of my life, filled with lies, and did so with a maniacal constancy.

I let myself relax, now we're on the bus with our kids, twisting on the road between the cliffs and the sea, towards Arguineguin, my little home town from ten years ago.

I need to meet Marco face to face.

I recall the previous day's bizarre events that started to unfold the moment I entered in that old, familiar shop – the *Supermercado*.

I stood at the counter and Jorge handed me the phone.

"Epa? Is that really you?" Marco's familiar voice asked from somewhere far away. "*Conyo**, I'm at the doctor's in Las Palmas exactly on the day that you finally fall out of the sky again!" Laughter disperses all tension and unites us. Another quick visit from Djellah: yes, a man, with whom you can laugh with all your heart...

We scattered excited and awkward sentences into the phone line. Then it was time to get to the point, the thing that had put me in this uncomfortable situation:

"Marco, I'd like to have my journals back! You remember, that bag I left here with you."

A moment's pause followed. "Oh, that bag."

"Yes, that bag. You promised to hold on to it, remember, we had a deal that even if it was ten years. And this summer it's going to be ten years." My tone had forcibly retained the laughter from a few moments ago, it was impossible not to suspect the worst.

Marco tried to keep the levity in his tone as well, but there was no lack of tension on that end, "See, Epa, I gave that bag to your uncle Harri three years ago. I held on to it for seven years."

"Harri?" I shouted into the phone. "But where is Harri? I haven't seen him for ten years!"

"See, that's something I don't know. The last time I saw him, he took your bag and left."

If Marco lied about not knowing where Harri is... If he thought that I would just let it go – he didn't take into account the possibilities of the Internet, or my zeal.

Half an hour later I was sitting at an Internet cafe and sending out pleas for help into forums and blogs. With the help of fiber optic cables

---

* Cursing in Spanish.

my message flew under the oceans and over the mountains, past seas and lands and a few seconds later, my question was spread all over the planet. The wording of that searching message turned out in just the same style, carried the same desperation that my first message carried ten years ago: "Do you know a guy named Harri Hommik?" This time my question was almost identical. "Does anyone know anything about the world traveller Harri Hommik? Could someone please help me pin down his location?"

Harri.

Yes, whenever I take off in planes, I always recall our first departure together, the one that took us above the field of pink clouds. And I probably also remember him for an instance, when someone offers me meat or alcohol, or when someone talks about war, or camping in the field, or genetics, or breeding. He shaped my world during those four months. But I had never looked for him since we lost sight of each other in an incredibly silly and almost random way after the trip that was so full of inspiration and conflicts. I know that he's alive and continues to supply the small jewellery stores in Tallinn's Old Town. But where could he be now?

After shooting out that message into the wide world, I walked along the sunny street, told my husband and children stories like, "See, this is the corner where I used to sell my stuff." All the while thinking about where in the world could Harri be? He's probably in South America somewhere, testing his markets, after all, that's the direction in which he was planning to go...

An hour later, I looked to see if someone had sent me a hint.

They had.

I read the messages and couldn't believe my eyes.

Two people wrote me the same thing, independently of each other: Harri Hommik had recently been seen in the town of Puerto Rico, on the island of Gran Canaria.

Right here? I knew that bowl shaped fishing-village-come-tourist-trap with white houses all too well – I'd sold jewellery there with Harri ten years ago.

I couldn't have suspected something so simple and so close.

Why in the world did he come back? That time, ten years ago, he damned the local markets to hell!

And is it really possible that Marco didn't know that Harri works and lives right here, in the next town, fifteen minutes away, on this same little island?

I fog up the bus window with my breath. It's all been too confusing.

Yesterday's events rolled out in front of me like a carpet I had to step on. Another thirty minutes after receiving the message yesterday, I passed a row of shops in Puerto Rico and arrived... in front of Harri's place.

He looked exactly as he did ten years ago, only now his sales counter was a big, fancy shelf, not a cardboard box found beside a dumpster.

"Hi, it's me!"

It's funny to see people's reaction when a ghost from years ago reenters their life. But I have to give it to Harri, he didn't even bat an eyelid. He looked at me and replied in his clear, sharp voice, "Hi yourself! How's it going?"

"I'm doing well... See, these here are my children and that's my husband... My new husband, Justin."

"Great!" said Harri, scanning my close ones with his sharp eyes, probably trying to determine how alert they were. "Justin? What's his nationality then?"

"American."

"I am an American, but I speak Estonian too, I learned it," Justin told Harri in Estonian and held out his hand for Harri.

"Well now, American – that's no more a nationality than Russian is!" Harri remarked and extended his hand as well. "Do you know who you really are?" Justin nodded, "Of course!" and earned himself an uh-huh of approval. When they shook hands, a broad-shouldered, olive-skinned, tall young man and a short, sandy-bearded old man with long locks down his back, I noticed how badly I wanted Harri to approve my choice of mate. Once upon a time, we stood next to each other at the market, with him eyeing the masses of tourists passing by and saying, "Not one of the people I see now would even hypothetically be suitable for you, it would be a waste of your genes. I know what I'm talking about, I've bred fish! There are those kinds of fish, for whom it is very difficult to find the right partner. But when you do find one that fits, the next generation is a bullseye, excellent specimens!"

The only time he ever saw my first husband Tom was when he was waving to me at the bus station in Tallinn, Estonia. He refused to "diagnose" him...

I shook myself back from the fog of recollection.

"Harri, I came here for my bag," I continued, a little awkwardly, getting right to the point. "Marco said he gave it to you."

Harri looked at me for just a split second and then fired, "He's lying, the son of a bitch Spaniard. Lying! You tell me, why should *he* give *your* bag to *me?*"

Harri and I talked about many things last night. What became of his financial state after we parted ("I went through the biggest financial crisis of my life with you, but I'm on top again now and spreading out my network all over the world!"), his new travels ("Now I've pretty much explored all of South America too!"), the latest in world politics ("Through my stories, by the way, a couple of ideas have gone from Israel all the way to the US administration!"), my kids ("They look like you, you have good genes, I told you so!"), and Justin ("Well, quite alert, I'm not saying the most alert, but still, quite alert."), his own lost children ("Yes, yes, they finally found their way back to Estonia, no wonder they did, they are alert!").

And, of course, about why he came back to the Canaries – because the climate is good and it's still a pretty good way to make money, so that's why he's kept coming back for all these winters and he is now living and doing business here completely legally and planning on, surprise, building an elaborate aquarium fish store right here, in the town of Puerto Rico. "Actually, I'd prefer to do business in Israel more, I kept going there for years too, but after the spot I sold at got a bomb threat and the bomb squad came to investigate, I saw that things had gotten too uneasy and got out of there."

"I went to the Canaries market here yesterday, recognized all the smells – but not a single face, not one of the merchants!" I shared what I'd seen. "Remember the ones who were selling embroidered linens? One of them looked at me for a bit longer, but..."

"I never go to the market anymore, that's bullshit!" Harri shot back.

"Do you remember that Palestinian man who sold toys? I wonder what's become of him? He gave me work a few times, when he saw that I had money trouble. What was his name?" I concentrated. That man's face was right before my eyes, I could have even remembered some of his sayings word for word, for example, he'd say, "Girl, you deserve a better life!" just as he would let me off at that gas station after a day at the market, dropping me off – but yeah, what was his name? Samil? Basil?

Harri shook his head. "No, I don't remember any Palestinians!"

"And then there was a guy, I think his name was Ali, this big, stocky guy from Iraq, who sold swimwear here – he gave me work a few times too! Do you know anything about him?" At this point I'm not going to recall out loud how actually those two men also offered me steadier work, but for some reason I couldn't break free from the promises and plans I had with Harri.

"Oh, you and your Arabs! I don't remember them!" Harri had, in fact, spoken to them as well and repeatedly so. How could it be possible that he didn't remember? I saw in front of my eyes how we argued with him, how he accused me of anti-Semitism, just because I was also friendly with Arabs. I also remembered how we got into a fight on the first night of our trip, in the holy city of Jerusalem, because I wanted to stay at a cheaper youth hostel, run by Arabs, and he stomped off, to the Jewish quarter, because his principles were also worth something.

I wasn't going to talk about all that. It was just a very good feeling to be friends with Harri again and I didn't want to spoil it. A period had been put at the end of that sentence with this meeting. But, just in case, I asked again about what was weighing on my heart, "So you're absolutely sure that you don't have my bag, or at least the journals? Those journals, by the way, have your life's story in them, the way you told it to me back then... The whole story of your lost children and how you were committed and how you escaped..."

"Well, that's all very interesting, but I just don't have it. Marco had the bag thrown out. He told me three years ago that he wasn't waiting for Epp anymore and I guess he threw it out. And now he's like a little kid, pointing the finger at me!"

"Does... does he know, by the way, that you're selling here?"

"Of course he knows! He even helped me with my *residentsia* paperwork!"

I guess that means I'd caught Marco in a lie... Unless Harri was the one lying.

Because of all that, I have to go back, to the western part of the island, to places that hold certain memories for me, and speak with Marco face to face.

I press my forehead against the cool bus window. The touch of windows has always calmed me. And just like back then, I like to get in the seat closest to the edge of the cliffs. Little Anna is sleeping in my lap and I'm lapping in the mysterious force of the mountains.

Is my bag with Marco or Harri? Those two men are at present living ten kilometres away from each other and hopefully somewhere right in this radius I'll find those journals, filled with my small, dense handwriting from that confused spring of 1999.

Life on the stormy sea

Ten years earlier. March 1999
Between Israel and Cyprus

I curl myself up into a ball on the ship's deck that reaks of vomit, somewhere in a crevice between the sea and the seat. Maybe it's warmer there? A desolate, depressing storm rages all around, rain and gusts of wind, and this so-called ship is basically lacking any kind of interior space. As a result, the passengers are crouched on the deck, just a few of them lucky enough to have landed one of the few seats available. In my heart, I'm cursing Harri, who's to blame for buying us the cheapest possible tickets to get to Cyprus and also for me not having a sweater anymore!

"You have too many things," he started lecturing me already at the airport in Riga before our long trip began. "You should lose at least half of those things in order to move around comfortably." He doesn't use verbs such as "to travel", because moving around for him is a lifestyle that doesn't need to be encumbered by such nuisances as a spare set of clothes – the only thing he's willing to carry around are heavy bags of jewellery.

All right. As it turned out on my first night at the youth hostel in Jerusalem, there were boxes for travellers in places like that, where you could pick up things left by other travellers and leave things that had become redundant for you. So I left my cosmetics and dresses and sweater right there, full of childlike delight over the feat. In reality, all you need in life are two pairs of pants, a few shirts and a comb to make yourself look decent every now and then, right?

Harri's wardrobe consists of only one shirt and a pair of pants. Whenever he washes them, like in a hotel shower somewhere, he puts them right back on, because that way they can just air dry. He hasn't brushed his teeth for decades and apparently they self-cleanse through a natural balance, as he claims. "I don't want any chemicals, I just rinse out my mouth with water!" Lucky for me, he hasn't forbidden brushing teeth altogether – I suppose it's because that doesn't really mess with your spirituality or pollute your genes, as he claims eating meat and drinking wine does.

I quit smoking voluntarily before the trip, but now under Harri's watchful eye I'm also a vegetarian and a non-drinker. Eggs are allowed only if you know that the hens that lay them have led a free and happy life – "Regular factory hen eggs are full of toxins and stress, the life of those chickens is so hard, they can't even stretch out their wings for a moment, they're crammed into these tiny cages and they lay eggs on a conveyor belt that takes the eggs away immediately, so that they wouldn't feel satisfied and so that they would start laying another one as soon as possible!" I notice that after hearing that, I really don't have a taste for eggs anymore. The same goes for meat.

I hope this new diet will leave room for a new freedom to grow in my heart and all that inexplicable bitterness from the past will disappear. Harri explained very logically, how the meat we eat contains the last desperate sensations of the animals taken to slaughter, so people just eat it all up and start gathering hate against the world.

It's cold! The waves lap over the deck. Who would've guessed that the Mediterranean Sea in March resembles the Baltic Sea during December? I huddle up, shivering. Harri's sitting on a bench a little farther off, his beard pointed up, back straight, eyes closed (probably for meditation), wearing only a short-sleeved shirt. He's used to wearing next to nothing in all kinds of weather. According to what he's told me, in Soviet times he was committed for refusing to serve in the Soviet army, so he escaped and lived in the woods, hitchhiking around all of Siberia and Central Asia. That's when his body grew accustomed to severe changes in temperatures. As for me, evidently, I have loads of room for improvement when it comes to getting used to the cold.

My feet are covered in blisters, just like when I went on a freedom walk from Tallinn to Vilnius as a teenager, walking tens of kilometres along the highways daily. Eight years have passed since that trek and after that I've mainly led the life of an office rat. Harri, on the other hand, is used to constantly walking in his everyday life.

"Keep in mind that I'm not going to look after you. You're going to have to keep up yourself," he announced with sadistic pleasure in the middle of the Tel Aviv airport just before taking off at a semi-jog: long grey hair and goatee trailing behind, wearing a wide-brimmed hat, taking enormously long strides, as if he wasn't carrying twenty kilos worth of jewellery on his shoulder. I noticed for the first time that his body is muscular like that of a young man.

And I learnt to keep up with his impatient tempo, what else was there for me to do.

"In a new city, it's good to walk around as much as possible, because that's actually how you experience real life," he shouted back to me while speed walking. "I've walked through most big cities in Asia and all the cities of the former Soviet Union!" At first, I thought that he was exaggerating, but as I followed him around at a nearly jogging pace through all the cities in Israel, I started to believe him.

Listening to Harri's stories, I tried to piece together the puzzle of this extraordinary path: at some point, after escaping from the mental institution, he got back to a normal life, married, and had children. Then, however, he decided to make a business out of his hobby of raising aquarium fish – so he left his wife and four children in Estonia and started flying all over the Soviet Union. In one place he'd have the fish hatchery, but the pet shops and the markets were somewhere else. But then at some point he had a falling out with his wife and demanded custody of the kids.

"Couldn't you have split the kids?" I tried to understand the situation. "Two for her and two for you?"

"No!" Harri almost yelled. "Split the kids? They have to be together!"

"And then what happened?"

"She gave me the kids. I soon found a stepmother for them. A Korean woman living in Siberia, who also took care of my fish..."

"A Korean? How did she end up in Siberia?"

Harri gives me a quick look of disapproval, "Don't you know anything about history? During the war they fled from Korea, over the border to Siberia, to get out of war's way."

"Uh-huh. But still – a Korean? You're the one who said that the Estonian blood has to be preserved. You said that we shouldn't randomly mix blood with strangers, other nationalities!"

"Of course we can't mix with just anyone! But Koreans are our tribesmen, I've come to that conclusion. I told you about that already too! The same principles that apply to multiplying aquarium fish, apply to humans as well: reproduction among distant relatives usually has a very good result. Besides, this woman was alert!"

At the moment, I haven't quite understood yet if Harri had any children with this alert distant cousin of ours and what happened to the children he took away from his first wife. But I can't push him, he'll tell his life's story at his own pace and in the sequence that suits him best.

Still, he's always more than willing to answer all my questions about selling jewellery. I've learned quite a lot on the subject: I can tell the difference between different precious stones and I can tell customers stories about Tibetan mandala boxes that open with a snap so that you can enclose a piece of paper with your mantra. I have my own favourites as well, the aromatic sandalwood necklaces and the golden, lustrous amber pendants.

So actually everything is just fine, I keep repeating to myself. So the sale of jewellery in Israel wasn't as successful as we would have liked, we had to run away from the police and people weren't buying much – but still, I got to see the Wailing Wall, felt chills while watching the masses of praying people, made interesting new acquaintances in the hostel... And every morning, without fail, I was surprised anew over how the air smelled of springtime tangerine blossoms, and how pink-tinted clouds formed in the sky in the blush of dawn. In addition to that, there were the stories about patching together the Arab and Jewish communities, a very interesting topic for a journalist, along with Harri's theories on the subject, of course...

March 1999

I look up at my employer, who's head is falling down and jerking up every now and then as he nods off, the wind blowing his long grey hair around. And I think: I'm so glad he brought me here. Even if it's so cold.

The cops are coming, run!

Two months later. May 1999
The market at Maspalomas, Gran Canaria

How should I start this story?

I hold my pen above the dusty notebook and let it touch the paper.

""It's the cops! Run! I'll watch your stuff!" my Arab neighbour shouts.

"I'm sorry, please come back in fifteen minutes," I tell the Brits who are looking at my silver jewellery.

"Oh, you've got trouble," they admit, their British propriety mixed with a greedy curiosity. I'm almost sure they'll be back. Because I'm exotic. Because once they're back home, they can say, "See, we bought this piece of jewellery from a young, blond girl at the market, who had to run from the cops while we were there."

I work my way through a wall of leather bags, then slip past a few weighty tourists and exit in another aisle. Any uniforms? They know what I look like and maybe they'll take me in now, like they threatened the last time. I walk as casually as possible. It was stupid of me to set up my goods so early! The cops hadn't finished their morning rounds yet!

Ten minutes later I see men in uniforms in an aisle that's already quite far from where my shop is set up. I sneak through a dividing wall covered in toys, hurry back to my spot and find the Brits already there waiting for me. The Arab guy is busy with them: he's holding my Tibetan mandala box and talking it up, "Good price, only for you!"

If someone had described this situation to me in Estonia two months ago, would I have believed them? Over these past weeks I've had to rethink many of my preconceived notions. Such as: there are much fewer thieves among people than I would have thought. Once, while I'm running from the cops again, I leave my cardboard sales stand without someone to guard it and when I come back, I notice that one little silver bottle is missing. Is it the first theft? No. Half an hour later, I find the little bottle under my foot in the dust."

I pick my head up from the notebook. Nope, nobody around! No police and, unfortunately, no customers either. Today's been a lousy day, and I have this crappy, out of the way spot...

Right here on this curb covered with dust from the market, it's suddenly very hard to see what in my life could be remarkable enough to write in the newspaper weekend section about, other than the police raid from yesterday. The market life that surrounds me already seems mundane. I rearrange the jewellery on the cardboard box in front of me. Should I describe these things and how I've grown to love them?

But let me just start at the beginning and see where it goes...

"It's the first morning on the big knick-knack market for the tourists.

"If you don't have a permit and a spot, you'll have to deal with the cops", the oldtimers warn us coolly. The community of market sellers, as it turns out, is just like the army: a closed system, where a newcomer is not easily accepted. Nobody is going to tell me when the uniforms will pass through, so I have to find that out through trial and error.

Challenges for asserting myself are plentiful here: I'm surrounded by dark-skinned salesmen on all sides. I have no idea what to do, when one of them pats me on the breast in the course of a conversation. I'm sick of this cops and robbers game I've landed in, I'm well aware of how

I'm actually not risking anything, because I can drop this market sales thing tomorrow and leave, do something else – so when the man pats me once again a moment later, I give him a well-aimed, moderately tempered, melodramatic slap across the face. At the same time, trying to maintain a smile *à la*, "Wasn't that funny?"

"Haha, what a *chica*[*]!" The roar of laughter extends far. It seems, however, that the guy actually liked the slap, and it was most definitely entertaining for the two other salesmen who happened to see it in person.

From then on, I have no more problems with male colleagues patting me anywhere. Do they really all communicate that much amongst themselves? Everyone seems to know about the slap and so they tease me about it, in a brotherly way."

Something makes me jump: I feel someone looking! No, it's not a cop, I sigh in relief. A little boy is staring at me hard, his hand in the hand of his father.

I think about how much I've adjusted over these past two months: is this the reason why I sense people looking at me much better than before? I also learn about which spots are the best for illegal sales in the market. I get to know each policeman and the times when they come on raids. And there's no denying the fact that the market crew has also accepted me, by teaching me sales tricks and Spanish.

The kid and his dad walk off. Apparently my box was just too low, too much in the dust for this father, and he didn't feel like bothering to lower his eyes that much. I can't wait for tomorrow, when the market is in Arguineguin, I know I can borrow a good table there from a cafe nearby. I curse today: all right, I'll give it an hour. If nobody buys anything, I'll pack things up and go see if one of my friends around the market is willing to give me a little work at his booth today. That would get on Harri's nerves, but I don't have to tell him. As far as I know, he's about thirty kilometres away at another market at the moment.

"Sales work is much harder than I could've guessed at home," I lament in my notebook, continuing with the article. "In half an hour, my nose,

---

[*]   "Girl" in Spanish.

eyes, hair and skin are covered in the dust that whirls around the mar-ketplace. I become obsessed by the idea of stepping out of this dirt sauna for even a moment and getting some fresh air...

On some days, all kinds of buyers will just pass by my little sales table as if I were invisible. If only that Spanish woman who bought my ring with the onyx stone knew what a good deed she was doing for me – she immediately doubled my intake for the day. Struggling with depression, I'm trying to come up with different tricks for capturing the clients' attention. I don't know how to scream like the Arabs – and I, frankly, don't want to either. But the buyers walk by and I have a critical two-second window of time in which I have to capture their attention. Ah-ha! I grab a bamboo whistle from Indonesia and start blowing it – luckily it's something very easy to do. And tourists can't resist the urges that have been passed on to them from the animal kingdom. They stop and start looking around to determine where that strange new sound comes from.

A few days later, I perfect my strategy. The moment people stop and look at me, I yell, "I'm a Canary," as a joke. It's amazing to see the thought process play itself out in tourists' heads: indeed, a bamboo whistle is a perfect souvenir to take back from the Canaries, because it makes a sound like a Canary bird! Unfortunately, quite a few whistles are left on the table, when people find out that these instruments are not local at all but come from Indonesia instead. Ha! If only they knew that nearly all of the things on sale here at this market are not local! All the tourist destinations around the world are full of goods imported from cheap places like China and gullible tourists buy them thinking that they're local and authentic... I already know that the same "local, hand embroi-dered" parasols are on sale on the Canaries, in Italy and also in Cyprus. This mass produced item actually comes from Thailand.

What should I do? I don't really want to lie.

"Look," I say. "This instrument is made out of Indonesian bamboo. Bamboo grows on the Canaries too, but here it's too small and soft, not suitable for making a whistle."

A few buyers who are about to leave go for this explanation and buy the thing. A necessary parallel has been drawn.

But in no time at all, I start telling people that it's a local bamboo whistle. This comes on a recommendation from Ali, an Arab with lots of sales experience. "You're not hurting anyone with this little white lie, you're only giving them something!" Yes, I guess that could well enough justify quite a lot of lies let loose around the world...

When my sales table gets banned and then gets banned again and again, I help out a few of my neighbours for pocket money. Ali gives me a few valuable lessons on sales. He has a sales booth for swimwear and children's clothing and he's well versed in the Arab art of getting clients. At first it leaves a bad taste in my mouth, but then I start to notice the spark in people's eyes. In fact, I think most tourists like the way Ali runs after them and shouts, "Hey you, wait, you tell me the price then, don't leave this business unfinished, don't insult me!" Theatrical gestures accompany this process, such as throwing his hands toward the sky, or beating his chest. And if a person stops just out of pure entertainment, Ali will most likely get him or her to start moving towards his booth step by little step. After all, they've come on this trip to gather a few cultural experiences, they remind themselves, so they decide not to resist the *force majeure* and start bargaining. By the way, Ali has plenty of room for that – the starting price of the clothing includes, as he's confessed to me, as much as a nine hundred percent mark up.

"And get it straight – dealing with parents is always much more important than fussing with the children!" Ali teaches me, when I start spending too much of my time in conversation with the little ones. "In most families, the kids are not the deciders: you have to charm the mother or father, so that they'll decide to buy from you. And then you can play with the kids!"

My second teacher, the hippie world traveller Harri represents a totally different sales strategy. He knows that with his Jesus Christ locks and blue eyes he looks interesting enough, so he lets his appearance do the work. When someone passes close by, Harri just raises his voice a bit and tells them in a friendly voice, "Hey, these things here – I've collected them from Indonesia, India, the Philippines, all by myself!" That's when an instinct is activated in the passers-by, the instinct that also rears its head whenever we watch documentaries about interesting places and crazy travellers, and there they go, already slowly moving in closer."

I smile to myself. This passage describing Harri, I think, turned out pretty well. In the end, even if I have problems with money – and the heart – here, I've still come out of it with an invaluable treasure: what people, what stories and what knowledge!

"We have bracelets made of tropical grass that come from the Philippines," I continue writing. "At first glance, they're just plain boring: little knobs that look like deer droppings. But these are the things I run out of first, because a little spark ignites in the eye of each female customer when I tell them about the bracelet. "It's really small right now. But you have to put it in water for five minutes, then it grows, and then you have to put it on right away..."

When the bracelets are all gone, an English girl comes up to me: her girlfriend bought a bracelet here that you're supposed to soak and now she wants one too! Are there really none left at all?

Women like it when you have to do something. They like experimenting. Aromatic necklaces made of sandalwood start to sell better, when my boss Harri tells me there's something you can do with them, "In order for the perfume in this wood to come out, these necklaces have to be left under a burning lamp bulb for a few hours and then they'll give off their aroma better..." The female buyer listens and nods avariciously. I imagine how she's already waiting for the first chance to test this out in her hotel room.

With a little bit of courage that I've gathered up now, I start to think up and offer all kinds of experiments for the tourists, even though I'm not sure if they'd work. For example, we sell tiny boxes made of sandalwood. – "If you put some lotion in here, it takes on the smell of sandalwood in two weeks and becomes like a perfume!" These kinds of half-truths, or rather unproven fantasies are part of my newly acquired market sales mentality. Everyone around me is lying a little bit, after all, and the wind carries these little white lies right to me. "Believe me, madam, this carpet will retain its colour for a hundred years..." and, "These pieces of jewellery are made of rare stones..." Stupid is the tourist who believes everything.

With my I'm-a-Canary-bird style of self-deprecating humor, I succeed especially in attracting British clients. They seem to have had enough of the screaming Arabs and for them I'm something refreshing. Sometimes, when I'm in a good mood, I sing traditional Estonian songs, to make myself stand out even more among all the other salesmen. If nothing else, my singing makes some people stop to just ask where I'm from. And in praise of the British it must be said that if they've spent five minutes of a salesperson's time on talking about random things, they will be polite enough to buy something and usually not try to talk down the price.

Germans are different. They like haggling and as a result, they may just walk off in the end. The British, on the other hand, never haggle – if they like something, they'll buy it.

But a typical Irish tourist will stop and chat not only for a minute, but sometimes for an entire hour. He will tell you the life story of his aunt Mary, who once bought a foldable sombrero back from the South Seas, just like the one I'm selling here now... The Irish love tales. They listen, heads cocked, when I tell them about the background of the different items, "This here is a Tibetan mantra box, where you can put letters addressed to God." – "Ooh, lovely, lovely!" they say and take two.

And then, of course, there are the rich Scandinavians, who have bought or leased property on the Canaries and are now spending their retirement years in the South, visiting relatives and friends in the "real" Europe just a few times a year. "Ooh, you're from Estonia! How's the weather over there?" a caramel tan Swedish lady is delighted and buys a pair of earrings "to support a girl from our parts," as she puts it. This support is constant during the days when I'm selling at the market in her hometown. Seems that such conversations with me provide entertainment for her that's sorely lacking in her normal daily routine of tanning and relaxing.

Some days there are masses huddled around my table. I find confirmation of the well-known psychology rule that applies to relationships between men and women, as well as to doing business at a market: popularity comes in waves and people act as masses. Only a person with a very independent mind dares to stop and look at a product that has no other interested parties looking it over. Most people will come running if they see that someone's looking at an item on my table. It's almost as if they're not interested in the product, as much as in the interest of the other person.

If one interested browser has inadvertently attracted others to come, my task is to keep at least one human being at the table, so that I wouldn't have a situation where there's an "empty table". Even if I see that a person won't buy anything, it's necessary to keep him or her there to initiate another wave of interest.

At the height of these waves, the salesman's life is tough. There are people swarming all around you and it takes real effort to try and remember whom you've shown what already. In addition, there's also an intuitive game to play: what kind of an item would most interest a certain type of person? Should I offer conservative silver earrings or tiny Tibetan perfume bottles that would go well around the neck of a bohemian type?

At moments like these, I have to show six items at a time and speak in three different languages, as well as keep an eye on things, so that nothing gets stolen. At the same time, I have to watch that I don't start talking too energetically (this will scare off some of the clients) or too lethargically either (in which case customers think I'm not really interested)...

And if I have to go in the middle of all that?

Then I have to yell for the salesman at the next table and tell him I'll be gone for three minutes. He will keep an eye on my things and maybe even sell something. At first, I was afraid that maybe that neighbour would take something. Later on I'm ashamed of my fears. This network remains vital only thanks to its mutual solidarity."

Sigh. Is it really just a bad day today or do the forces above want me to write instead and is that why I'm not being sent any customers?

I put away the pen and paper. "*Mira!**" I call out to the group of dark-skinned tourists passing by. I already know that this will make them turn their heads.

---

*   "Look!" in Spanish.

While my daughters are sleeping

Nine years later. May 2008
Barcelona, Spain

The girls are asleep in the bed of our rental *apartamento*[*], tired from the morning flight here. My husband is off at his conference and I have an unexpected free moment to look out the window and inhale the surrounding scents.

Just like old times. With two little kids, these kinds of moments are few and far between.

A warm breeze blows in from the balcony, and shouts in Spanish rise up from the street below. I look at my daughters – sleeping kids are always the most beautiful and peaceful.

Our rental apartment is in the same quarter, called Barceloneta, where I once sold on the streets illegally and darted away from the cops. Right now I look back at that time just as I look at my children: with incredulity, fear, and hidden admiration. How is it possible that it all really happened?

I once read an analysis about the pink-covered Barbara Cartland romance books: how can a heroine get into such whirlwind situations,

---

[*]   "Apartment" in Spanish.

though the storyline is still more or less believable? Because ninety-nine percent of the time Cartland created her main characters as motherless, which meant that they lacked a personality in their life that would have balanced and quieted things, someone who'd have said, "No, you should not do that!"

In my early twenties, I was definitely like a typical Cartland heroine. My mother's early death could explain quite a few things, among them my quick wedding, as well as the dash to take a trip around the world. My mother would probably have been the one to say through her actions, as well as maybe directly in words, "Calm down, think about things, don't rush your decisions."

However, who knows, maybe she would have been the one to egg me on?

I remember one night a long time ago.

My mother is still alive. She probably already has the cancerous growth inside of her, but we don't know it yet. The two of us are watching the evening news, it's springtime and there's a breeze coming in the window, just as it is today in Barcelona. The news is showing a freedom fighter and journalist, a Lithuanian who grew up in the US, a man by the name of Paulius Klimas, who's initiating a freedom walk "Baltic Freedom Now" that will go from Tallinn, Estonia to Riga, Latvia to Vilnius, Lithuania. Along the way, he plans on organizing meetings and inviting people to come walk with him, and each day he plans on keeping contact with the Voice of America radio station and reporting on the day's journey, as well as the situation in the Baltic States. All who wish can join him for a day or longer on this protest walk.

This is what the news report is telling us. The camera shows the protesters' flags blowing in the wind on Toompea hill, the seat of Estonian government in Tallinn.

It's spring 1991. A few months earlier, some people guarding the television stations in Vilnius and Riga were killed, and those stations are still controlled by the Soviet special forces. The newspapers say the so-called "political climate" is explosive.

I'm sixteen years old. "Mom, I'd really like to go on that freedom walk with those other people," I tell her.

"Good idea," mom replies. I don't remember any doubt or fear in her voice. "That really could be interesting for you. Just think of it, you can practice English with that American and get all kinds of new experiences..."

How did she manage to let me go so easily on that trip, where the possibility of dying, or at least getting in trouble, was so high?

In any case, it was my mother who told my father that, see, Epp has this idea and why not let her go and explore the world a little? The next day she also managed to convince my friend's mother to allow her daughter to join the walk, and helped us talk to our teachers, so that we could get our exams out of the way early. (Does that sound familiar? That was the first time and after that I've done it time and again, thinking that travelling is the perfect opportunity and excuse to get all my work done ahead of time. And that exceptions from the general system of things should be allowed for me, for some good reasons.)

And that's how they let us go on a political protest walk against the Soviet Union. We joined Paulius a week after the walk's start, on the west coast of Estonia.

"Hello, Paulius," I approached him – we were waiting in the middle of one little village, as we had been told, and saw the approaching group carrying the national flags of the Baltic States. "We... came to join your walk."

"Oh yeah? Great," Paulius smiled.

"We'd like to come all the way to Vilnius! We just have to go back to school for one day next week and take this exam, but we'll be right back!"

I remember the look in Paulius' eyes.

It held consternation, surprise, fear of responsibility, but maybe also curiosity and trust – if that girl knows exactly what she wants then she has to have that chance.

And maybe that's a part of the reason why my mother let me go. A mother's heart senses the possibilities of her child's course of life. For some inexplicable reason I had been sitting in our little local library and reading old issues of *National Geographic* copies that had been discarded from one British library, smelling the foreign scents in these old journals, writing out words in English on a piece of paper and admiring the landscapes in the travel photos. Surely my mother saw which road I was meant to take.

During the next month, my friend and I were protest walkers. At a time when just five months had passed since "bloody Sunday" in Vilnius, we walked along the highways in our seven-membered group, flags waving. People from the villages lining the way gave us gifts of homemade cheese and bread, there were also some that joined us for a day-long walk. We slept in hotel rooms paid for by the Estonian-Latvian-Lithuanian Popular Fronts and proclaimed a message of freedom that was also covered by the foreign media. My friend and I even managed to give a couple of interviews in our stumbling English.

As we feared, the situation escalated. Three days before reaching the border between Latvia and Lithuania, Soviet forces attacked the border control station. In the course of an anxious early morning meeting, our leaders, the Lithuanian politicians Paulius Klimas and Petras Gražulis decided that "the kids would stay home today," and so we played board games at the hotel. The next day we were allowed back on the road and we were joined by our bodyguards: four Lithuanians from the "Lithuanian Rockers' Union", dressed entirely in black leather, riding ahead and behind our group. Gun holsters were strapped to their belts. I remember the startling, yet exciting sensation I felt when I noticed that. Even though we didn't talk much with those young men, the story soon reached us that one of their best friends had died defending the television station during "bloody Sunday" in January.

Would I let my sixteen-year-old daughter go on a trip like that in a similar political situation? Would I go to her friend's mother, who probably has fears and a rational, adult way of thinking, and convince her that we should let the kids go...?

I don't know.

There were more of those kinds of moments along the way that years later make me shake my head when I try to imagine my own daughter doing the same things. How would I feel about it all?

There's a day that still gives me chills, even if I just briefly recall its events. My age: already twenty-four. Place of residence: Gran Canaria.

I've left the southern part of the island, where I spend most of my time, to visit the capital city of Las Palmas in the northern part of the island, where a great fair is being held.

After the end of my day of work at the fair, I go to the public beach, where I undress with ease and settle in to enjoy the sun with my breasts bare. Yes, topless. Because over the past weeks I've already grown accustomed to the beaches on the southern side of the island, where it's common among women to do it this way – more so than tanning with a top on. I've adopted this habit after getting over the first shock. Tanning with a bare torso seems so much more natural: honest and direct relationship between sun and human body.

I don't even think to look around before lying back, however, had I done that, I would have discovered that the tanning habits of women fifty kilometres apart can be vastly different.

"*Privet!**" someone wakes me from my nap. I open my eyes to notice that I'm surrounded on all sides by young men. I'd seen them that morning at the market. Russian sailors on land leave here for a few days.

"*Privet!*" I cheerfully reply and start talking to them. Why, they're almost my compatriots! Soon enough some of the guys invite me to go swimming and others offer to watch my things. Sure, why not? Alone on a beach, one of the biggest problems is not being able to go swimming. There's a good amount of jewellery and a little money in my bag that I couldn't leave out of sight.

A wind blows inland from the ocean, whipping up great salty waves. We jump in the water, dive in the sea...

I lose my balance for a moment and one of the men grabs my hand to help. It's Yura: a tall, blond, wide-shouldered man, friendly like a teddy bear.

"Do you want to pick me?" he suddenly asks in a rushed manner, breathing in my face and throwing furtive looks towards his friends. The waves crashing around us are so loud, nobody can hear us.

"What?" I ask, still smiling.

"They're planning on getting you on the ship... But if you choose me, then I can protect you. I can even pay you. Come with me! I can get your things and we can get out of here!"

---

*   "Hello!" in Russian.

May 2008

In a flash, everything around me has changed.

I turn to look at the beach to see that my little beach towel has been taken over by the men and one of them is holding my bag between his legs. And I can see that they're wolves, baring their sharp teeth in a smile, and I've turned them into these animals, because as far as the eye can see, I'm the only topless woman on this beach. And they're sailors who just docked yesterday. They're probably even ready to rape me. Or at least they think that I'm kind of like a prostitute.

And there's nobody on this beach to come help me if I was to step into the middle of that gang of sailors and started demanding my things back.

I jump in the waves, the smile frozen on my face, looking at the apathetic mass of tourists on the beach, trying to figure out what to do. Who to bet on? Would someone come help me out or would I just end up making an awkward scene that wouldn't help me get away from the sailors?

The waves keep crashing around me and there are four men around me, one of them looking a little more expectant than the others now. We've got a secret. He knows I understood what his offer meant.

"Yes," I shout to him, more on instinct than as the result of an analysis, which I was incapable of at the moment. "I agree!"

An instant later and we're out of the water. I'm shaking, wrapping a beach towel around me, and clumsily trying to get my clothes on.

At the same time, Yura is telling the others something in a super-fast and incomprehensible mix of Russian and Spanish slang. I can't understand what he's saying and can't get my head to work right at the moment. Have they manipulated me into some sort of a trap? Is he still trying to promise his friends something? Have I so easily lost my ability to think clearly...? What should I do?

One thing is clear – we're all trying to outplay each other here.

For a second, I think about trying to pull my bag from Yura's hands and screaming, "Help! I want to leave!", but I just don't have the guts. My sense of embarrassment has reached epic proportions.

Yura and I are walking down the street now, his strong hand tightly wound around me; we look like a couple. In his other hand is the bag with my jewellery, and I already regret not making a scene on the beach. Maybe one of the people on the beach would have come to help me and I could have got my bag back? But that moment is gone now.

I try to quickly figure out what to do. A part of me is panicking and another is totally apathetic at the same time, just willing to give up, go along with Yura to wherever fate will take me. If I only could be sure that he will be alone, maybe it wouldn't be too bad... But I don't trust him. Blood is pounding in my ears.

All the same I don't trust the world around me either. We walk down the street, here and there we see some locals in office clothing walking at a quick pace and some tourists in crop tops and shorts loitering around, everyone busy leading their own lives and I'm too scared to start screaming.

The only thing I dare to do is pray, "Dear God, wherever you are, whoever you are – and I apologise for neglecting you for a while – please, please, give me a way out of this. I know it's asking for a lot, but I'd like to get out of this with my bag..."

We're probably somewhere near the port now, I can see ships at the other end of the street. We stop at a hotel, and Yura pulls me inside, the bag too. The street in front of the hotel is lined with palm trees and to me it seems like a tunnel from one place to the next, all I have to do is rise up into the air and fly into this tunnel. I sneak a peek at my bag and place another call to God...

The bag bounces to the reception on Yura's arm.

"A room for two hours please," he says.

"Yes, your passport please," the smiling girl asks, just going through her daily receptionist's routine, not knowing that something is about to happen. I know that I'll have to make a scene right here and now. This is my last chance, unless I can just run away.

The bag. The bag is on the floor for a moment.

I grab the bag, run out of the door, slamming it shut behind my back, into the tunnel-like street without looking behind me, running faster than I've ever run before. I feel how the chemistry released inside my body is bursting to get out, I run so fast... until I'm in a park somewhere, trying to catch my breath, head spinning, with the taste of blood in my mouth.

I slump down on a bench and just let myself cry.

Marco lives an hour's bus ride away, Harri is selling his things somewhere on these streets, Tom's waiting for me in Estonia, but I'm just a stupid girl, all alone in the world.

The flow of tears, as we know, leads to the release of a happiness hormone in the body, I've read that somewhere and know it from previous experience as well. That's good to know. Little by little the sobs subside, the world around me stops spinning and a new state of mind arrives. It's peace, maybe even happiness; it's a state where there's nowhere to rush, and where I finally recognize a thought that's been rising up inside of me: yes, God does exist. God saved me. I don't have to prove this to anyone. Ever. This is something between me and the universe. Just because I dared to believe that the powerful force upstairs would help, I got through the tunnel and away to freedom.

When I meet Harri at the place we agreed to meet earlier before returning to the southern part of the island, he looks troubled. On the outside, I've calmed down already, but my heart just may be beating faster than usual.

"Did something happen to you?" he asks anxiously. "I was so worried about you today, like something had happened to you!"

"I... got a little smarter today. Nothing special. I don't want to talk about it."

From then on, I gave up topless tanning on the southern beaches as well.

Every time I get undressed to sunbathe now, I still feel the same shiver, even if it's in the safety of my own backyard.

But now, years later, the scent of adventure is in the air again. I'm back in Barcelona with my two children. At four years old, one of them is in a moody, world-conquering phase and wants to do everything on her own; for example, to walk across the street without holding my hand. The other is nine months old and tries to pull herself up wherever possible and pull down anything she can get her hands on, which can be something as dangerous as hot tea. She's also liable to fall down from high places, such as balconies.

Nowadays the risks in my life are on a completely different level than when I first stopped here as a young, fearless market peddler. What happens when my kids get sick? Get lost? Will I manage when my husband is away at his conference and I have an extremely complicated situation: my big kid wants to go to the bathroom while we're taking a walk, but she doesn't know how to wipe herself. At the same time, I can't leave the little one by herself, but all three of us won't fit in a bathroom stall together. What will I do?

These are the kinds of adrenaline-filled moments that now wait for me.

Three days later. The kids are taking a *siesta** right here on the balcony and I'm breathing in that specific, warm scent that garbage-strewn southern streets give off, something that I've always found pleasing.

Suddenly, I'm reminded of an old saying, "We all learn our whole lives long, as we get into new situations in old roles or into old situations in new roles."

When I was walking back along the beachfront promenade in Barceloneta towards the main esplanade, La Rambla, I noticed a man ahead with a light blue uniform: a cop! I couldn't have imagined that it would still stir the same reaction of excitement and fear in my belly. When black guys with big bundles over their shoulder speed-walked past us a few minutes later, I knew: they're looking for a place where there aren't any police, to quickly spread their merchandise out again. After all, I was their colleague here in Barcelona back in the day.

I fish out a photocopy of an old article from my bag, written at that time about my daily life in the markets. I packed it along for the trip to get the most nostalgia out of the moment. What kind of a life did I live back then?

"At the central market in Barcelona, the policeman politely lets me know that the next time he catches me, he'll confiscate my goods," I read from the article. ""Illegal sellers like you are usually on the beach,'" he drops us a hint, "however, if you get caught there, you didn't hear it from me!"

A day later I'm trying my luck in front of a shopping centre on the beach. This is where men, women, and boys from faraway Bangladesh are selling their wares. Every one of them has a sheet spread out before

---

*   The afternoon relaxation time, common in most Spanish speaking countries.

them with a certain type of product, for example, a stack of silk scarves. I put my sheet over a nice big cardboard box that I find next to the dumpster. I fuss over the display, making clusters of clasps with leather flowers on them... Oh, and I've got a few sewing pins in my bag, so I even affix my sheet to the box so it doesn't blow away.

After all this I understand why the others are selling on the ground. A police car suddenly pulls up to the shopping centre, spilling out men in neon vests. All the sellers instantly pick up the four corners of their sheets to form a bundle, throw it over their shoulder and disperse into the wandering tourists.

Pride and flight are battling it out inside of me. The sheet is attached to the box with pins, so I don't have enough time to run anyway! I stand there proudly and stammer in my pathetic Spanish, "Why can't I sell here? Don't take my things!" A group of curious tourists is gathering around us and they seem to be making the police feel a bit uncomfortable.

I get off easy and the men drive off, but not before I've gathered up all of my wares.

A minute later, all the others are back. This time I follow their example and spread my sheet out on the ground.

Half an hour of selling goes by. I forget myself in the stories, telling my clients about our goods, when suddenly there are three men in neon vests standing behind me.

"We won't let it go a third time!" they declare.

When the market closes at midday, the sales move to the beach area. The beachfront is full of restaurants, where young black kids dart between the crowds, holding gold chains or sunglasses in their hands. They approach the tourists and shout, "Good price, lookie-lookie!" On the insistence of my boss Harri, I try this a few times too, waving a bunch of foldable sombreros around. "Look, people, at first it's just a sliver, then you make a fan out of it and then *voila*! I pull it open all the way and close it with the velcro tab: see, it's a beach hat instead!" I clear my throat, trying to attract more attention from the tourists walking by.

However, all I end up with is a strong inferiority complex. I admire the black salespeople around me, who can retain their entrepreneurial spirit and good mood even when the tourists snap at them with a disdainful "No!" and turn their heads. When it comes to me, there's something else besides agitation that I see in the eyes of those people: it's curiosity mixed with racism and sympathy, "Excuse me, but why does this blond girl, who looks like us, have to do work like this?" During these weeks I get quite a few job offers: as a waitress in restaurants, a public relations person (that's what they call the poor soul who has to stand in front of their establishment and bring in people off the streets), a hotel receptionist, a timeshare salesperson...

I'm not taking any of these jobs, for starters, but I also give up on the active sales work near the beachfront restaurants. I find a spot near some more modest black women, who are selling on the steps.

Tourists pass us by with veiled stares. I try to put myself in their place – what would I do, if I walked past a set of steps where illegal salespeople have spread their goods? A short time later, I discover that I can't put myself in the shoes of a white tourist anymore. It's too distant.

Little black kids keep a lookout at the top of the stairs. When a cop car stops, they whistle. We pick up all our things and step away quickly. Policemen hurrying down the stairs shoot malicious looks at us, but there's not much else that they can do.

One day we don't hear the whistle. Suddenly the cops are right there. The black women's wooden elephants and drums are confiscated and put in a large bag. One of the women starts crying, "I have five children!"

I give the policemen a look that's as sincere and ignorant as possible, "Why can't we sell here? There's lots of room, the stairs are wide!"

He looks at me with astonishment for a moment, probably wondering to himself whether a half-wit tourist has decided to do something extreme for entertainment. Then he snaps, "It's not allowed. You have to apply for a permit! If I see you one more time selling, I'll take your things, too!" The next time I see this cop is at the market. Once again he only threatens me. I still suspect that he's a racist: I'm spared a fine and the confiscation probably just because of my light skin and blond hair."

I look up from the article. So what do I feel here in Barcelona besides nostalgia? Things that were once romantic now seem somehow ridiculous, stubborn and incomprehensible. If my own daughter wanted to try her hand at a career on the market, I'd tell her – now – that there's no point in it, what are you going to achieve or prove by doing that?

Yes, then and now. There wouldn't be one without the other, if there were no experiences then no wisdom would be gained.

Life in its entirety is actually one long series of "then and nows", or rather, that's one way to look at life. For example, I now have the chance to make one of my dreams from back then come true. Walking around here in Barceloneta nine years ago, in the narrow streets of this fishing village's old town, a bag full of jewellery on my shoulder, I wanted to know what kind of life was being led behind these balconies full of laundry hung out to dry. Now we have just that kind of a home for one week, a small rental *apartamento* on one of these tiny streets. And it's just the way I thought it would be. The windows and balconies of the opposite building are so close that our most intimate neighbour is the one across the street. For example, a lady with two poodles lives in the balcony across the street from us. The day before yesterday she did her whites and yesterday her colours. Her laundry flaps around outside, almost at a hand's reach.

When I was here nine years ago, I really liked "people watching" from behind my jewellery stand. Today, I know what a luxury that is – to have plenty of time to spend on just watching people! Right now I'm more in the category of those rushing around and putting on a show for the watchers.

Imagine: "A young woman with two children enters the beach area. She tries to drag the stroller through the sand, but then abandons it in the middle of the beach and drags her kids to the waterfront. The older one runs head first into the waves – and while the woman runs in after her, the smaller one, who's alone now, is happy to work through the sand and stuff cigarette butts she finds into her mouth. 'Noooo!' the woman desperately screams and runs towards the baby. At the same time, the older one is off into the waves again... Poor things," I would've thought back then. "Is that happiness? Am I actually lucky not to have any children?"

Or a scene from the eatery at the zoo: "A woman arrives with two children, buys food and sits down to eat, with the smaller one in her lap. But then the older one starts to whine and runs to the toilets around the corner. A short while later she cries for her mom, and, man, does this kid have a set of lungs! Mom hurries to answer her call, carrying a twisting and screaming baby under her arm. By the time she makes it back with them both, a flock of doves and sparrows has helped themselves to their lunch, and all of us, the people sitting around them, we smirk as we look on, while the mother yells to try to chase off the birds. Their food is spoiled now anyway or, well, basically just devoured! But I'm surprised that she left the stroller and her purse here just like that. Isn't she afraid they'll get stolen? Or does having two kids really make you that crazy?"

Maybe the 1999 Epp would think these thoughts when looking at the 2008 Epp?

I remember feeling a twinge of jealousy looking at those well-off middle class families back then, the kind I am now myself. At that time, I belonged to the class of poor backpackers.

Now I walk along the main street of Barcelona with the children and Justin, dropping money in hats here and there, and suddenly I recognize it: here's that youth hostel that I lived in back then. That's probably where that group of young break dancers is staying, the ones performing right in front of the building. Back then I shared my room with young mimes. Oh how they went on about their lifestyle: you get to travel around with your own gang, from city to city. Except you have to be ready to swallow your pride and walk around with a hat in your hand after the show.

And for some reason that hat-in-your-hand-life makes you a bit bitter towards those whose life seems problem free, rich and beautiful. Children and money and look at them, they even hauled their stroller here from the other end of Europe...

I'm rolling my daughter's stroller down La Rambla street on a Saturday night, it's getting darker, the night comes on so quickly in the south, and I feel the sniffles coming on. My nose is runny and I'm sneezing every few minutes. Maybe I caught a cold yesterday at the beach, while running after my two little escape artists?

And there, nose dripping and eyes watering, under the palm trees, I suddenly understood why I had to come along with Justin to his business trip. Life is a spiral and I'm back here, not just physically, but spiritually as well, back on the ground from the heights of my illusions. The runny nose was needed to remind me of all the other sniffles I had during my travels.

"Remember it well: travelling is difficult and, to a large extent, pointless," I write the words in my journal, as if they were dictated from above, that's how sure and right they suddenly seem. "Travelling should be avoided at all costs and undertaken only when there's no other recourse! Much more time and energy should be invested into living a stable life, than to looking for a new one all the time."

It feels as if I've just made a long leap in my personal development. This is me, one of those thousands of young people on this Earth just dying to travel. These kinds of people have always been around – my grandfather, for example, apparently went into the army to satisfy this longing, that's how much he wanted to get away from his home village. However, the way things are in the world today, this satisfaction can be appeased for masses of people, more than it ever has been. It's an appropriate thing to do for a young person in the Western society to go backpacking. It's even strange if a person has never been travelling. Just as it is perfectly acceptable for a young woman with children to take her kids and go away for a week or two to satisfy her thirst for the world.

But these trips also make us feel the other side of the coin. The intensity of travelling is tiring. I remember how long ago at the beginning of the journey with Harri an experienced backpacker at a youth hostel told me, "Don't be surprised when at times you get tired, you're sick to your stomach, you don't want any new experiences. You'll ask yourself: why are you doing this? How many museums can you visit? How many new people can you meet? How many new sensations can you soak in from new places, until your pores get clogged? That's when you need to take a day when you don't do a thing, you'll sleep in the hostel bed, for example, or just sit in a park – you'll have a day of fasting from experiences, so to say."

When I got back to that youth hostel in Jerusalem four months later, I knew exactly what she was speaking about and passed on the

same recommendation to two kids at the beginning of their journey.
I feel good embracing these memories. The first adviser was a white girl from South Africa, just finishing her year long trip, but those for whom I recommended this down time – that was a couple from the Czech Republic. Where are those people now and what are they doing? An array of faces and fates runs through my mind. I think of another Czech girl, with dread locks and bare feet, who sold jewellery on the markets in Gran Canaria, like me – and who suggested that I go to India – "I think you'd like it!" Or the Californian girl I met in Israel, who told me about her travels and got so carried away in her storytelling that she even started to cry. With eyes teared up she told me, "All the places I've been were completely different from what I imagined before. I've changed so much and I can't imagine how I can ever go back home now, after Indonesia, the Philippines, China and Vietnam!"

I think these people I once met would agree with me, when I say that travelling is a kind of job. A beautiful and satisfying one, but in a way hard: gaining this understanding of the world and growing personally can be painful. You're constantly hurt physically and mentally. And when a moment of happiness arrives, it is intensely luminous, but you've paid for it with the masochism of the previous days or hours. Whether it's physically conquering a mountain top and then looking down, breathless, or just another feeling that's hard to explain, but you know it has hit you, the sensation of really understanding something new about a culture unfamiliar to you.

After pain, there's happiness – that's a rule of life that can be experienced especially intensely during travels, and maybe remembering that was why I came on this trip. Suddenly I remember so well how I woke up once in a hotel in Gran Canaria, sneezing and miserable, stared at the grey concrete wall of the hotel room and the onion-honey-lemon concoction I had mixed together in a jar. Once the congestion let up, I sat at the open window, just intoxicated by the air and the morning sunlight. Without that painful night, this intoxicating moment would certainly not have been as great.

There have been some other interesting memory tricks. Yesterday when I was already getting sick, I headed for the store and suddenly discovered that I could still ask for everything I need in Spanish. *"Miel? Cebolla? Limon?"* If someone had asked me a week ago how to say "honey", "onion", or "lemon", in Spanish, I could not have answered.

Now I remember it all.

Toughening up on the other island

Nine years earlier. May 1999
Puerto del Rosario, Fuerteventura

So here I am! Sitting in one of the most beautiful places in this hemisphere, the Canary Islands – merely pronouncing these words evokes dreams, luxury, sunshine and joy. My Estonian friends are probably jealous, because they know I'm on a sun-filled trip in the south, where besides seeing the world and learning languages I'll even manage to make some money. At least that's what they think. If I described this cafe with bamboo walls and flower arrangements for them, their jealousy would probably not subside for some time.

Especially if I leave out the part about not having enough money for a cup of morning coffee, should the waitress ever come around. And I have no idea, how the hell I'm getting off this island. My bankcard is way out of reach, a boat ride away in Marco's hotel safety deposit box on Gran Canaria. Why didn't I take my card with me? Because I wanted to save that seemingly symbolic sum of money that was still left in the account... But why did I chase off this guy named Jonai? Now I'm all alone.

Two days ago, a boat brought me here to the island of Fuerteventura. One of our market colleagues told me that there was an international handcrafts fair going on here. I arrived on the first day, on a reconnaissance mission, and I was supposed to call Harri at Marco's hotel to let him know whether it would make sense for him to follow me or not.

However, I didn't start towards the port of Gran Canaria alone. At the last possible moment, a strange young man I had met a few days ago, and who had told Harri and I how to get to the neighbouring island, jumped on the bus. That's how come he also knew what bus I was planning on taking to the port.

"Hello! I'm coming to Fuerteventura too!" he said panting and crashed down in the seat next to mine. Before I could even express my surprise, it became even greater: a strange squeaking sound was coming from the young man's backpack.

"What…?"

"I found some kittens and bought a feeding bottle and milk for them," he explained in all seriousness and carefully pulled a week-old kitten out of his bag.

"The poor thing, its eyes aren't even open!"

"Yes, but they're not newborns, see, their eyes are about to open. By tomorrow they'll see the world."

"So how come you took them, where's their mother?"

"I'm sure their mother has died. I watched them for a while before taking them, went to peek at them every few hours and saw that they were squealing louder and louder."

And so we all rocked in the boat all the way to the new island: me, Jonai, the four kittens we fed from the bottle, and, of course, my big bag.

Why did he decide to come with me? He wasn't even trying to hit on me, at least not in the way the other locals did. This tall young man with brown, curly hair and strangely lit light green eyes bought a sandlewood necklace from me at the market – "It's really aromatic, especially if you heat it up a bit," I told him what Harri had taught me. The young man listened to what I was saying, paid, and then asked me for help with putting it on.

He bought it for himself? Funny, I thought that he was getting it for some woman, but why not for himself, sure, it really wasn't a very flashy necklace: just a string of small sandalwood beads. I fiddled with it and got it closed. Seeing and accidentally brushing the nape of someone's neck almost gives you a secret power over them. Maybe I accidentally enchanted him and that's why he came along with me? Or maybe he was just bored? He's been living on this island for his whole life and one day he meets someone, who just happens to be planning on going to the other island nearby?

"My ancestors, as far as back we know, are from right here, on Gran Canaria," he proudly tells me about his genealogy during the boat ride. "I'm a Guanche, do you know what that means?"

"Eh... so you're a real Guanche?" Harri had told me about them. Before the Spaniards and Arabs made it to the Canaries in the Middle Ages, a race of mystical origin, with light skin and blue-green eyes had inhabited the island.

"For us Guanches, genealogical research is very valuable and it's even been recommended for us to intermarry, just not too closely..." The strange young man bottle fed his kittens and talked about reproduction in the same skewed way I had gotten used to with Harri. All right, if you say you're a Guanche, then you're a Guanche! I wasn't going to tell him that, according to Harri's theory, the Guanches were actually Estonians who circled Europe during their Viking expeditions and found these great little islands off the coast of Africa, and that Estonians, in turn, were former gods who arrived in the Himalayas. I sighed and decided to give my head a rest from Harri's strange but captivating theories.

"I'll help you. Where do we need to go?" Jonai found the right bus near the harbor and brought me to the fairgrounds. He helped me find cardboard boxes and dragged them where I told him to.

I felt especially lousy, without any new reasons. Yes, of course it was complicated to sell illegally on a piece of cardboard you found next to a dumpster, while other salespeople had nice setups and numbered booths. But I should have already been used to the feeling!

The kittens were mewing. Jonai sat next to me and fed them one after another. I looked at the landscape stretching out behind us – yes, desert-covered Fuerteventura is closer to the African coast than my home island – and then looked at the fairgrounds once more, just to check. There were people there, but nobody came to us.

And then a policeman's light blue shirt appeared!

"Let's go!" I shouted to Jonai and pushed all my jewellery into the bag. "We can't sell here and I can't afford a fine!"

I felt such shame, as we speed walked out of there, to the tune of the kittens' mewling and under the policeman's dumbfounded stare. It must have been at that moment that I started to hate Jonai a little: yes, he wanted to help me, but I didn't need it and I didn't want him to witness my shame!

And when he pulled out a joint in that desert landscape and offered me some, that's when I said, "Listen, maybe it would be better if you left now!"

He followed me around for a few more hours before leaving, the smell of marihuana around him, the kittens still squeaking in his back-pack. And that was the last I saw of him. I don't know if he's still here on Fuerteventura, or if he's made it back to his home island already. I tried selling one more time last night, with no luck, spent the night under a bush, and now I'd love to get back to my island. If only I had the money.

Being without money makes me feel as if I were inferior to what I was before. I rub my face. Remember this feeling, girl! I tell myself. Even if you get off this island today, the same thing is waiting for you on the other one.

It's the feeling of walking for kilometres on end behind Harri to go sleep in the mountains because you don't have any money. Only a short time ago you were working as a white-collar journalist, you had the power and the glory. Now you're going to the last bar on the edge of town and asking, "Where are the toilets?" and pretending as if you're not bothered at all by the herd of dark-eyed men leering at you, dropping lewd comments in Spanish and cheesy compliments in English. You pretend as if it were also completely normal that you use a hotel bathroom to brush your teeth, but then leave without buying anything at the hotel cafe.

"This is my uncle," your introverted look should be telling them. "I'm actually from one of the richest and most dignified families in Estonia. This guy is our family's black sheep, but I decided to come on this trip with him for the experience!" After all, this is what you've fibbed to a lot of your colleagues at the market.

Sometimes there are luxury hotels on the periphery of the city. That's when you tell Harri: "Wait outside," and he gets a little mad, but still agrees. Then you pass the doorman with a bounce in your step and a movie star smile on your face. "Oh yeah, these dirty and ripped jeans, it's the latest fashion thing, and of course I'm staying at this hotel," is what your smile says. And you go to the bathroom with its shiny glazed tiles to look at yourself for a moment in the mirror.

Who are you? Where are you? What have you got yourself into? What's going to happen now?

And then you're in the mountains. A spider is climbing all over your face and you know for sure that during these past weeks you've changed, because you just calmly let it climb on. A strange apathy has started weaving its web inside of you. Why bother twitching? Why bother hoping? There's nothing you can do about it anyway.

This is what life is like today. It's the one you chose.

I run my fingers over the cafe's bamboo walls and stare out at the sea. On the other side of this paradise blue gulf is Gran Canaria. Who's waiting for me there? Just one angry man who looks like Jesus Christ gone wild, one eccentric sea captain, and one crazy world-travelling hippie chick. And actually I'm totally lost. I don't really know which direction is home. Just drifting.

I've toughened up. I spent last night in a sleeping bag in a copse of cacti, and I really slept. Even though I may have gone a bit too far with toughening up on more than one occasion on this trip and consequently caught several colds, I do feel myself getting more resilient with each passing day. I remember my colleagues from work, at the office. The comfortable, pleasantly scented and safe sterility, pretty things, a clean, dry and predictable world. "Like abroad," is what that lifestyle was called in the Soviet era when I was little.

The real abroad, though, has now turned me into a girl who can carry twenty-plus-kilos of baggage around daily without a problem, find a place to sleep outdoors, can sleep on the floor, wash under a cold shower on the beach and drown all of the available sugar in coffee when at cafes, to get the extra free calories...

When it comes to money, I've become used to taking it one day at a time: if there's enough to pay for a room and buy some milk, bread and an avocado, I don't have to worry. Oh, how long has it been since I've thought in terms of "payday" and "x amount of money in my account"?

How incomparably different is this life from the one I led in Estonia. Sometimes, for example, when writing e-mails back home, I get images of my former life. I wake up in the morning, walk to the car, drive to work, discuss the current news and gossip with the ladies at work, have some coffee, make a few calls, go to lunch, maybe shopping, chat with the ladies some more, check my e-mails... The day goes by to the tune of the steady hum of computers and air conditioners and then it's done. On the way home I pass by the store, buy some food, watch TV for an hour, and then it is time to go to sleep. And then you wake up in the morning astonished: is this it?

Yes, it is.

A comfortable circuit, everything is predictable. Choices are made on a simple level: should I move to the competing magazine or not, should I go to the countryside for the weekend or not, should I buy a new washing machine or not?

However, the nauseating choices I have now could very well belong on the pages of some romance novel that I'd read on Sundays while lounging in a hammock and thinking, "Hah! Boy, is this story line over the top! Who's stupid enough to believe in some crazy hippie's promises? And once she's already there, why should she stick with him? They're not engaged or anything! Why doesn't she just take off on her own and start a new job?"

Yeah, why not?

I stare at the sea, thinking.

Why won't that girl leave the old hippie?

I suppose I'm somewhat dependent on Harri's stories and his unique charisma. I can't stand him for too much at a time, but there's no denying the fact that the daily doses of his life's story and apocalyptic tales have captivated me. I can't give him up.

There's another reason. I think I like feeling what the world is like if you quite literally don't have any money. After all, there must be things I've come to understand better by sleeping under bushes.

How much did I take for granted in that white-collar life six months, or a year ago? Hairdresser. Cosmetician. Manicure. Depilation. Slimmer. Anti-cellulite treatments. A part of me is longing to get back to those safe pleasures: laying there, the masseuse's hands manipulating your body, while you just remain there, enjoying the expensive procedure that you can afford.

But then I remember that hollow feeling that overcame me in the midst of all those procedures. Is this life? Why did it seem to me that my life was slipping away somewhere and hiding its real significance farther and farther away from me? In that women's magazine factory, finding happiness was done according to a certain set of ways. One of those ways, for example, was the slimmer – a machine that showered your stomach with electric shocks, creating minispasms and involuntarily making the muscles work. Another way was called the tanning bed – a machine that covered you with a growl and taught you a new kind of trust. How are you supposed to get out of there? What happens, if the electricity goes out? I would lay there frying and worrying. I didn't know how to enjoy spending money on my body, because my body never became ideal. I wasn't perfectly beautiful and definitely not perfectly happy, just throwing a lot of cash into the wind trying out those happiness machines.

I knew instinctively that one way to understand the real meaning of life was to let out some of the biological pressure that was building inside. I needed to become a mother. I even sewed baby clothes, just in case, but the one thing that wouldn't show up was an extra line on the pregnancy test. I went to regular doctors and witch doctors, bought a fig tree for my house because it's supposed to increase fertility, made a fig and vodka concoction for myself and my husband. But still, nothing. Life remained empty. Luckily I could go to a restaurant, go to the movies or get a manicure. Or just go to work... I think I came on this trip also to get out of that nightmarish circle.

May 1999

In its own way, my new life has become a new nightmare. The days are becoming a soggy, soupy mess, filled with resort pleasures, an uncertainty that the multitude of choices brings, and inferiority complexes due to unsuccessful sales... And the Spanish lifestyle, of course, is to let the days just roll along and develop on their own. None of the days have gone the way I planned them the night before. This is something painful for a person who's used to planning, it requires adapting... But I don't regret a single thing.

I see myself in a dream. It's an image of the future, of a woman: she's quite similar to her older friend Djellah, but she's taken her best experiences and learned from her mistakes.

She's freckled, her hair tousled, in jeans and a blue and white striped sailor's shirt that is slightly worn at the elbows. She's on the water, in a boat, heading somewhere. Make up? Cellulite? Career? If you ask her about all that, she'll nod. Yes, she remembers the years when she worked as a a chick in the women's magazines, even though those years are becoming more and more obscure in her memories and are at best just a good, compact background story for a future novel. From time to time, she'll run down to a small table down in her cabin, pull out a notebook from the drawer and write something down. Her skin is more inured and the corners of her eyes boast of stronger tan-smile-lines-crow's feet than her former university mates, who still work in a sterile office and pay their weekly dues to the cosmetic industry. The soles of her feet are black like soot!

But she is happy, because she's living life to the fullest.

Does she have a man in her life?

Yes. This is something she's learned from Djellah's experience. She has a man. He's not ideal and he's not the perfect man, but our main character has learned that happiness is first and foremost inside one's self, so her man's faults are just an accepted and appreciated part of the package. Thanks to that, the acceptance and appreciation is reciprocated from the other side as well.

Do they have children?

This is where I lose my train of thought. The souls of children need space to move. They have to be enticed to come, like backyard hedgehogs with milk in the fall: you put out the bait and just keep going as if you weren't even thinking about them anymore.

"I let the world go free!" I remember Djellah's shout.

I fish out a pen.

"One pulsating planet and a small, two-chambered heart," is the short sentence I write in my notebook. I know that later on it will remind me of all the important things I have thought about today. Slapping the journal shut, I stand up. After all, I have to go sell things in order to make some money so I can somehow make it back to Gran Canaria.

The decision to go back

Ten years later. January 2009
Tallinn, Estonia

I'm sitting in front of the computer screen and fiddling with last-minute offers to the Canaries, as I tend to do a few times every year. After the trip to Barcelona last spring, I know that there are things inside of me that can be activated. I once came through a very intense period of life and these memories and experiences are still inside of me, locked up in a drawer, but at least they are still there.

I wanted to go back already in the fall of 1999 after returning to Estonia, to reclaim my bag and my memories, to see Marco and the other locals again. I even looked up ticket prices – but didn't make that last click of confirmation. Instead, I went on a long trip with my husband Tom, a new escape attempt that turned out to be embarrassing and morally instructive. I've seriously considered returning to Gran Canaria about five or six times over these past ten years, but each time I put it off.

Every time I click on those travel offers, I return to my memories. Once more I see those mountainous landscapes, remember exactly the people and the street corners. I even remember the times and the locations of the big markets. I remember quite a few of the faces of my colleagues, who'd sell in a new place each day. Ten years is a long time, but it's also quite short. Will any of them remember me? Remember a blond girl, who sold Indian and Indonesian jewellery with an old man who looked like Jesus? And how that girl was constantly writing something in her notebook, whenever she had the opportunity.

What did she write? Something like this, for example: "I was playing on the beach with the children of the boat dwellers, they're incredibly alert. In his five short years, this little one has lived on three continents and speaks three languages. This is something I need to think about. Do children like these need a regular, traditional education? Do they have to become anchors for their parents' lifestyle, or are there other solutions?"

Or this: "A traveller named Javier lives in the hotel room next to mine. We went out for tea, and the talk somehow got very personal. I told him that I'd had no luck becoming a mother and he, in turn, confessed that he once had a baby with a woman, but then they separated and she wouldn't let him see the child anymore. It pained him so much, that after long weeks of deliberation, he went to a clinic and got a vasectomy. He doesn't want any more children. "Do you regret your decision?" I asked and he replied, "No." But I didn't believe him. Can any sort of tampering with nature make a person happier? Can letting go of pain before it even happens lead to bliss?"

Or this: "At the market I was talking to Christian, a German traveller. He was very much in love and expecting his girlfriend, who was supposed to arrive in a few days. He asked, "Tell me, have you ever really been in love in your life? Do you understand the profoundest meaning of 'falling in love', when you're deep in a hole and there's no way to get out, but you don't even want to?" I thought about that and remembered an old cliché that I could never understand: "Freedom is perceived inevitability." Is love that same kind of perceived inevitability? Have I ever been down in that hole? Or not yet?

These kinds of meetings and horizon-widening questions were something I encountered daily on that trip, sometimes even on an hourly basis. These recollections, however, have been written down in hindsight, after I left the Canaries and I realized that my old journals, with all the exact descriptions of the people and the places... stayed behind there, waiting for me.

Sometimes a strange curiosity grips me, a wish to return to the places I have been, to reanimate the past and catch a reflection of old relationships.

Harri's been in my dreams sometimes, maybe you could even say often. One dream definitely recurs: Harri's running in the mountains and I'm following him. Something terrible has happened in the world, it's either a climate catastrophe or a nuclear war. I don't know. Sadness intermingles with excitement, there's the acknowledgment of the inescapable nature of the event and a sense of happiness to have survived. From dream to dream, I try to keep up with Harri, but an eerie sensation comes over me at some point: what now? Do I really have to blindly follow him? I squat down between cacti somewhere in the mountains. I think. I look down the mountain and wait. Is he even going to look back and notice that I'm not there anymore?

At some point I realize that he's not coming back. I'm all alone now. The panic starts to subside and I thank the world again that I'm still here, even if it is alone. That's when I wake up and know that I've had that "Harri dream" again.

Maybe he's haunting my dreams because we never properly got to say goodbye?

The same way I didn't say goodbye to Marco. I dream about him every now and then as well. These dreams are nightmarishly confusing and usually he's running late or forgetting something. "Do you still have my bag?" I sometimes ask him in those dreams. Sometimes I see that moment again, how I waited for him until the last moment of the last day, and then just ran off to catch the bus.

My gaze returns to the computer screen. I click on.

"Confirm your purchase."

The unfinished story

Two weeks later. February 2009
Maspalomas, Gran Canaria

Crickets are singing all around as I sit in the dark, warm night, in front of our bungalow. My family sleeps behind these walls. I try to calm down, but the volcano I reactivated by returning to this island has begun to stir.

Today I was brought back together with two men who played an important part in my fate ten years ago, two people with whom it seems I share some kind of karmic connection.

Marco and Harri were both important for me, but in completely different ways. Today, however, they're in exactly the same position for me: they're mirrors reflecting back an image of myself from ten years ago.

Harri's mirror reflects an adventurous, curious student, but what about Marco's?

I jump up and walk between the bungalows. The thing I realize now, ten years older and wiser, is a slight shock for me. That whole time I had been focusing on one guilt and one sin: what I did to my husband Tom back then. But the way I wouldn't let Marco close to me, how I wouldn't trust him, how I left him here to wait. That sin is probably just as big.

Now I'm a full-figured mother of two, seemingly mature and balanced, with the beginnings of a double chin and a soft belly. Ten years ago I looked like an angel: blond, with a taut body and a gorgeous smile unframed by the signs life leaves behind. But on the inside I was a sick egomaniac, who only acted on her own impulses and wasn't capable of loving anyone else. Why? I don't know. I just wasn't equipped with that simple ability. It wasn't until later, while living in an ashram in India that I found out what love means. Ten years ago on the Canaries, all I knew was how to do was escape, seek, fantasize, sympathize, listen ardently to people and their stories and write them down. But loving? That was something I didn't know how to do.

What would life have been like with my first husband if I'd had that simple ability back then?

Or: what would my life have been like with Marco?

Marco.

He was the man a psychic predicted for me, at least that's what I decided back then. In that week in the winter of 1999, I went to see a psychic before leaving Estonia. It was just a few hours before I bought the tickets to Israel that Harri was urging me to get.

The imposingly large woman, with a dark, ominously bottomless stare, laid the cards out for me and peered at me through half-closed eyes as she told me,

"You're going to leave the man you're with now, unless you succeed in dragging him along to reach the next level. If you don't succeed in getting him to come along, you'll completely lose the lifestyle you've led until now, and the rest of your life will be spent searching, moving, on wheels, on waves, in flight. Your new partner will be connected to water in some way, you're going to see water from your bedroom. He's much older than you and has two daughters your age..."

Why did I go see that witch? I suppose it was to find something to grasp onto in this befuddling world, and – in the long term – to learn my lesson.

For some reason, I read the prediction to mean that the trip and the stormy life that followed were all meant to be for me – after all, she said that I would lose my homeland and my husband, if I didn't manage to drag him along, and I couldn't do it, so that was clear enough! And, of course, the whole time travelling through Israel, Cyprus, Greece, Italy and Spain, in my heart I was waiting: where is that man of the water older than me and with two daughters my age? Where are those bedroom windows to the sea?

When I met Marco – a former sea captain, divorced with two daughters – I knew instantly. Not just because of the demographic data that matched (for some reason that information came out immediately, in our first conversation at the hotel reception), and not only because of the view in the hotel room to which he led me. It was his scent, his way of speaking, the look in his eyes, something so exotic, yet it felt so much like home.

And then what?

This wasn't a fate I desired. I could have stayed on this island forever, but back then I thought, in many ways due to the influence of Djellah and Harri, that Marco was not serious about me. Now I understand that the mantra "he's not serious about me" was just a form of self-defence. It allowed me to not notice my own cruelty. I didn't even leave Marco a note with my coordinates, because I was so upset about him being late to our last date before my departure! I just left my bag at the store with Jorge, asked him to tell Marco that, see, Epa waited for you here for two hours, but you were late again, so *adios, amigo!*[*]

I understand now that it's hard to come up with something that could be crueler. He was just a simple middle-aged man, who, first of all, probably couldn't even remember the complicated last name I had back then and, second of all, didn't know how to use the Internet. How was he supposed to find me again? At that moment, when I was so insulted that he was late, running to catch the bus to the airport, I didn't even know that in the frenzy and confusion of packing I had left my journals, my notebooks and my phonebook in that bag. I thought that if the mood struck me, I could just open that phonebook and call. That was a luxury I was not to have, but I do know that if I'd made any effort at all, I could have gotten the contacts information to his hotel or the supermarket easily. He was findable for me, however, for him I probably did just disappear into the thin air.

---

[*]   "Goodbye, friend!" in Spanish.

And so he stayed behind to wait for me, with my bag as ransom. Interestingly enough, the whole situation seemed totally normal for me – I was going back to my husband and somewhere on an island there's an old captain, who is probably going to wait until I decide to show up again. In the end, I hurt them both and paid for it dearly.

I am walking through the southern night, feeling the scent of the island, its energy. The island is bombarding me with memories. Little flashes of images, in some I see myself through the eyes of a stranger, in others it's that old world through my own eyes.

How Marco would shout in his loud captain's voice, for the whole street in front of the hotel to hear, "Epa! *Donde estas?**" and how he kept trying to only speak Spanish with me, so that I could learn it faster – "The first two months are difficult, but in a year you'll be fluent!"

Or how I went with him that first night to his house in the mountains, because he had to fix a pipe there and then the plan was to take me out with his friends on that Friday night. We had met at the reception desk that same day and he'd been a little awkward asking me what I was planning for the evening – "I could come out with you, for example," I snapped back and we both started to laugh. And how I looked at his body, leaned over to work on the pipes, the nape of his neck, and finally understood that "this is my fate!" How that scared me and how I ran away, down the mountains to the big road and towards the sea, finally out of breath and realizing that I had no idea where to go from there. How I turned around and walked back. "Crazy girl!" he laughed, still working on those pipes. "Where did you rush off to? Hold on a minute, I'll just finish this and drop you off downtown, or wherever you want to go!" And that was the first night I stayed at the villa. We never made it down into the town.

Or how a few days later I made my own creation of mashed potatos with avocado for his visiting friends and got high praise for it from his friend Giorgio's wife Isabela, "This girl has style, she knows how to mix tastes!"

Or how Marco and that same Giorgio and I used to go to a Cuban salsa club on Fridays to dance and have dinner one or two hours after

---

*   "Where are you?" in Spanish.

midnight, as is the custom around here on weekends. How I learned to curse in Spanish and add "*conyo!**" to the beginning and end of each sentence like a Canarian, making the men tear up in laughter. "Epa, you've become a Canarian, keep talking like this and you can never leave this island!"

How I learned to love this island that lives its own life despite the tourists. How Marco took me to a commune of hippies living at an old banana plantation. Or how we walked around in the mountains somewhere in the middle of the island, where most tourists will never make the effort to come, because all they want is a market, some sand, palm trees and the sea.

But there are darker flashes as well, from this same island. The time I was so broke that I'd stay overnight at Marco's villa just so I could shovel in as many free calories as possible for breakfast. How I was too ashamed to tell him that I couldn't afford a room at his hotel at the moment – I couldn't pay for it, but I was too afraid to ask for a free one. He was probably also afraid to offer me one, proud and peculiar as I was. That's how come often times I just made him think I was off to another town and another hotel, while in reality I was sleeping outdoors in the mountains with Harri...

And how I was chased away from the markets and how Harri would get upset with me because I couldn't sell anywhere.

The main topic of our fights with Harri was, of course, Marco.

"I am responsible for you! Your husband put you in my care!" he screamed in his high-pitched voice in Estonian, right there in front of the hotel that belonged to Marco, after I had admitted to him where this trip had led me.

"Nobody has put me in anyone's care," I hissed back. "My marital crisis is my own personal matter! You have no idea what the emptiness is like inside of me when I call my husband in Estonia, you can't see into my heart!"

"What are you getting so dramatic about now? Why didn't you just find a new and better man? What are you messing around with this Marco for!"

"It's my choice!"

---

*   Cursing in Spanish, but a regular filler in Gran Canaria.

"That damn Marco doesn't deserve you! He's just using you! I'm so disappointed in you for wasting your genes like this! First of all, you should have chosen a man with good genes. Secondly, he should have been an Estonian! And have you told Marco that you're still married to a man in Estonia?"

"Yes! Marco is divorced too and doesn't care that I'm still married!"

"That's because he doesn't really care about you! That's what it is!"

"It's none of your business, that's what it is!"

"And have you told your husband in Estonia that..."

That's the point at which I ran away, up to my hotel room. No, I hadn't told a thing to Tom, who was waiting for me in Estonia. But I was planning on doing it tomorrow, first thing in the morning, *mañana por la mañana*, as the locals said.

Harri wanted to fire me, but we were bound to each other: by that time I owed him quite a lot, because I spent all the money that I made, while in actuality only ten percent of it belonged to me. At that point we were also still waiting for our ship to come in, the one that would bring us containers from Hawaii, from Frank the promise master, "And see that's when we'll really get to selling, that's when we'll make a profit!" Harri kept predicting.

"Leave that crazy old man, so what if he's your uncle! Quit that useless illegal loitering in the markets," Marco would try to convince me. I was waiting for him to finish the thought. Would he ask how much money I owed Harri by now? Would he offer me anything else in place of the market sales career: love, his heart, his hand, or at least a stable place to sleep or work? No, none of that. I did clean his mountain villa every week and he'd give me money for it, looking aside as he handed it over ("Umm... I'd give this money to a housekeeper, but she doesn't need to come, since you've done such a great job here yourself!"), but our strange love affair never made it to a more steady track. Or perhaps was it that I didn't know how to read him, didn't know how to be more self-confident and assertive?

Where did that invisible line pass that prevented the psychic's prediction from coming true? Was it the day that I agreed to Harri's plan to buy tickets and fly back to Cyprus and Israel, instead of staying on the island? Or was it the following week: on our day of departure, when Marco was late and I had to run to catch the bus to the airport without seeing him, with Harri's angry screaming voice calling out, "We're going to miss the bus!"

As the plane took off, I could hear my heart beating. At that moment, I was probably flying in two parallel dimensions: I had taken a new direction in space, as well as fate.

From then on, I lived as best I could, blocking out all thoughts of Marco as well as the bag that was left there to wait for me.

When there's no one to blame

A day earlier. February 2009
Arguineguin, Gran Canaria

I'm sitting in front of my one time favourite eatery – it's the Italian style pizza place in my former "hometown" of Arguineguin. When I had money, I came here to eat. When there was none, I'd just enjoy the smells and sit here on the stone wall, writing... Now my family is there enjoying their pizzas, while I said that I need to meet the past and went to call Marco.

I lean against the stone wall and look at his little shop and hotel. That could have been my home too. "Yes, Epa, I'll be there in three minutes, wait for me in front of the pizzeria," he told me over the phone in his commanding captain's voice.

So this is where I'm sitting, writing down questions I'd like answers for, just to pass time. Did you take me seriously back then? Maybe you know where my bag is? Do you have a new woman? Have you forgotten me? Are you happy? How is your mother? What kind of cancer took Djellah? Do you know where is her grave?...

Three minutes become ten and then fifteen.

I'm reminded of how that typical conflict between a northerner and a southerner used to drive me up the wall: how we could never set a time to meet, because he would always be late and the times of his promised arrival all had to be multiplied by ten, in order for me to have some idea of when he was actually getting there.

He's not perfect. It's just that there's something in this subtropical air that we have yet to finish and it needs to be concluded today. What remains is my guilt over leaving without saying goodbye, maybe also his guilt for letting me go. We have to forgive each other as well as ourselves.

All right. Another half an hour has passed now and the tragedy has become a farce, as I'm still sitting here and waiting. Bloody Spaniard! to use Harri's expression. History repeats itself: this is exactly why Marco and I didn't meet that last time, because he showed up several hours late, true to his style.

Ok. Calm down. I'm sitting here in front of my favourite pizza place, in my favourite little town, on my favourite island. My family is below in the cafe, enjoying their lunch and I'm waiting for a former lover who doesn't know how to tell time. Why not just make the best of this situation. Why not look back to the past.

Right here next to me there are those cliffs where I once photographed Djellah for the magazine.

"Do you know," she informed me, "that at a certain age you shouldn't photograph a woman's face too close up. You go up on that cliff and I'll stand below, right here... When you're my age, you'll want people to take pictures of you from above too!" Her voice was so raspy that if I hadn't known her, I would have thought that she was angry with me.

Right here on these cliffs is where I had my first glimpse of the timeshare sellers' subculture. There was a redheaded young man from Holland, who was probably trying to either get it on with me, or just prove to himself that his life was all right after all.

"I'm not an addict, I just use occasionally," he said and offered me a joint. I refused, because I had never tried anything like that and I was more and more happy with the "clean life" that Harri was preaching. There wasn't any room for intoxicating substances, so I'd even given up drinking wine with Djellah lately.

"Sure you don't want any?" The redheaded Dutchman puffed away right here on the cliff by the sea and told me about his work. "It's very simple, we just have to sell lottery tickets on the streets or play an egg hunt in the sand. The kids love that... And each ticket and each egg is, of course, a winner!"

"And then what?"

"Then I send them to a reception area, where other people take over, my colleagues. I've done that job too. Basically, you just have to get them to sign a contract that they'll take a room in the hotel complex for a week or two out of the year. And they'll get to use it for the rest of their lives."

"Oh really?" I vaguely remember hearing something about this.

"Yes, it's totally legal and a very common deal, we've got nothing to be ashamed of. You just have to convince people that living here is so great that they'll want to come back every year and get them to fork over a ton of cash all at once. I think that you'd be great at this job. You know how to influence people and you look all warm and fuzzy and trustworthy!"

That Dutch guy was definitely not the last timeshare sales person I met here and certainly not the last one to invite me to work there. "Why are you selling at the market for next to nothing?" a young British guy told me, walking past me once at the market. "With your appearance, English language and sales skills, we could really use you and you could make lots, I mean, lots of money! These shares are not hard to sell at all. We're all dedicated to just one step of the process. For example, I deal with the people who have already made it to the presentation. And it is so easy to talk them into the next step: what we have here is so cool, this paradise island, it speaks for itself! And when you get tired of living here, we have a whole network. You could go somewhere else in the world to sell timeshares."

I tried to imagine it: I suppose there is a certain excitement to the work. A community of international young people, who apparently had their own parties every week, their own rooms right here at the giant island paradise hotel that they were selling shares for, and after all, the work wasn't so bad, so why couldn't I just sell hotel rooms instead of jewellery?

"Epp, I just wanted to warn you, don't go work there!" I was told by the owner of the Internet café: blond, blue-eyed Norwegian guy, Djellah's fake-groom, whose name I have forgotten, but whose deliberately and passionately presented warning may have changed the course of my life.

He had heard through Djellah that I was considering taking the job. "You know what, it's hard to explain, but – people change when they start selling hotel shares. Even the most wonderful and normal people somehow get twisted. I've seen it so many times here." Djellah and Marco were just as skeptical – you could sense that for these native islanders, the hotel share sales people were considered to be outcasts, people who sell pipe dreams.

"But they're just doing their jobs too," I tried to argue.

"Yes, they are," Djellah replied, "but I'm sure that they know that what they're selling isn't necessarily what people end up getting." When I mentioned the timeshare salespeople to Harri, he was instantly irritated and started cursing them, "They're just catching gullible people here on the streets and beaches – a person will pay the money and then all of a sudden their bank accounts will start dwindling! Whether it's renovations at the hotel or maintenance costs and in the end they won't even be able to choose the two weeks themselves! I've heard people bitching and moaning about how they won't be able to vacation anywhere else in the world, it's like they're forced to stay here!"

After all these accounts and opinions, I still decided to go to a time-share sellers' party at Amfi del Mari, a castle-like hotel complex, just to get a closer look at that crowd.

Amfi del Mar was – and, of course, still is – immensely large, built of huge cobblestones, right here near Arguineguin. It's basically a small town in and of itself, with its own shops, cafes and restaurants, surrounded by magnificent cactus hedges and a warm private bay. The salespeople themselves lived in the same complex and, of course, were selling timeshares to that same little wonder-town.

There was a little island off the bay, as I recall, and that's where the party was held. In the middle of the day, with the sun almost at its zenith, it was strange to see the crowd of jovial, intoxicated people dancing to blaring techno music. Shouldn't these kinds of parties happen at least at dusk or when it's dark already? I sat there awkwardly and held the glass of punch I was given, not that I wanted any. Yes, they say that a sober person can also, so to say, "let loose" among a pack of inebriated partygoers, but for some reason I just couldn't. I looked at the tanned bodies writhing around me to the beat of the music and felt that I just didn't belong here – so why would I even pretend to "let loose"?

"You wanna come powder your nose?" a blond girl called out to me. I can remember neither her name nor her nationality, but with that question she left a strong impression in my life.

"What?"

"Do you powder your nose?" She swiped two fingers across her nostril. At that moment I did get it: she was talking about cocaine. With cramped smile on my face, I shook my head, and finally did let loose, which in my case meant leaving.

Every so often I raise my head and take a look around. No. Still no Marco. Three minutes have become forty-five already. Was freeing myself of illusions the ultimate reason I had to come here?

But some illusions are still there. The images are running through my head. Our bodies in his mountain abode, in a bed next to an opened window, covered with a fine layer of sand by morning, because a sandstorm or a *calima*, as they called it here, swept over the mountains overnight. Us, at home, sitting and eating a breakfast of *gofio* – that local, bitter-tasting flour made of roasted corn, mixed with sweet condensed milk and hot water. I've forgotten that taste over these ten years. Or another morning, when he's dropping me off at the market gates and I see that the police are on the move, so we sit at the market cafe and eat *churros con chocolate*, a local cafe-breakfast, long pastries that have to be soaked in hot chocolate before eating.

"Crazy girl," Marco shakes his head, criticizing my readiness to go sell on the market as soon as I see the police car pull away.

"I don't want to leave things I've started unfinished," is how I try to explain it to him. "And I don't want to break promises I've given. I promised Harri that I'd help him sell that jewellery over here!" I can't even begin to tell him or myself, for that matter, what binds me to Harri. Is it the need to hear the rest of that life's story that Harri tells me when we have down time: the one that leads him from one continent to another, one sharp turn in life to the next one... Marco's life's story, after all, is just as interesting. As the captain of a ship, he also lived his life from one continent to the other. There are falls along his path as well, when he invested most of his captain's salary in a plantation in Ghana, only to lose millions after the *coup d'état*.

But the way Marco told his stories was somehow reluctant and uncomfortable, they just didn't sound as interesting, as I recall, still sitting in front of the pizzeria, looking towards his hotel and letting the past carry me away. Marco was a simple man, who lived without much talking, so he was never as much of an inspiration and enigma for me as Harri was. He just felt very familiar, he was my "possible present and potential future" – the kind of person whose scent lets you know that this is a person to grow old with. Something akin to what I've felt with my first and now, of course, my second husband...

It's strange to sit here and line up men like that. But it's not bad for passing time and when you've made arrangements with a Spaniard, what else are you going to do but try to have a little fun to make time pass faster?

Then I see him. He's approaching with a small, scruffy dog bouncing along on a leash. Finally. He's the same as he was ten years ago, a straight posture and a sharp stare, except there's a hint of grey in his black hair.

"Epa!" he gives me one, two, three neutral kisses on the cheeks. Just like a relative from far away. I recognize his smell.

"Well, Marco, where were you! Three minutes, Marco, three minutes!" All of a sudden I'm gesturing like a local, I laugh nervously and he laughs back.

"I'm sorry, I couldn't get away sooner! My woman is so jealous! She won't let me out of the house alone! Finally, I took the dog and came out with him to take a little walk!"

"You have a wife?"

"Well, a girlfriend, a Romanian, Gabriela," he speaks in his usual choppy way. "We've been living together for three years, moved to the top floor of this hotel after my mother died. Gabriela wants to have a baby, but I don't think I do, I don't trust women... Where did you disappear to, Epa? You were never jealous! Did you even care about me, huh?"

These phrases are all spoken in a light manner, not really demanding an immediate answer, but still...

"Did you even care about me?" I throw his question back.

"But of course!" He lands his fist on his chest with a thud. Well, yeah, a Spanish man's word of honor in love... There's too much of that northerner in me, each of his movements and statements first make me laugh for a brief instant, even though I'm not really in a joking mood.

"Marco, but what's the matter with your heart?"

"The doctors are analyzing it... *Los problemas*, that's what they say. My heart hurts. My father was already dead by the time he reached my age. I'm fifty six now already!"

"Your father died of a heart disease? I didn't remember that."

"The heart, yes."

We walk down to the sea and talk. Now I'm the one who's letting my people down, sending Justin a message saying "ten more minutes", while it stretches on into another half an hour.

"Tell me, Marco. Did you call me *la rusa** behind my back when I was here? Djellah once told me that. She warned me about you. For some reason, I didn't make a scene about it back then, but it really did get to me. Do you remember?"

"Yes, of course I remember, I did call you that! How could you think I wouldn't remember? I remember everything!"

"But why *la rusa*?"

"What of it? You were the one who told me your grandfather was Russian. I was just proud that I had a half Russian girlfriend... or whatever you were to me!"

He looks at me, standing with his feet apart in his captain's stance, hands folded on his chest, a pained stubbornness in his eyes. So that's what he's like. I didn't even remember that he had silver fillings at the ends of his front teeth. He's actually not such an attractive man. But there's something very, very familiar about him.

Maybe he really did care about me much more than I realized?

Maybe I was the one who was disconnected and easily manipulated by others, the scatterbrain who couldn't see what was what: were he got *la rusa* from (indeed, my great grandfather really was Russian!) and why didn't I think to tell Djellah that? Would she have accepted my choice more then? Or was she trying to plant inside me that same seed of disappointment in men that she was nurturing in herself?

"You were just so damn independent," Marco says. "You never did anything I suggested for you. You were just as stubborn and crazy as Djellah, and you're the one who ran away."

---

*   "The Russian" in Spanish.

"Yes, Marco. I regret disappearing like that; I've matured a lot during my life and learned how not to hurt people. Back then I didn't know how to trust or care for people."

"You wouldn't let anyone give you money, you acted like a... I didn't know who you were to me. Gabriela is crazy and jealous, but you know what, she moved in with me like it was just the most obvious thing to do, can you imagine! There was something wrong with you in that sense, or maybe you didn't want me...?"

"I was stupid and proud! I couldn't ask you to buy my freedom from Harri, I owed him so much money! I couldn't tell my ex-husband either. I just kept struggling all alone..."

"I thought about you a lot after you left. Every day, all the time I thought about you! I asked myself whether Epa was still alive and whether she finally had a *bambino**. I couldn't forget how you were worried about that. I was so happy, when Jorge told me yesterday that you even have two blond *bambinas* now, like angels! And you have a husband who's darker than you, yes? I wonder if you would have had blond *bambinas* with me too, Epa?"

My voice breaks a little, as I try to leave the slippery ground of emotions and get to the most important topic of all.

"Listen, Marco, but tell me, where is my bag? Harri told me you still have it."

"Harri told you...?"

"Yes, he's selling right here, almost around the corner, in Puerto Rico! I found him yesterday!"

"Oh really... Well yes, that's where he was for a while, but I thought that he was gone now... Epa, I waited for you for seven years. But then I started renovating the hotel and I felt that I needed to let you go. I kept one item of clothing, umm... bikinis... from that bag, as a souvenir."

"My bikinis? But did you see the journals in there? My journals? The blood of my heart?"

I remember how he liked the way I was so dramatic, like a Spanish woman. It still seems to me that I have

---

*   "A baby" in Spanish.

to earn those journals on this island somehow: talk, perform, plead, gesture, as long as I need to get them back.

Marco sighs. "Epa, if those journals were so important to you, why did you just leave them here like that?"

"It was an accident... I was crying that morning when I was packing and I mixed up the bags. I didn't notice that I'd left them here with you until I was unpacking on Cyprus."

"And then?"

"I'm not normal! Who else would leave a bag here with such important things alone for ten years?"

Marco sighs again. "Well... so after I had waited for you for seven years, Harri came into my store, three years ago. He still came around, at least once every winter. Every time I asked him if he had heard anything about Epa and he answered that he hadn't and that he's not in Estonia that much anyway. Tell me, Epa, how come you never called me?"

"My phone book with all my numbers was in that bag too, by accident," I admit, "and I think I blocked you out, tried to go on with my life. First with my old husband we ended up in new crises, and then my new life came on like an avalanche, I travelled around the world so much, one country after another... And I really have a hard time putting time in perspective, it's really unbelievable for me too that I let ten years pass by somehow! But listen, last year I did look up the hotel's phone number online and called, several times. I kept getting the answering machine."

"Yes, I was living with Gabriela by then. She was really angry when she heard your messages and asked me what bag, Marco, what girl, what bag? I just couldn't call you back."

Something in the way Marco is talking is making me wonder if Gabriela had something to do with my bag...

But before this thought can develop further, Marco starts cursing Harri.

"And can you imagine, he picked up the bag and said that this time he's flying to Estonia with next to nothing and can drop it off for you. Why doesn't he want to admit this now? And what has he done with your bag? I really don't know!"

"You are never going to know which one of them is lying," Justin says after hearing my story. "You're just going to have to let it go!"

We're in a bus bounding back towards our bungalow, the kids squealing in our laps, and I'm looking for a place to fix my eyes on, be it the mountains, the sea, or the sky. It's so beautiful here. Why worry about an old bag and three notebooks?

There have been other instances in my life, when there's no use in looking for someone to blame. Why did my father's home burn down and why did I have to lose all my childhood photographs and writings in the fire? Why did someone break into my house and steal the computer that held my first attempt at writing a novel? Why did my mother have to get sick and die?

Now that list also includes the lost journals. It's just something in the past and the time has come for it all to move along.

But for now, I can still vividly picture it: how the pages filled with my small handwriting are gathering mould somewhere around here in a landfill and waiting for me. There would still be time to read them, before they turn into soil that covers this ground.

Does history repeat itself?

Two days later. February 2009
The dunes at Maspalomas, Gran Canaria

I'm lying on the ground, the morning sun stinging and caressing me, I can almost feel vitamin D being generated under my skin. I'm completely naked, half-sleeping and meditating in the sun, trying to let go of those damn journals. I guess either Harri or Marco threw them away three years ago, but it feels like I lost them yesterday.

We're at the southern end of Gran Canaria today with the family, at a nudist beach, which here means that you just find a free spot to lie between the dunes, where nobody can even see you. The dunes are sprawled out on the ground like a giant woman, with a tiny ant of a man or even a whole colony buried in a secluded zone between each fold of her skin. That time ten years ago, Marco and I took a walk here along the sea. We strolled through the nudist beach to the nudist gay beach and after a few more kilometres we arrived at the so-called "public sex beach", where the unwritten law said that anything goes, the kind of place where "exhibitionists and voyeurs" meet, as Marco succinctly put it. I just wanted to leave as fast as possible, before I could see anything. I remember the emptiness that scraped at my soul that day.

Already years ago I had a feeling about what would make me happy and I was right: children. Djellah never got to experience it and in a way it's probably for the best that we didn't meet again. Seeing me and my happiness with children would probably have been painful for her.

I'm sun-dazed and on my back now, running my hand through the hot grains of sand and listening to the musings of our five year old Marta, "If I counted up all the grains of sand on this hill I'd be a hundred years old already..." In the meantime, eighteen month old Anna brings us enthusiastically some sand from the other side of the dune. "Bring some more!" I ask, and off she goes again.

"Mommy, come run with me!" Marta jumps up and starts climbing up the sandy slope. For the first time, I notice how feminine and beautiful my five-year-old daughter has become. She's like a young gazelle.

She runs up the hill, out of our sight.

"Mommy! New sand!" little Anna arrives again. Looking around for Marta, though, I get a shock. She's still not back.

I stand up and stagger up the hill through the soft sand.

Even there I can't spy my five-year-old beauty anywhere, as far as the eye can see. By then Justin has also gotten up and we're shouting and looking for our girl.

Suddenly, far off, at the other end of the sandy plain, we notice a naked man shouting and pointing at something.

My insides freeze: has something happened? What is this man trying to tell us? Did he see someone take Marta and is that why he's pointing? I try to run, slipping back in the sand with each advancing step.

"Hah! Mommy, you didn't see me!"

She's jumped in front of me, the little tan tomboy, laughing like crazy. Yes, we didn't even think about the possibility that she could be hiding, she did it so well just by lying on her back behind one of these humps.

The day goes on as before, except my heart beats faster than usual for some time after that.

"I'm going to travel too," Marta promises, while we walk back towards the bungalows.

"Oh yeah, where do you want to go?"

"I want to come to Africa again! And to India, like you!"

It was just yesterday that I was reliving my memories of how I travelled here as a young and reckless girl, living on a knife's edge.

"There are lots of gods in India, right! You said so. I want to go visit those gods!" my five year old tells me, tirelessly stomping through the dunes, her body glittering with grains of sand. At home (well yes, this little bungalow is our home already, that's human nature), we have to take a bath and try to get rid of those little grains, but I know that's impossible. They will be found on our bodies long after we leave the island...

"And I want to go on a long voyage on the sea!" the child continues. "Daddy said that you can take a boat to America, too!"

And then I realize that I really have no chance of keeping history from repeating itself. The world is replenished with more and more bold girls and boys, who have to see for themselves whether the Earth really is round.

Where does it start?

Memories of my childhood are stored inside of me. Of how my grandfather loved collecting maps – just for pleasure. "What are you poring over again now?" my grandmother would huff, but he and I were hunched over the table, passing the magnifying glass between us and just looking and looking.

"See, this is where the Sahara Desert begins..." I hear my grandfather Papa say. "It goes through lots of countries, see, here..."

Papa also collected language textbooks. He was especially excited, when he could buy something that had strange writing on it, for example, lemonade from Georgia or condensed milk from Latvia. That same magnifying glass in hand, he studied the tiny words on the label and looked for their meanings in his dictionaries and textbooks.

I don't know why some people, for example my sister, just believe that the world is round and why others like me just can't accept that knowledge and have to see for ourselves.

I remember when my sister and I were teenagers. All of a sudden we had grown to the point where freedom begins – and where travels start.

I cried in my pillow one night, when I found out that mom and dad wouldn't let me go on a hiking trip to the deserts of Kyrgyzstan. My sister asked, "But why do you want to go there?"

Why indeed? I still don't know the answer. But I know how to sense that urge – the urge to leave. Not a day went by before I was reproaching my mother for their decision: how could my friends go on the trip and I couldn't. It's like I was living in a different dimension and there was me and there was them. How would they manage hiking there? Maybe my mother felt guilty and that's why she let me go on the political protest walk along the roads of the three Baltic States a year later? It was the first time in my young life, when that "leaving" I so longed for actually came true. From then on, leaving has become a pattern.

And here I am now, my Papa's grandchild and my daughter's mother. The same urge to seek meanings and explore deserts is still inside of me. Have I passed that on to my fiery daughter?

An awkward ride

One hour later. February 2009
Puerto Rico and its surroundings, Gran Canaria

Back from the beach, I'm itching inside and out and a cool shower has not helped. Once again, we're heading out with the family to see my old stomping grounds, back to the western part of the island. After the talk we had last night, Justin knows about my past with Marco, but it doesn't seem to be bothering him at all. He's more interested in the past I shared with Harri.

"So how could you sleep in the mountains, weren't you afraid of snakes?" he asks. And, "So he really seriously thinks that Estonians are gods descended on earth?" These are the kinds of things he wants to know.

"No, I wasn't scared, there are no snakes on this island," I answer. And, "He really does believe the story about the gods, Harri's definitely not lacking in imagination!"

"But have you ever thought that he might be lacking in some other departments?"

I think about that, face pressed against the bus window again. "You know what, in a way he does have a lack of empathy for simple and stupid people, or maybe even for all people. He would love to toughen people up and breed them. His worldview holds no place for the weak and the stupid. They are the ones who should die off. There's an air of... fascist Germany about him, you know?"

"Is he insane?" Justin tosses the question up like a ball in a game.

"No, he's smart, in his own way! But I have thought about it, what if they did something to him at the asylum back then that... well, kind of messed him up a little?"

"What do you think – were you under his influence back then? Or are you still?"

"Sure!" I chuckle, as I bounce the toddler in my lap. "I think I understand those who lose it and just join a sect or a criminal group all because of the influence of a charismatic leader... A part of me believed him completely – or still does – and the other part of me was probably just using him. I have a feeling that his incredible life's story was like a prize for me to win for having the courage to run away from home, or, well, from the life that did not suit me. I'll never meet anyone with a fate as strange as his, even if I live to be a hundred years old!" Justin nods with a hungry curiosity, his eyes are also shining with a writer's yearning for new stories. I can now verbalize yet another thing that connects the two of us. When we see an interesting situation, we run towards it, even if it may be a little frightening.

In Puerto Rico, after arriving at the bus station, we walk. Just like yesterday, the streets of this little town fill me with nostalgia. I wonder, is physical distance always necessary for generating this bittersweet feeling? Would someone who's lived in the same place all their lives find themselves struck with this painful feeling while walking down a familiar path and think: here's where...?

"So this is that cafe," I show Justin, "here's where Harri told me about his idea for the first time. He wanted to build a giant aquarium in Puerto Rico, or actually more like a pool, where water would cascade down from level to level and where different fish would be on each level. And I know that this aquarium doesn't exist here, but I can just picture it, you see, right there, that's where I imagined it back then. Isn't it strange how things imagined in the past, whether they're someone else's or your own, stay with you and almost turn into real memories?"

Justin himself nods, but doesn't even get a chance to respond before I shout, "And look! Here on this corner, this is where I used to sell my jewellery. And on this corner too." Words cease. I remember how I sat on this sidewalk and once wrote in my journal for two hours straight – the one I've probably lost now.

Harri's booth can be seen from far away, he's talking to someone, beating his drums and bouncing figurines made of dolomite from the Estonian island of Saaremaa. I'm happy to admit that the risk of coming back unannounced paid off – after all, we couldn't call him ahead of time because he doesn't have a phone, which is convenient enough for him, but not for the rest of us.

Marta runs ahead and shouts, "Uncle Harri, we've come to see you again!"

"Hey!" I give Harri a slight nod as I start to look through his display and tell Justin about the items in a lowered voice. Some things look so familiar. Maybe this pair of silver earrings with blue stones bounced around in my backpack long ago and now still holds some of my angst from back then? I don't know, but I swear I've seen them before.

"So where is this new husband of yours from?" Harri asks after the tourists have left with a large Kenyan drum. For some reason, he's asking me and not Justin himself, who's standing right here next to me and replies himself, "But what do you think?" in Estonian.

"Yes, guess!" I remember playing a game with Harri in buses and at markets, where we'd look at the strangers around us and he'd guess where they were from – after travelling through so much of the world, he has a pretty good basis for determining different nationalities.

"Let's see then..." Harri looks at my green-eyed husband and his brown, almost black hair. He thinks for a moment and then announces in a certain tone, turning directly to Justin this time, "Your genes are from Persia, man. Persia! It's obvious looking at you that you're from the areas that are now Iran."

"Persia? I don't think so... My ancestors are from Italy."

"Huh? Nothing to be surprised about here, you just have to know your history a little! The Persians came to Southern Italy through Albania, so many people in those areas have those dominant Persian genes..."

Justin is surprised. "From what I have found out so far, one of my grandfathers is from a village in Italy that was settled by Albanian immigrants..."

"See, there you go!"

"Justin and I met six years ago in Finland, he's American," I start telling him. "We backpacked around Europe, lived some time in New York, and after that Justin moved to Estonia, learned the language..." Harri's face starts taking on a much more positive expression and he announces very categorically, "The main thing is that the children live in Estonia. Your genes are dominant in them, but it's also necessary for their upbringing to be Estonian, otherwise they're lost for the country!"

Suddenly my phone starts beeping. Harri clamps his mouth shut, giving me a very judgemental look. Yes, I know, I'm wasting my energy again, sorry...

I'm not surprised when a local number shows up on the telephone screen. I did give my number to Marco yesterday.

"Epa, where are you? I got the day off today, so I can show you and your *bambinas* the island!"

I guess we're probably not going to be talking about the bag anymore? The thought passes through my head.

"And to your husband, of course," Marco adds.

All right then, we won't discuss the bag, but... another thought starts to form...

"That sounds good to me!" I answer. "We're in Puerto Rico again, can you come here?"

"You're here? To meet Harri again? But what about me? "

"Why not you, too? I was afraid to call, because you said you have a jealous girlfriend at home! In any case, why don't you join us here, on the beach promenade where Harri is selling!"

I realize it's actually good that we haven't talked about the bag and my old journals today. Let these two men think that I've forgotten the matter. Maybe I can pull off something out of a classic police movie, where I pit two people against one another to see which one is not telling the truth. Which one of them?

February 2009

Half an hour later.

"Hey, Marco, why did you tell Epp that you gave me the bag?" Harri jumps up to meet the approaching former sea captain. He's probably anticipated my plan. Marco looks around nonchalantly as if he's either been caught in the act or just can't see through other people's plans enough to outwit them.

"What bag? Epa's bag? But I gave it to you!" he shouts to Harri.

Neither of the men makes eye contact with the other.

It's a long, awkward moment that stretches on and reveals nothing. I realize that my plan is a failure, unless I want to grill them both a little more and make things even more uncomfortable.

"Don't run so far away!" I yell at my kids instead. The moment of silence has passed, the strained energy around us dissipates and everyone starts talking at once. A couple of retirees with flip flops and wrinkled bellies walk past us, stopping to see what all the commotion is about. Why has this small, strange little group of people gathered in front of this sales booth? They don't seem to be interested in the jewellery and the drums. Why are they all arguing about something?

"Hey, line up!" Justin shouts above everyone else, trying to calm the awkward moment with the flash of a photo camera. "Wait, Epp, why don't you pick up Anna, look over here!"

Another long moment. The burdens of the past are flanking me on both sides, someone's lie is hanging above our heads, a baby is screaming in my arms, and I am trying to smile for the camera.

We're sitting in Marco's car and the situation has become even more of an absurd comedy. Marco has promised to take our family to the mountains. "It would be interesting to see your mountain villa again," I spontaneously replied to his suggestion, so that's where we are headed. I still don't understand why Justin doesn't seem to be jealous at all. He's just sitting in the front seat of Marco's car and observing everything around him, looking highly amused. We've driven along sandy mountain roads lined with cacti, through little villages, where Marco stops his car every now and then to shout something in Spanish out the window, which generally gets reciprocated by a head stuck out of the window of some little house or another. "*Conyo!*" is the only word that I recognize. Here and there Marco leaves us in the car without any further explanation and steps inside a random building to "take care of some things"...

Then we wind up and down the mountain roads with enough speed to make little Anna nauseous and I have to catch her vomit in a baseball cap I find on the backseat.

"Oh, just throw that out!" Marco yells and points to the window.

"No, I don't want to!" I shout back, baffled. Why should I pollute the mountains? I stick the sour-smelling cap into a plastic bag I find on the car floor. The rocking of the car takes me back to that twilight zone where memories, reality and its alternate versions intermingle.

Finally, we arrive, at the beginning of a familiar driveway. A long time ago I ran away down this path, the very first night I met Marco. I stare out of the window, a wooden cross swinging in my line of sight – probably the same one he had hanging on his rearview mirror ten years ago.

Why am I here in front of this house? Why did I let this happen, why did I end up here with my family like this?

I realize that I'm a hair away from bursting into tears. No matter where I set foot outside of this car, there is no safe ground anywhere: one man from my present, another one from my past, and the house that symbolizes stolen happiness from a long time ago. There are the windows that let in the sandy wind... For a moment, it seems that I'm in a time warp and catch a quick glimpse of a girl at the window. Is it me?

Is it really me that lived here once – or, let's say, spent her evenings, nights and mornings here?

I feel my temples pulsating. A person's blood, I am reminded, is supposed to be in a constant state of renewal. Skin cells die and fall away. Hair grows and falls as well. All in all, I'm not at all the same person I was ten years ago. I have new blood, new skin, new hair, so the bulk of me is someone completely different, not the girl peeking out of the window.

But something inside of me, the chemical reactions in that same old grey matter are still keeping it all fresh. As if it was still the same me who had a right to enter this house.

Luckily I am a mother who has to keep an eye on the children, who are now darting out of the car.

"Marco, what are these trees here called?" Marta calls out. Exactly the same question I asked him about the same trees back then.

Marco doesn't respond. He's squatting by the front door and inspecting the contents of all his pockets laid out on the ground.

"*Conyo*, I don't have my keys!" he curses.

"So we can't get in?" The thought is at once a relief and a disappointment.

Now he's looking through his car, patting down all his pockets one more time. "I don't come here very often. I don't carry the keys with me all the time... I forgot!"

It's for the best, I realize. This is a line that should not be crossed.

Justin walks around the garden, I'm about to go join him when I remember something.

"Marco, what am I going to do with this cap that my daughter threw up in? Do you have a trash can somewhere in the garden?"

"Just throw it anywhere in the yard, it doesn't matter!" Marco swats his hand indifferently through the air. "I have a gardener who comes to water and weed the plants. He'll take care of it!"

A thought runs through my head, but it's just a sliver and I can't catch it; the confusion is too great. I decide to leave the bag in the car and wash the cap at our home bungalow. There's nothing I can do about it, I've been raised the northern way, and I can't just throw trash anywhere on the ground, much less into a manicured garden!

My family, having taken a walk in the orchard in the meantime, now gathers by the car. The sky has clouded over and it's getting darker.

"Do you want to see the zoo?" Marco asks, as he settles into his car seat. He's a bit tense – I'm not sure if he regrets bringing my family here to the mountains or whether it's just the way he is. I don't really know him, have not known him for a long time.

"Sure... if this zoo is not too far?" I slowly force my answer.

"What do you mean – the zoo?" Justin asks.

"Come on, let's go!" Marta is already shouting louder than all of us.

And we're off. We turn back to go down the mountains, the rear of the car scrapes the foot of a cliff... We drive along and past a wall constructed of huge stones meant for catching falling debris. "All this is my property, as far as you can see," Marco points proudly towards the mountainous landscape, covered in reddish brown sand and solitary tufts of cacti. "And see this wall... this is where my new house is going to be."

"A new house? What for?" I ask, before realizing how impolite it might sound. "I mean, you already have a house in the mountains that you practically don't use at all?"

"But there's a neighbour right next to that house! Here, it's completely private!"

We bump further down something that slightly resembles a road until we arrive at a strange place fenced in with barbed wire. Dozens of wooden sheds can be seen through the fence. Marco rolls down his window and yells at the top of his lungs, "*Gordo!*"

A fat, stocky man staggers out of a large shed. "God damn it, drunk again," Marco comments, shooting me a look in the back seat, as if there should be some background knowledge we shared here. Why?

Do I remember this man with a large build who's approaching us, should I remember him?

Memory is a strange thing. Maybe I really have seen this man with rotten teeth and a beer belly before, but maybe what's recognizable here isn't the man, but Marco's attitude in a similar situation, something I've seen before – the loud, arrogant way that he behaves, almost sadistically enjoying the role he's playing. Or maybe this recognition comes from a past life, an emotion that suddenly came on in an intense flash and then slid back into its hiding place in the subconscious. Something that really had nothing to do neither with me nor Marco?

There's just this angst. This sadness that reveals itself in the darkening mountains, where the present and the past, reality and the world of dreams mix together like the mountains melting into the sky along the horizon.

Gordo opens the gate and we walk in. Marco is yelling at him, it's hard to say whether he's truly upset or if this is just the way they communicate. Birds are making noise all around us: geese, ducks, and white doves, all of them thrashing around their wire cages.

"Maybe they're hungry?" I ask, turning to Marco.

"Yes, sunset is their mealtime," he answers and shouts an order to Gordo.

---

* "Fatty" in Spanish.

"What is this here on your land anyway, some kind of business?" I probe further. "Do you eat these birds? Did you have this back then also? You did eat meat, right?"

"I do eat meat, yes..." Marco begins to answer my barrage of questions, but then my impatient daughter drags him away by the hand, "Hey, come this way, can I go near the birds?"

Reeking of whiskey or something else rather strong, Gordo sways a little as he's standing next to us and speaking in Spanglish, "No, we no eat them! They – *pffft!*" he runs his finger across his throat in a gesture that doesn't leave much to the imagination and then throws his hands up towards the sky.

"They get killed?"

"*Sí*. Yes!"

"But why? If you don't eat them?"

"We no kill them! We sell them to *cubanos*."

"Cubans?" Well yes, there are quite a lot of them working on the island, as I recall. Jorge, for example, the one who works at Marco's store...

"But why do the Cubans *pffft* them?" I ask throwing my hands to the sky as well.

"For God! For the spirits!"

I see. So the purpose of this so-called zoo that Marco finances is breeding white doves for some strange rituals? I feel a wave of nausea coming on. I look at Marco playing with my daughters and the doves farther off. There's nothing really wrong here, thousands of birds and animals are killed for food every day and why should these ritual killings for the spirit world be any worse than the slaughter of animals for food? Every person leads their own life and makes their own decisions...

But still, a suffocating angst has come over me. As if I was somehow responsible for these doves.

"How come you don't seem to be jealous at all?" I ask an hour later, when the taillights of Marco's car disappear and we stumble towards our home-bungalow, each carrying a sleeping child. It has been an incredibly long and strange day that started off idyllically enough with the whole family naked and on the dunes, but then took us almost accidentally to my ex's abode in the mountains, then on towards old memories being ripped open and to new bloody revelations.

"Jealous? I don't know... This just doesn't seem like a possible future for you," Justin says. "It's a distant past and that's exactly what it seems like. But you know what: I feel sorry for you. I can see that it's like you're here and in the past at the same time, you're fighting these demons of the past and reliving everything again..."

"Yes, I guess that's how it is. I'm so glad that you're here with me."

"But you know what, there's one thing I can tell you. I'm ready to bet on it. The one who threw away your bag with the journals was Marco."

"What do you mean?"

"Remember the way he told you to throw that hat away? He's just that type of person: the guy who throws things away! I don't want to say anything bad about him. I felt that he respected me much more than Harri did, for example. But if you ask me, which one of them swung your bag in their hand and let it fly towards a dumpster... I can just picture him doing that!"

I pause to think. Justin may be right, but maybe not: often life is a master at bluffing and in the end the cards play out completely differently than what you expected.

From the asylum to the road

Ten years earlier. March 1999
Haifa, Israel

"Let's go back to that Christian hostel," I shout ahead into the darkness, where Harri is trudging along.

"Impossible!" he shouts back. "It's all the way on the other side of the city!"

We've been walking around this suburb of Haifa for quite a while now, looking for a place to spend the night. One hotel we find is all booked out, we haven't seen any more, and the chances of finding another one are getting slimmer. It's night now and everything is quiet around us. We stayed at the library for too long, because Harri was looking for "his signs", reading and drawing at a frantic pace, but it still took him several hours.

"We're staying here overnight!" Harri calls out, turns off the road and starts hiking straight up a small mountain. He found large cardboard boxes near some dumpsters before and is now dragging them along.

An instant later, I'm looking down at the city lights. That feeling of joy and freedom that came over me that first day when we arrived here ten days ago still hasn't left me. Everything is balanced perfectly on the edge between beautiful and dangerous. To spend the night here, outside, between cacti, acacias, olive trees, and aloe bushes? Harri has spread out the pieces of cardboard, I spread out my sleeping bag on top of them – after all, this is why I brought it along from Estonia in the first place. Already way back then, I dreamed of the chance to spend the night beneath the starry southern skies, listening to the chirping of crickets and the whispering treetops. True, in those dreams I did picture a balcony, but if it's the mountains instead, that's all right with me. It's eerie here, but wonderfully, beautifully, extraordinarily eerie.

"Are there snakes here?" I ask Harri cautiously.

"There can be! I'm not afraid of them, but... do you have something made of wool?" he asks in turn. "Snakes can't stand the smell of wool. It's an old trick to wear something woollen or to surround yourself with a circle of woollen yarn. That'll make the snake hold his breath and slither away!" He laughs at my anxiety while I'm rummaging around in my bag. Yes, there it is. In the bottom of my bag I have a scarf that I wore as I left the wintry spring of Estonia and Latvia ten days ago. A shadow passes across my mind, as I think of Tom waiting for me back there, of the witch's predictions, and of the fact that I haven't been able to write to him in the last two days.

It's a good thing this scarf is made of wool! I arrange it in a semi-circle around my head and crawl into the sleeping bag.

"Do you ever just get the urge to travel?"

I can't sleep. Besides, in the dark night, with the background of flashing city lights, this kind of silly, yet important questions are easier to say out loud than in the light of day.

Harri clears his throat and turns around somewhere on the other side of the aloe patch. "I didn't begin travelling because it's fun. It was more because of the practical, physical need to survive!"

I look at the city lights and listen.

Tonight's story starts in Soviet Estonia, in the coastal town of Pärnu, and the year is 1971. The sixteen-year-old, savagely talented Harri completes three years of high school in one year, walks around with long hair trailing behind him in the breeze his pace generates, barefoot and wearing a loose robe. This is also what he looks like when he walks across the stage at his school to accept the diploma, shocking his teachers one more time. He passes all his exams with A's, except the final essay, for which he chooses to write on the topic "Estonians in World War II" and, in his opinion neutrally describes a small people, drawn into a war by two opposing sides that pitted brother against brother. It's probably this ability to think independently that puts Harri at odds with his Estonian language teacher, whose husband works for the local KGB. This, in turn, foils the young man's plan to take off a year before starting university studies to breed aquarium fish and earn some extra money. "Can you imagine it? I got drafted at a time when officially I should still have been in high school! They simply wanted to take away my chance to go to the university at all!"

"And then you ran away?" I've heard some details about Harri's weird odysseys under bushes all over the former Soviet Union, but I still haven't heard about how that journey began.

"I didn't even bother going to the commissary to argue with them and say, 'What do you mean you're drafting me? I should still be in high school!' because I figured that in that case I'd never get out of there. But I wrote a statement accusing the Soviet Union of being a system that is anti-progress, anti-humanity and anti-evolution, as well as a system that has become distanced from its basic ideology. I also added in the statement that due to these reasons I refuse to serve in the Soviet army."

"And you signed your name?"

"Yes, I sent it all off to the army commissary, got on a train and escaped from Estonia! I left word for my mother that I'm leaving, don't look for me, my father had died by then."

From there, the story turns to Karelia, on the Russian-Finnish border, I turn in my sleeping bag and listen on. Young Harri had decided to go look for work on a nature reserve in Northern Karelia and then, when opportunity will present itself, to swim across the border to Norway. He took a collection of old coins from home with him, and plans on putting it inside his coat while he swims across, to convert it into money in the free world and use it to start a new life.

"Well, do you know off the top of your head what the map looks like up there?" he asks from the other side of the aloe bush. "You know, there's this little island between the peninsulas of Rybatchy and Kola, and right beside that island is the Norwegian coast!"

For a month and a half, Harri manages to live and work quietly on the nature reserve near the border, while planning on going through with the swim, but then...

"But then I made a stupid mistake. At the same time, I don't know, maybe the Soviet state would still exist if I had gotten out and not been able to influence the course of things!"

"What mistake was that?"

"I wrote to a friend of mine in Estonia, asking for a detailed map of the entire Karelia border area – I knew that he could get his hands on it, but there weren't any in Karelia."

The next scene brings us back to the night, where Harri is sleeping in his forest cabin and hears a car pull up outside, steps approaching, the door being kicked open...

"They all jump inside, guns aimed at me, screaming, 'Don't shoot, we'll fire!' So I don't move a muscle, just lay there in the bed, looking at them... It's the local police, under orders to apprehend an especially dangerous criminal! The letter I sent to my friend ended up in the hands of the KGB!"

Then we're in jail, where Harri's hair is cut for the first and last time in his life. Shaven, to be more exact. ("But they were decent people, they didn't hurt me!") A day later we're in a prison rail car, making our way through the Kola Peninsula to Leningrad, to the toughest prison in Russia, where only political prisoners were kept ("Katarinsky Kresto, you don't get sent there on a field trip after a misdemeanor! I shared a cell with people who worked with those guys who doused themselves in gasoline and set themselves on fire to protest against the Soviet state. It was really an interesting crowd in there, university professors!"). A few weeks later, Harri's road takes him back to Tallinn, to the solitary confinement cell of the Battery Prison, where he's held without hope of any kind of investigation even being initiated. It's not until he goes on a hunger strike and promises to end it only if an investigation into his case is launched that he's taken to meet an investigator.

According to the way Harri tells it, this man is rather confused about what to do with this strange young rebel who is completely outside of the system.

"We understand that you're young and emotional, but you refused to serve in the Soviet army. And you've also previously committed crimes against the Soviet state," Harri imitates the investigator for me. He's come out from behind his bush, now squatting beside me with the past casting a fire in his eyes.

"Crimes against the Soviet state? Did you really?"

"Well, yes! During school there were some red flags burned, a bomb got thrown into the window of the Komsomol* committee window, a couple of slogans written in paint on the highway – later on the whole school was out there scrubbing with brushes. Oh, yeah, and once the Estonian tricolour made it to the top of the local church somehow!"

"So... what exactly did this investigator offer you?"

"We'll give you two options, he said. First: give up your rejection of the army and we'll send you off to the unit, we'll just pretend it never happened. You're a smart person, we've got plans to send you on a submarine and educate you!"

"Were you tempted? I mean, you were so interested in fish, didn't the world under water...?"

"What?" Harri shouts, before continuing with his role of the investigator. "There's a second choice, young man: I guarantee that you'll get the death sentence for attempting to cross the border..."

"But you didn't even attempt anything?"

"Well, I did ask for a map of the border areas! And refusing to serve military duty?" Harri lets out a defiant laugh and he continues his story, now playing the role of himself.

"Go right ahead, if you sentence me to death, it's your loss, not mine! After all, it's only possible to win if the opponent comes over to your side!"

"That's what you said?"

"...and then they sent me back to my cell. Ten minutes later, people in white smocks came in. I already knew that much – people who are potentials for the death sentence go through a psychiatric evaluation before the court order, to the psychiatric ward at the prison."

The next scene unfolds in this department. Even though the laws state that the evaluation should take place within a month somewhere on the territory of the prison hospital, something happens just three days later. Right before lunch, a nervous nurse approaches Harri and tells him to

---

* The youth wing of the communist party in the Soviet Union.

eat and drink as quickly as possible, because a car will soon come to take him to the main psychiatric hospital on the other side of the city.

"But the way that nurse was behaving, the nervous looks she was shooting at my glass, and the way she was rushing me to drink up... I realized that something had been put in there!" Harri talks and plays the whole scene out, squatting with an imaginary plate of porridge and a glass right in front of him. "See, there was this epileptic right next to me, eating his porridge. I just mumbled lightly to the nurse, something like all right, I'll drink it, took a tiny sip while she was looking, maybe two spoonfuls... Then she looked aside for a moment and right at that moment I switched glasses with my neighbour, and kept drinking the new stuff. By then though the cramp hit me!"

Harri is leaning over to one side now, twitching, rolling his eyes and panting. "Like this! My whole body on the right side contracted! At that time, right after the hunger strike, I only weighed forty kilos, so two spoons of that stuff were enough for me. I tried to force myself to relax, just pure willpower, and in the end it passed."

"Didn't you worry about that epileptic man?" I cry out. "That man had to drink your poisoned drink!"

"Well, if he did drink it, I guess he got his stomach pumped!"

That poor fellow prisoner with his unfortunate choice of seat bothers me for a moment, but the action just keeps coming: Harri's story has taken him to the hospital car, where he goes through two more spasms as they drive through the city, and then to the psychiatric hospital, where the doctor first tells him to stop pretending, but then realizes the seriousness of the situation and gives the young man medication to help relieve the cramps. "It was clear that it had all been planned out on the prison side: get the drink in him, put him in the car real fast, and oops, guess he didn't make it, kicked the bucket half way there!"

But it's not that easy to get rid of a nuisance like him. The next episode takes place at the small insane asylum where Harri is sent next. During the first month, there are no evaluations, no medications, "but then I somehow happened to be included among those who were getting insulin treatment. People would get a shot of insulin, they'd fall into a coma, then they'd get a shot of sugar and were brought out of the coma, but meanwhile they got tied to the bed, just in case, because nutcases in comas tend to thrash around. If you're normal, you stay calm in a coma. I didn't get into these fits and didn't thrash around, so that meant my nervous system was completely fine."

"So they just put you in a coma?"

"Yes, a few times. By the way, when you come out of a coma, you really feel like your brain is incredibly well-rested. I saw people who had had about thirty comas. They had turned into extreme pacifists! They were simple, lethargic creatures! It was a good tool for keeping political dissidents under control."

"How terrible!" I look out into the night and an involuntary shudder passes through my shoulders. Being committed is one of my secret fears, the lack of control over what's injected into your body... "You tried to stop them from giving the injections, right?"

"Of course! I would beg them, tell them that I feel lousy, and when I came out of the coma I pleaded for them to not do it again. I would say, 'See, I'm not crazy'. But there's nothing you can do there. The only thing you can do is escape! And then I started getting them used to the idea that I'm a type of specimen who can sometimes be out of sight. For example, I'd go sleep under the bed. It was mimicry, see! To divert their attention."

"You were thinking about escaping already?"

"Of course! When we were let out in the back yard for a walk, I noticed immediately that there was a rowan tree right where the yard ended – it was so far that we couldn't go there. And I'd tell all the nurses every day that I wanted to eat those rowanberries, get them for me, or I'll go get some myself. Crazy people can say anything they want! I figured that when I try to escape, I'll go to that tree first and if they catch me, it's

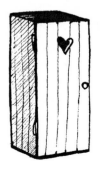

not like I'm trying to escape, I'm just going to pick some berries!"

"Was the asylum surrounded by a high wall?"

"No, it was a regular small fence."

I can see it all in my mind. The following scene as well: the daily walk outside, the laziest pair of nurses... The day has come! Harri shuffles off to the outhouse in the yard and hides behind the door. He's so skinny that he manages to push himself up against the wall and go unnoticed when the nurse comes to check. From there, he darts quickly to the main building, where the door has just slammed shut, listens for a moment: everything has been calculated. He has to make it to the rowan tree and then straight over the fence during the two minutes when the nurses are following the crazies up the stairway inside the building and haven't made it to the second floor windows yet.

"How did you get over the fence?" I ask.

"Ha! It was just an easy jump! First I – crack! – broke off a branch with some rowanberries and then went over the fence and then... oh gosh, I ran as quickly as my legs could manage, over the field, into the woods! It was the end of August, the nights were cold, and it was already starting to get dark. I ran through the thickets and the woods, until I got to a highway. I looked around: the cops were already out there! Then I noticed it: a barn. The hell with it, time to take a little nap! I was so tired from the stress and the running that I just crawled in the hay and slept for a very long time."

Then it's night. The young man, dressed in striped asylum clothes, has finally woken and shivers as he speed walks through the woods along the highway, towards his hometown, one night walk away from where he is. At the first farm, he sticks a hand inside the front door to find a farmer's work clothes, but has no luck. He finds a coat in the second farm he comes across. In addition to the coat, he steals a bicycle. Pedalling through the night, he reaches a village built around a collective farm and thanks his luck again: the dogs are sleeping, and someone's laundry has been hung outside to dry, it's just flapping there in the wind! He gets rid of his striped costume and puts on proper clothes, even finds shoes in a hallway behind someone's door, pulls up some carrots from someone's garden to eat, and keeps pedalling towards his hometown. Just before reaching his hometown Pärnu, he abandons the bike, leaving it in someone's yard and dives into the bushes by the road again at dawn, to avoid the police...

"I went down to the river and waded through there. But I didn't go home! A friend of mine owed me money."

"You trusted him?"

"Well, yes. What else was I supposed to do? I had to trust someone. But when I got to his house, I saw that there was a car waiting out front. I sneaked on through the backyards and gardens, and saw that there were cars in front of all my friends' houses. Then I remembered a guy I knew, but almost never really talked to. I trusted him very much, because we had organized anti-Soviet protest actions together. And there was no car in front of his house! I knocked on his door, slid inside and told him, 'I need the following things double quick: a map of the Soviet Union, a comb and 25 rubles'".

"A comb? But you had been shaven?" I notice an inconsistency in the film running in front of my eyes.

"Almost half a year had passed by that time! I started growing my hair out again... So, that acquaintance of mine gave me everything I needed. I had just barely left his house and started walking, when I saw from across the street that – boom! – a car pulled up to the house, four men jumped out and ran inside."

"Someone had snitched?"

"Don't know! In any case, I got lucky by about three minutes. Of course, I high-tailed it out of there, taking back roads and going through the backyards and gardens where I'd played as a kid. And then on to the highway... I stopped a random car and decided that my direction was, in brief, Siberia. But that's enough for now! The next part is already the next chapter of my life's story. To be continued tomorrow!"

"No, please!" I beg him, enraptured by the story. "Tell me more!"

"It's a long story, I can't tell it all in one go."

"It's like a fairy tale of One Thousand and One Nights!" I laugh. "I'll follow you around until you tell me your whole story. But, come on, please tell me some more tonight!"

"Well, all right..."

Now Harri's taking random cars, first to the south and then towards the east of the Soviet Union: Riga... Daugavpils... Vitebsk... Smolensk... Oryol... Tula... Ryazan... Penza...

"Where did you sleep?" I interrupt Harri's list. "Where did you get food?"

"No, listen to my itinerary now! Do you know the map? From Penza to Kuybyshev, then Ohrenburg, to Kurgan from there, to Omsk, Arabinsk, Novosibirsk..." He carefully counts off the names that, honestly, don't really mean that much to me, but he's got a story to go along with each of these places. Fantastic.

"But where did you sleep then?" I interrupt him again.

"Always in the woods! The car would take me to a new city and I'd start to walk out of civilization. I never used public transportation, because I was sure that I had been listed as wanted all over the Union – and taking the bus could have gotten me attention I didn't want."

"Didn't you get cold sleeping under bushes?"

"Well, I'd cover myself with patches of moss... But yes, in Siberia it did start getting cold, so I just headed farther south."

"And where did you get food?"

"I stretched that 25 rubles worth of bread over ten days, ate very little. In ten days I arrived at Novosibirsk. I didn't want to steal anything, so I was hoping to find a job."

"Did you have any documents?"

"Everything was left behind at the asylum! But that acquaintance of mine, the one who gave me a comb and some money, also gave me his Komsomol identification card." Harri cackles. "I had to keep reminding myself that my name was Paul Peterman now! I invented a story for myself too about how I came to do construction work in Siberia for the Komsomol, but my passport and wallet were stolen, so I only had that ID. I asked drivers I met if there was any work around, so that I could buy a ticket and head back to Estonia."

The story has taken us to the oblast of Novosibirsk, where Harri manages to get work for a week as a miller, except there's a minor formality to take care of – to request a permit at the local police station. But a wanted criminal is not going to go ask for a permit just like that, is he? Harri weighs the situation, marches into the police station and gets his permit, using the Komsomol ID and playing the part of his friend. The following job he happens to get is at a turnip harvest, "And can you imagine, I got a special prize from the Komsomol for being such a diligent harvester!" Harri snickers.

"But in reality, you probably didn't belong to the Komsomol?"

"Of course not! I've never been part of any organization in my life!"

And he goes on talking. The next page turns and reveals a mountain village in Kazakhstan, Central Asia, somewhere west of Almaty, that Harri has reached on his hitchhiking tour. Winter arrives, he gets work in a settlement full of Kazakhs and Ukrainians, fixing harrows at a blacksmith's workshop and is even given a little house to live in on the edge of the village. Little by little, the young man starts explaining all kinds of pan-Soviet and international news items to the villagers. "The director of that *sovkhoz* noticed that I was reading the news and telling other people about what I read, so pretty soon he suggested that I become the village's political informer!" Harri's shrill laughter rolled down the mountain. "Can you imagine that! So I started organizing meetings in the mornings, before people went off to work, I told them about everything that was written in the papers, but from my own angle... But that really is enough for now! We have to get up early tomorrow and go sell stuff!"

He gets up and stomps back to the other side of the aloe bush, to curl up on his cardboard bed.

So how long did he stay in that Kazakh village? I wonder at this while looking at the olive branches against the night sky, and trying to fall asleep. Another question lingers and won't let me fall asleep.

"Hey," I call out into the darkness, "but still, you forgot to answer my first question. What do you think? Would you have become a traveller if you wouldn't have been forced into it? Do you know what the urge to travel feels like?"

No answer. Harri is probably already far away in dreamland, wandering around the Kazakh steppes.

---

* A Soviet state-owned farm.

From the road to the asylum

The next day. March 1999
Haifa, Israel

I awoke today morning excited: hopefully Harri would go on with his life's story right away! His story had deeply touched something old and forgotten inside of me, bringing together all my childhood fears, urges and dreams.

Harri was already awake, sitting under the aloe bush and looking pensively down at the city. "I was meditating and analysing," he started. "It's time to move on from Israel. The sales here are just not good enough!"

I rubbed my face, trying to understand if I was awake or still dreaming: the first leg of our trip had been finished here and now, just like that? We're just going downtown to the port and buying a ticket to Cyprus? Really?

I have a small pocket atlas with me that was given to my grandfather as a present and that Papa let me borrow for my trip. He handed it over with a wordless, conspiratorial smile... So now I'm sitting on a grey, concrete bench at the port of Haifa, waiting for Harri to return from his ticket hunt, and studying the atlas. Yes, Israel and Cyprus are actually quite close to each other. The boat will sail north from here, and we're currently situated on the eastern coast of the Mediterranean Sea.

There's a special charm in studying a map. You feel so small and so big all at once, like a speck that can just be blown around the world on a whim, or like a powerful controlling organism that has an overview of everything...

"We're leaving on a boat this evening. The night boat," calls out Harri, who has now come around the weathered concrete wall and notices my little atlas. "Let me see that for a moment! Look, let me show you where I hitchhiked that time, remember, like I told you yesterday?" His finger starts drawing enthusiastic lines and circles on the map, along Russia and Central Asia, "See, I was here and here..."

I look at him and smirk: does he seriously think he's hasn't been infected with the travel bug?

So this is our last day of sales work in Haifa, and we're back on the same familiar beach promenade. Luckily there aren't many people out by the sea today, so I can continue to watch the film about Harri's life.

"So what happened next, when you stayed at that Kazakh village for the winter?" I ask.

"Well, spring came and I told the sovkhoz director that I was ready to move on."

"But why? You were doing so well there?"

"That's exactly what he asked! God damn it! I can't live in the same little Kazakh village forever! Of course, that's not exactly the way I worded it when I told him."

"You could have led a peaceful life there, could have even been there now!" I tease him.

"Yes... He kept on probing me about why the hell I had to leave, said that I was the soul of the village, the person who educates everyone and gets people to come together. You want a passport, Paul? We'll get you a passport! I still didn't want to stay. So then he started offering me other things: Paul, my dear, I have two daughters, one's at the university, the other is in high school..."

"Choose which one you want?"

"No! He was a Muslim, he said: I'll give them both to you! Just stay here. I guess he realized that I could improve his gene pool. And then he opened this chest and it was full of money! Packs of 25 rubles!"

"That much money?"

"Well, yeah, the herd of sheep at the sovkhoz was essentially his personal property and he had tens of thousands of sheep there."

"And you?"

"I had to go. My intuition was telling me so. He wasn't offended, wished me all the best and told me that intuition is something that one has to listen to."

"Have you ever gone back there?"

Harri shakes his head and starts to laugh, "That would be something! I'm sure someone in the village would recognize me and yell, 'Hello, Paul!'"

We sell a few items, but then we're back in the reality of twenty-five years ago in Central Asia. Frunze... Tashkent... Katta-Kurgan... Samarkand... Rebetek... Still hitchhiking, stopping random cars for rides, walking for some distances ("I decided to walk on foot beside the train tracks through the desert of Karakum in Turkmenistan!"), and with a clear destination: Harri has decided to head to the Turkmen capital of Ashgabat and the Caspian Sea from there. He's heard that from there it's possible to escape across the border to Iran.

"And can you imagine it? I'm in a car, heading for Ashgabat, when – boom! A barrier in the middle of the road! Border control! A total catastrophe!" Harri's gesticulating wildly. "The driver, an old Turkmen, shows them this rag of a document that has the photo page hanging from the rest by two threads, half of the passport is gone – basically, the remains of a passport. But they're fine with it! I show them my Komsomol ticket with Paul's name, the employment record book from Kazakhstan, tell them that my passport is gone and so on. So they discuss it amongst themselves and then decide, 'Get out of the car, let's go to the border control office and check out who you are.'"

"How did they even check anything back then without the Internet?"

"They sent a telegram to Estonia! The reply came: Paul Peterman does indeed exist, but he lives in Pärnu and has never been to Kazakhstan. So the border control officers stared at me and their tone was already a little angrier when they asked again me who I was. I thought about telling them that I was an American spy in Iran and accidentally crossed the border, wondering if they would then turn me over to the Americans. But I wasn't sure whether the Americans would want me. So I decided what the hell! I just tell them the truth!" Harri cackles. If there's one thing I especially like about his storytelling, it's that he never really takes himself too seriously. Now he's channelling the Harri from twenty-five years ago, sticking out his chin and declaring, "My name is Harri Hommik, I refused to serve in the Soviet army, they stuck me in a madhouse, I escaped and got my friend's Komsomol ID and now I've been hitchhiking around Siberia and Central Asia for a year!"

"So what did they say?"

"Their jaws dropped, just watching the show I was putting on for them! They had a map of the Soviet Union hanging on their wall, so I started showing them the exact locations of army bases, where according to my observations there were tankodromes and airports – just showing them the cities, telling them that see this, here is where I passed through and here..." Harri laughs again and straightens his beard, raising his voice to new heights, "And they were like, 'Sure, yeah, we believe you. But who are you really?' They did send out a data request with my name. Three days later a telegram came from Estonia: 'Send that nutcase back to Estonia to be committed!'"

"Really?"

Harri's squealing with laughter. "I heard the border control men discussing it amongst themselves: 'Man, what a mess, why did we have to bring this guy in? We just ended up catching some lunatic! What if we just left the door open and let him escape?'... However, the next morning they did end up taking me to the psychiatric hospital in Ashgabat, where the chief resident just blocked their way in and said, 'Listen, this is a hospital and we don't take political prisoners, take him back to your station!'"

Once again a couple of passers-by have stopped to watch us: Harri's shouting in a strange language and his imitations of different characters definitely provide an attention-catching show.

"Man, were they stuck with me, huh! They couldn't take me to the police, because I was sick, and the hospital wouldn't take me because I was political! In the end, it turned out that one of the officers at the station knew someone in the hospital, so through this contact they somehow sneaked me in through the hospital back door a few days later. What a circus that was!"

So a new page finds us in a new psychiatric ward. Here, however, nobody has any plans to poke or prod the young man any further. First of all, they let Harri stay officially under "evaluation" for a month, which meant sunbathing in the lovely Turkmen climate, eating and drinking to his heart's content. Then a committee of psychiatrists assembles to discuss the question, "Do we think that refusing to serve in the Soviet army can be an indicator of mental disease?" Roaring laughter rings out in reply. The answer is: no. If this young man indeed had a mental disorder at some point, then it is the opinion of the psychiatric committee of Ashgabat that he is completely cured and ready to assume his normal life. However, since the threat of a relapse into this supposed disease still looms, the committee decides to release the young man of army duty, permanently.

I laugh wholeheartedly at the end of this chapter, eyes on the horizon and wind in my hair. How could it all end up working out so well!

How to lose children

Two weeks later. March 1999
The Mediterranean Sea between Greece and Italy

"Maybe you could go on telling me your story?" I ask. Harri and I have plopped down on chairs in the waiting room of the marina. Our trip has lasted almost four weeks now, through Israel and Cyprus, and during that time I've been writing down and saving the stories of my crazy and charismatic boss on the pages of my journals.

We've spent the last day and a half on a ship's deck, drifting across the water from Cyprus to Greece via Malta. All kinds of stories are drifting around us as well. There's the curly-haired, energetic Russian Irina, who is running away from her husband. I'm playing with her doll faced, two-year-old son and thinking how these stories flowing all around me usually don't have happy endings. Irina fell in love, got married, and then her Greek husband first became annoying, then suspicious, and finally violent. What's going to happen to Irina now? Does she really think things can be settled that easily, that she can just pack up, take the kid and run away? On the other hand: wouldn't I solve that situation exactly the same way?

And then there's Gustavo, a long haired, blue-eyed ("Polish descent" Harri secretly pegged him) Argentine man, who'd taken a year off to travel around the world. We met for the first time at the youth hostel in Israel, where he had just arrived from Egypt, proudly showing off pictures of the pyramids. The second time I saw Gustavo was on that boat between Israel and Cyprus, where he was shivering in the midst of the storm with the rest of us. The third time chance had us meet in Cyprus, in a hotel in Larnaca. When we left there to go to the next town called Nicosia, the pony tailed traveller Gustavo was just ahead of us again!

And by the fifth time we met, right here on the ship from Cyprus to Greece through Malta and then on to Italy, I ceased to be surprised. Was this series of coincidences meant to be? And if so, what were we to learn from it all? Or is it just something usual that people travelling in the same direction keep bumping into each other?

There's something special in Gustavo's blue eyes, so I take great pleasure in seating myself next to him to practice my Spanish pronunciation: Gustavo would say a word, I'd repeat it, and his mane of hair would tickle me when he moved. We're going to get to Spain at some point, as promised, so why not learn some more of the language and with a slight Argentinean accent? Gustavo is in no hurry to leave our tandem and neither am I, so here we are repeating words, until minutes become an hour or two, and the words blanket themselves around us.

There are other pleasant blue eyes on this boat as well, two pairs even – religious Germans, with young, tanned bodies, blond locks and brilliant white smiles. A pair of handsome brothers who spend a few months out of every year in Israel doing volunteer work, in order to atone for the sins of their forefathers, as they say – were their grandfathers in the army of the Third Reich or do they mean "sins" on a more symbolic level, that's something I tactfully omit from my questions. They're just on their way back from the two-month atonement trip, carrying with them a German-English pocket dictionary that's been read to shreds. "Let me learn some German," I ask them and randomly open the book to slowly read, "Today is the 26th of March" – but wait, it is the 26th of March today! This book has today's date in the sample conversation?" What does it mean? What is this type of coincidence good for?

"This is a sign from God," one of the brothers says in astonishment and the other nods along. But a sign about what?

In addition to all these small enigmatic stories around me, another bigger one is being told – Harri's past unravelled bit by bit through the different years and at various angles. For example, he's explained to me in detail how he travelled around Siberia selling fish with his six-year-old son, and told the story how his jewellery selling business got started. This was after he'd left his kids somewhere in Soviet Union and was struggling financially in Estonia. He decided to take the last money he had and fly to Singapore and Thailand to purchase goods to sell. That's how it all began.

We've also gone through the asylum where he was brought back to Estonia under the surveillance of a Turkmen doctor after his initial escape and after the rehabilitative decision of the psychiatric clinic in Ashgabat. He took tremendous pleasure in describing how the chief of staff at the nuthouse exclaimed, "Now we've got you!" upon first seeing him, and then had to admit defeat when he heard the decision that declared Harri's rehabilitation. The KGB gave an order prohibiting the acceptance of the young man to study at any university in Estonia, but that's when Harri cleverly stepped through the door of the zoology museum at the University of Tartu, organized a spontaneous tour for its guests, shook hands with the director an hour later and got an excellent job that, among other responsibilities, also allowed him to breed fish and organize fish-breeding clubs and seminars all over Estonia. Even though the KGB was annoyed by the director's actions, the man was unwilling to give up such a talented employee, so that's where Harri stayed. In his wild course of life, this seems to be the most stable page of them all – three whole years of totally normal employment. "The first and last time I worked for someone else than myself. Never happened again!"

I sense that the most painful experience in my travel companion's life still hasn't been told.

"Listen, so how come you left your kids in Siberia, how did that happen?" I ask now after working up enough courage, on the boat, stretched out over the seat.

"Not to Siberia, but to Tajikistan!"

"Yes, sorry!"

Harri grows silent and looks off into the distance. Then he starts to speak.

This time, the story takes us back to a time about twenty years ago, after the period of escaping from the mental institution, when he starts living with Maarika and has four kids in a row, one each year. He's just given up his job at the museum of the University of Tartu, because they didn't want to give him vacation time for visiting the fish market in Moscow, even though he had been working without leave for several years.

"And, see, that's when that certain balance in my life was lost," Harri tells me. While the KGB had been checking up on him frequently at his job at the museum, now that he was breeding fish more intensively and travelling between Estonia and Russia with his suitcase-aquarium, they had no tangible control over him. That's why the KGB started calling him in more and more. "For instance, they got me back in a mental institution again to check up on my health. The doctor told me to not even bother to try running away, "We won't give you any medications. You'll just spend a quiet week here." The secret police wanted to scare me and show what kind of power they had over me!"

However, since the fish business had started to earn him a decent bit of money, Harri hatched an ingenious plan: he hired a KGB agent, paying him twice as much as he was getting at his KGB job. "And that man brought me photocopies of absolutely all the letters that had been written about me, since the time I was still in high school. There were about a thousand of these letters. All from people I know: classmates, people from the university." Harri is silent, collecting himself before he continues, stressing each word, "But one of those letters was from Maarika. And that meant our life together was – finished!"

Maarika. They met during the university entrance exams, which Harri wasn't allowed to pass, and soon enough Maarika also abandoned her studies and started raising the kids. That's how much I've gathered so far. When talking about Maarika, Harri has mainly emphasized her good genes that he was intuitively sure about right away. But now I'm observing a moment, when it turns out that the partner with good genes wrote a letter to the KGB about her spouse.

"So what was in the KGB letter then?" I try to understand. "Was she giving them information about you? Betraying your secrets?"

"No, well, there wasn't anything special in the letter. She was just describing what she knew: how I travelled back and forth between the fish market in Moscow and to other places she knew about, where I'd gone to sell fish..."

"So she actually wasn't telling on you? Maybe she was just forced to write the thing?"

"I'm sure she was. But she should have told me about it, said that look, I was forced to do it and I wrote this thing. What kind of trust is there otherwise? I only deal with two options: trust or mistrust. I'm not okay with hiding things behind each other's backs and trying-to-more-or-less-somehow live together! And I told her that the only thing left for us to do now was go our separate ways!" Harri talks at length about how he was slowly edged out of his life in Estonia by increasingly numerous KGB controls, so he swiftly and secretly moved his fishery in Tallinn to Siberia in a rail car and from there into a large apartment he bought on the spot, "Because there was plenty of money and I had no other choice, I had to go!"

It seems that the events of those times still weigh heavily on him.

"But then... your children stayed with their mother?" I ask. "Why did you have to take the kids away from Maarika?"

"Maarika couldn't handle it!" he says with a voice full of despite. "She was an aristocrat, she needed a servant herself! When I went to see the apartment she lived in with the four children... Public restrooms are cleaner than that! I realized that the children would be better off with me."

Life isn't simple, not just black and white. There are many half tones, I think while listening to my travel companion's story, trying to understand and see behind what happened. Harri's Siberian-Korean friend died and his widow Tanya first started taking care of Harri's fish, then became his partner and soon enough the new extended family was living all together in Siberia: Tanya with her two sons and Harri with his four kids. Except that Harri wasn't home very often because he was flying guppies all around the Soviet Union. The plans, as I gather, were grand indeed: with the money he made, he bought his own personal island in the middle of a water reserve in Tajikistan, organized twelve large rail cars with timber from Siberia to be delivered there and was planning on building a three-storey home for his whole family. But then a huge falling out took place between him and the locals, after which Harri left for Moscow. The story is still a bit unclear for me, but from what I understand, Harri really wanted to fly back from Moscow to Tajikistan for his children, but he didn't have any money left – everything he had was invested in several bags of an expensive black matter called mumijo.

"Mumijo?"

"It's a type of resin from the mountains of Central Asia, a miracle cure," Harri briefly explains. "A guy in Moscow ordered large amounts of that stuff, I went to deliver it, but he bailed on me and I couldn't get rid of the bagfuls, and I didn't have enough money to get to Tajikistan..." He explains at length how his passport was then stolen and how he tried to start over with aquarium fish in Tallinn to make some money. Then how he tried to do business in Hungary and Finland with the little money he had left over, and then in Singapore and Thailand. Because then the borders were opened, and the world opened up in new directions..."

"And by the time I had enough money saved up for a plane ticket home, a few years later, I flew from India to Tajikistan. Once there, I asked the people in the building about my family, but they said that they hadn't seen my kids in over six months. They moved away, but nobody knew where! At the same time, there was a civil war in the area."

"And you haven't heard from your children since?"

"No, I haven't!"

"So they could be dead?"

"No, they're not dead! That much I just know, I can sense it, you know, I feel it in my blood. They have good genes and they'll manage just fine. Wherever they are right now, they're just being toughened up for what lies ahead."

The last bit of it sounded ominous, but I've slowly gotten used to Harri's theories about the next world war. If it comes, it comes and hopefully I'll have toughened up sufficiently by then as well.

There was something else about this story that didn't sit right with me, but I just couldn't put my finger on precisely what it was.

"Epp, come quick!"

Harri has gone to take a walk on the deck after finishing another chapter of his life, and is now calling for me from the other end of the passenger lounge. A group of passengers has gathered there in front of a large television set. The Germans, the Argentinean, the Russian, all of our ship acquaintances are there, necks craning towards the television.

"Te US has sent its bombers over Belgrade!" The reporter is anxiously relaying the news...

At the same time, we hear shouts from the ship's deck, "Come see what's going on! They're here! The planes are here!"

We practically run over each other trying to get up the stairs.

Yes. There they are, the triangular planes appear over the horizon.

"They're probably coming from the NATO bases in Italy," someone comments in a loud voice over the general hum of the crowd.

The bombers are heading straight for Belgrade, right above us. War! It's the first – and hopefully the last – time in my life that I see with my own eyes the planes heading out to drop bombs.

I shiver as it's suddenly so damn cold. There's something deeply painful about war, death and chaos, something that I almost seem to remember, but at the same time it holds an equally powerful attraction, an excitement that also somehow seems familiar from a time long ago. Perhaps it comes from the stuffy-nosed mornings of my childhood, the sheets soaked in flu fever sweat, when mom had gone to work and I was home alone, reading books about heroic pioneers and partisans. At our kolkhoz˙, they sometimes had these so-called drills for us. A fallout shelter had been built into the basement of our apartment building and during these drills we had to file in while the deafening sirens blared away.

At school, we also had drills from time to time and, of course, military education courses, where they showed us before and after pictures of the atomic bomb that hit Hiroshima. Maybe they didn't

---

* A Soviet collective farm.

show it to us every time, maybe it was just once, but it was enough for me. After that, I started praying to God every night that the Americans wouldn't drop an atomic bomb on us during the night.

I was a child with a vivid imagination in the middle of the Cold War. Maybe that's why I get along with Harri so well – his stories of the coming war land on soil in my soul that has properly been ploughed by the Soviet regime.

The next morning, when we have already arrived in Italy, the television news anchor speaks of the bombing in Serbia in the past tense. An accidental hit has also been made on the Chinese embassy, for which the NATO forces are humbly apologizing.

"Accidental, my ass!" Harri chuckles and strokes his beard. "The US military doesn't even fart by accident! This was an excellent show of power for them, because in one fell swoop they stuck it to Russia, as well as to China. Showed them that the US is a force to be reckoned with, right? But I don't think those two are just going to take it lying down! We'll see. Yes, we'll see how far away the next clash of the titans is! The first two wars started in Serbia, looks like the third one will too!"

With his beard sticking up in the air, he studies the sky with a hopeful air.

The prodigal son returns

Ten and a half years later. November 2009
Tartu, Estonia

It's a dusky fall afternoon, like any other.

"Hallo, is this Epp?" a voice asks me over the phone. "There's a person here named Arpo, who wants to talk to you. Let me give him... Here, go on, take it!"

A moment later, I hear a loud voice at the other end of the phone line speak with a strong Russian accent. "*Karotshe**, I mean is it true that you have seen Harri Hommik? I have this friend here, he helped me search on the Internet and we found your blog where you wrote about Harri."

"Yes, I worked with him, the last time I saw him was at the beginning of this year, on the Canary Islands."

"What? *Oy blyat***, where is he? I've been looking for him for twelve years! I haven't seen him for about twenty years!" The phone line relays a string of Russian curses to my end.

---

*   "In short" in Russian.
** A Russian curse word.

"By the way, I wasn't really looking for him that hard," I couldn't help mentioning, "and once I did properly look, I found him in an hour! You just have to use the Internet forums and blogs, get the message out there. I don't think anyone in the world these days can remain lost, if you have this person's full name!"

"What? An hour? I even put up a sum of money as a reward for the person who manages to find him! I found a trail, heard that he had been registered to live in Thailand, so I had people look for him there, but no luck!"

"Wait, your name is Arpo?" I remember the name vaguely. "Are you Harri's son?"

An hour later Arpo is at my place. A young man of short stature, with large muscles and a shaved head stands in front of me, looking much bigger and more belligerent than he really is. I try to find similarities between him and Harri, but I can't see any.

"I'm actually really surprised that you've had to look for him like this," I admit. "It was just at the beginning of this year, when he was praising his children when we spoke, saying how they all made their way back home themselves."

Arpo seems to be taken aback, but quickly regains his composure. "Well, I guess he has his reasons for not showing up to see us then."

"And I thought that you had all gotten back in touch already a while ago, that everything was fine. He was so happy and confident when he talked about his kids being back in Estonia!"

"*Nu vot, blyat*" Arpo curses. "Looks like you really don't know my dad at all then!"

We've been sitting at the table for the second hour already. I've been listening to Arpo's story and fitting new pieces of the puzzle into the background story of Harri's life. "We didn't have anything in Tajikistan, we were literally barefoot and starving, stealing food!" and "There are three mad geniuses in the world: the first is Hitler, the second is Stalin and the third is my father!" However, a moment later, when I'm almost certain that I should never get this young madman together with the older madman, Arpo sighs and says in a completely calm manner, "Basically, I just want to meet him and see if we can do some business together."

"All right, I think I can get you two together again," I say only to hear, "I'm strong enough to do business with that man! He was scared of me already back when I was seven years old. I'm the youngest of the four of us, but I was the only one to stand up and react to that crazy bastard. I'm sure there will be a proper reaction this time too; See, when you put nitrogen together with glycerine, you get nitro-glycerine, and both sides have their work to do!"

"That's... like an explosive, right?"

"Yes, yes! Seen a bit of that too!" and Arpo smiles his wide, devilish smile. My heart is heavy as I finally see him off: something tells me that this young man is not kidding when he says that he could kill his old man for the sins of his past, unless the old man meets his expectations...

We've agreed to go two months from now, when we both have time to fly to the Canaries. "I could just give you the directions too," I start to say, but Arpo nips that idea in the bud, "No, you should come. You're good at finding him!"

All right. I guess it will be good to have someone neutral along when this choleric duo gets together after twenty years of being apart.

A dead mother is a good mother

Two months later. February 2010
Düsseldorf, Germany

The winter has been uncharacteristically cold, even for Northern Europe. Now, on the landing strip of the Düsseldorf airport, it finally hits me: in a few hours we'll be warm again, back on my dear volcanic island... Strange, how time turns even the most complicated periods of life into "the good old days".

I've come to realize that Arpo has never been this far south and he'd love to escape into the warmth forever. Seeing the white blanket of snow in Germany, he lets the curse words fly again.

"Fuck, you fly and you fly and you still can't get away from the snow!"

"But this winter has been so beautiful," I argue. "Don't get me wrong, I'm definitely a warm weather person too. But it's just so special, when nature around you has gotten so wonderfully cold, every branch looks like it's a crystal masterpiece!"

"Bloody hell! What fucking masterpiece! I have everything: the energy, the time, the people, the tools, the training, a fantastic construction company – but I can't make a living in that fucking crystal paradise right now!" Arpo snorts in reply and continues just as heatedly, "You know what, I look around in Estonia, at everyone around me – nobody knows how they're going to be able to keep living! My friends were employers, shit, like Kolya for instance, he gave everyone the chance to work and make a living. But now he's out of money too! Fucking recession, it's the same story with everyone: the people who are still working, they've lost half of their wages in a year, but at the same time the prices all went up. And those who already lost their jobs, they're struggling, searching, crying. Everyone is thinking about leaving Estonia!"

"Would you leave? I don't think your father would like to hear that..." I interject.

"Fuck what he likes! What he likes! Umm, wasn't he the one who forgot that his children were somewhere thousands of kilometres from Estonia? He's the last person with any room to criticize! I'm going to get old, grow a beard before the situation will change in Estonia! People want stability, to have food on the table! If I had a choice between being Estonian and leading a normal life... What matters for me is having a piece of candy for my kids!"

"Is that why you want to meet your father?" it suddenly dawns on me. "To get him to help you find a job?"

"Shit, do I really have to have like a list of reasons for meeting my own father?"

Our trip started in the early morning, when we started off together from Tartu heading for Riga. There's some interesting symbolism here, Arpo, I thought halfway through my sleep while sitting in his car, listening to blaring Russian pop music. A long time ago, your father's and my trip together started from Riga, too. What has changed inside of me during that time, I really can't say, but I do know what I am looking for during this week – I'm still hoping to find my journals and I am trying to find similarities between people, and similarities between yesterday and today.

For example I'm hoping to feel that sweet nostalgia of recognition at the airport in Riga, when I see that spot where I stood eleven years ago on a morning in early spring with your father. I stood there at a corner counter writing an article, the last one of the series that the magazine publishers had already paid me for in advance. Our long journey was just beginning. "How to be happy?" was the title of the article meant for a family magazine and I was making a summary of research done by different psychologists: happy people are the ones who feel that they are in control over their life. Happy are the ones who believe in God. Happy are the ones who feel that their challenges are proportional to their skills.

But what is the challenge in your life, Arpo? Do you know what you are looking for on this trip? These were the thoughts that lulled me to sleep.

Walking through the Riga airport, my eyes wandered around hungrily, looking for a familiar place, but no such luck. Everything had changed. My thirst for nostalgia went unquenched, the little memory fragment of writing a piece on happiness rang hollow through the air, without finding a corner to settle.

"Do you have places in the world where you'd like to go back to in order to remember things better?" I ask Arpo as we wait in line at the airport café here in Germany.

"What's there to remember?" he laughs his unique, forceful and always unexpectedly loud way. He's started speaking to me in Russian. Maybe it's the culture shock of being in a German-speaking airport? I don't know how else to explain it. He had just told me before how at the age of seventeen when he returned to Estonia from Tajikistan, he didn't remember his native language at all and started methodically relearning it, writing hundreds of words in notebooks daily and trying to remember his lost mother tongue. With his brothers and sisters he still speaks a mix of Russian and Tajik – this will probably be like salt on a wound for Harri to find out...

"So would you ever like to go back to Tajikistan?" I ask Arpo.

He shrugs. "Not really, I know that it's dangerous there and I went through shit you couldn't even imagine... I'd rather go back to Siberia, the town of Neryungri!" He speaks of the place where his father first took them – he was six years old back then, didn't know a word of Russian, but learned it fast. Life was like a fairy tale, at times frightening and at others incredibly rich. "A regular person's salary was about two hundred rubles a month. But behind the aquarium we had, can you imagine, 267,000 rubles! I secretly counted it all," Arpo recalls and confirms all the facts about what Harri once told me about his get-rich-quick fish business and adds the same exact detail as his father did back then, "The ruble, by the way, was stronger than the dollar back then!"

"So what happened to all that money?"

"We moved on to Tajikistan, my father bought an island and a lot of timber, but war broke out there..."

"What do you mean war? Battles on the streets and all that?"

"Of course!" Arpo reluctantly replies and continues on a happier topic: the time when life had taken him to Siberia. Another film reel runs through my imagination, this one of a little boy – a six year old, the same age as my own daughter right now. What a cultural conflict that boy must have had to struggle through, when he was taken from Estonia and brought to live with his father and step mother in the middle of Siberia! How much does it haunt him? Has he accepted his past? This is something only Arpo knows, or maybe it is secret even for himself.

"Memory is a strange thing..." I try to coax more insight from him, and from myself as well. "As for me, I need some physical connection to certain places in order to get below the surface of my memories. That's why I want to go back to old places. I need to find these kinds of... umm... monuments of my memory, so to speak. For example, there was this woman on the island of Gran Canaria, she was much older than me, Djellah, and we met when I was selling jewellery on a particular flight of stairs. I have to go back to these stairs, because it's an important place for me, its a monument for me. Do you have places like that?"

Arpo listens and shrugs again. Then goes on with his story, "Well, for example, in Omsk, that cafeteria may still exist where I was caught with stolen money..."

"Stolen money?"

"Well, yes. I decided that I wanted to go back to Estonia to live with mymother. So I shovelled about five thousand rubles out of my father's bag and ran away. But the cafeteria manager, of course, noticed that I had way too much money for a six year old – a whole gym bag full of money – and he turned me to the cops. At the police station, I tried to get them to teach me how to shoot a gun, so I could kill my father and go back to Estonia!"

I am contemplating the last sentence I just heard.

"And that was just the first time I ran away," Arpo goes on. "There were more and more of these attempts, until he took off himself."

What a family!

My thoughts fly to Estonia, where my husband and children wait for me back home. I've returned to my old pattern of behaviour, but hopefully it will all work out. My whole life, so safe and secure, has been left behind again – but only for a week – and I'm flying towards strange adventures in dubious company.

Hopefully this adventure won't turn out to be too dangerous for anyone.

I noticed earlier already, walking around Riga airport, that we had switched roles – I was the one now walking in front, finding the right flight information board, the right gate, and mister Hommik is the one trying to keep up with me... True, it's not the same Hommik, but his son instead. However, I manage well in my leadership position, I've toughened up and I'm experienced!

Unfortunately, this burst of pride gets a severe blow at the security gate of the Düsseldorf airport. As it turns out I'm not that "experienced" after all!

"These are bottles? In your carry-on luggage?" The uniformed German woman with white gloves quickly finds a bottle of shampoo and sunscreen in my backpack.

"Yes they are, but look – there's only a little liquid on the bottom of both," I defend myself. I read that you can't take over hundred millilitres on board with you... Look against the light: I'm sure there is only about fifty millilitres left in each one."

"No, I can't let these big bottles through! It's my job! You have to put these bottles in a separate bag and check them in!"

A moment later, I'm running down the airport hallways with two bottles in hand. It turns out that I have to pay for an extra piece of luggage now. With my credit card in hand, I run to pay the fee.

"Yes, but you have too little time before the plane," the young lady at the counter announces, with that same German love for order in her voice. "You're going to have to take this extra baggage on board with you. You don't have any bottles in there, do you?"

"I do!" I reply, panting. "The bottles *are* the problem!"

I run back to the security check, pushing past people to get back to my bag. And my two pathetic bottles end up in the trashcan.

Arpo has been waiting for me on the other side of the security gate and now we run towards our gate. My heart is beating, rage and adrenaline pulse through my blood. Calm down, just calm down! I suddenly remember a moment from when Harri and I arrived in Cyprus.

"You know what," I tell Arpo, out of breath as we plop down in our seats on the plane. "A long time ago, your dad and I went from Israel to Cyprus, about a week after the Schengen countries became visa-free for Estonians. We were completely soaked, there was a storm out on the sea, but the first thing they did on the border was empty out our big bags of jewellery on their tables. Harri fibbed and told them that it was all for our personal use. Moreover, it turned out that they didn't believe that we had the right to enter Cyprus without a visa, we were bounced from one officer to the next one. Harri was so angry, he was screaming..."

"Oh yeah? I can imagine!"

I'm quiet now, trying to remember. "It's funny, but I don't remember how that situation turned out," I admit disappointedly. "I haven't told anyone about the incident before, never reran it through the sections of my brain that hold memories... And it's been erased, as if it never happened. The next thing I remember is that we've reached the Larnaca youth hostel, where we meet once again this Argentinean we know. But what happened to the material of several hours in between?"

Arpo is staring at me like I'm strange. I understand: most people are not so obsessed with the abilities or failures to remember.

"I did get a good idea, while I was waiting for you," he chuckles and changes the topic. "Could you imagine going through security with a sports bag, putting a couple of automatic weapons in there, a couple of regular pistols, some loose bullets around them and a hand grenade to top things off. And then you say: 'What, it's not allowed?' I wonder what they'd do then, huh?"

We laugh. I'm slowly getting to know my new travel companion and his peculiar sense of humour, one that formed and ripened in the midst of the Tajik civil war.

The plane has started its engines and pointed its nose south.

"Did you tell your mother that you were coming to see your father?" I start to probe a little.

"What? I don't have a mother!"

I hear another bizarre and painful story. His mother is mentally unstable, "registered as a local asylum patient, you know," Arpo says, bitterly adding that she can't be trusted and she can't manage her own life: she hasn't been able to hold down a job or pay her rent. She's been evicted from one apartment, then another one and another one, each apartment increasingly shabbier and in a worse location and nobody knows how it all will end. "It's because of Harri that she's sick," Arpo says through his teeth.

"How do you know it's because of him?"

"You imagine four kids being taken away from you and then having to go on with your life, what do you think that feels like?"

I do try to imagine it and I feel this grey wall looming nearby, moving in closer... That may indeed have been the wall that cut off Maarika from the rest of the world.

"And the fact that we didn't go nuts or that we survived at all, that's only thanks to the four of us being together in that shit, not alone! We were each other's mothers and fathers. Our sisters knitted socks for us, my brother and I, we went out on the town and in the mountains to try and find food... without a mother, without a father!"

I sigh. "I thought that my life was tough because I lost my mother when I was young, but my life is nothing compared to yours!"

"What the fuck, a dead mother is a good mother! But do you know any mothers who would just give their children away? Anyone who's ever asked me, I've told them that I don't have a mother or a father."

"No, I personally don't know any mothers who have given up their kids, but..."

"Me neither! Except for my own mother."

"Did she have a choice?"

"No." Arpo grows silent for a moment, very unlike him, but then rattles on, "If you've seen my father, that crazy power that he has, then you understand: at that time, Maarika didn't have any other choice! When we were taken away, my sister Rita ran back to my mother on the train platform, she was crying. But Rita was told clearly and from both sides that it was better for her. You have to go with your father! And there wasn't anyone who could do anything, because it was our own father who was taking us away!"

"But when Harri disappeared...?"

"...we called our mother in Estonia," Arpo quickly takes over again. "And what we got in response... *konets*, this is where we're staying. Nobody's waiting for us to come back to Estonia, there are too many of us and we're just a big headache for her. Why bother? Four kids who all want food and care. Mother got tired of us, then father did, but mother was still tired too – why the fuck they had to make so many of us!"

"Are you sure? Your mother didn't want you back?"

"Of course! My sisters called her, talked it over for a long time, discussed it and then told us the verdict: we're not expected back there. For days and days after that, we were in a big *dipressiya*, you know. Until that moment, we had been living in the hope of getting back to Estonia soon. But then we decided that we'd have to make it on our own in Tajikistan. Well, decide... You couldn't really call it deciding, did we have any other choice, all by ourselves?!"

"But your step mother? The Korean?"

"Step mother?" Arpo lets out a mocking laugh. "That woman sold all of Harri's belongings and the mountains of timber he owned and took off with her sons. I understand, of course. Her sons were a little older than us and would've been meat for the war in no time flat. But she could have helped us a little too somehow!"

I'm quiet and thinking.

"Why didn't Harri come back to get you? You said he left in 1992 and after that you lived in Tajikistan for seven more years before going back to Estonia – you grew up, became adults and you were still waiting for him to come back? He really couldn't manage to come get you...?And when he did come, as he told me, he couldn't find you anymore, because you had moved somewhere else in Tajikistan in the meantime?"

Arpo laughs. "No, really, he couldn't find us! Do you really believe this bullshit? We used to live in Nurak, we were notorious fighters and

---

hooligans there, known all over the city! And the fact that we moved on to the other city in Tajikistan, Dushanbe, and went to the university there, lots of people back in Nurak knew that! It's one of two options: either he didn't go back to look for us at all, or for some reason he decided not to ask around, because that way was more convenient for him – fine, let them be lost!"

"But maybe it is true? Maybe he really couldn't find you?" I carefully ask. "You know what? There was a sea captain, right there on Gran Canaria, who said that he couldn't find me for ten years..."

I hear Arpo's wordy response and curses directed towards his father, but my thoughts are starting to drift.

Marco.

The plane is heading south and we're approaching the western coast of Africa at breakneck speed.

I'm still not clear about whether I should meet with Marco again. Would that be polite or just the opposite, would it be impolite for me to let him know I was coming back to the island? It would certainly be a cruel way to rip the bandage off the past again, for me and for him, but at the same time it would be interesting. And secondly, is it still somehow possible that my journals from back then are in Marco's possession and he's holding on to them for some reason that makes sense to only him?

Or is it Harri who's still holding on to my old journals?

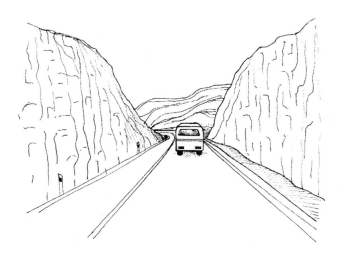

Back on the island

The same evening. February 2010
Puerto Rico, Gran Canaria

I'm running to catch the bus at the Las Palmas airport with Arpo trailing behind me, taking in great gulps of that wonderful, aromatic, dry island air.

We're here. The mellow evening sun shines right through our winter-weakened bodies, as we push and shove our way onto the bus along with all the locals and other tourists.

Sitting down on the bus, I notice a local man outside leaning against a palm tree, picking at his fingers, lifting his head every now and then to lazily look around and eye the passing buses, only to continue his picking a moment later. For him, this is just a quiet, normal day, while for someone else it's probably the most important day of his life. Like for Arpo.

Something is nagging at me and not just because of Arpo's strange search for his father. It's the kind of feeling that goes along with flying into a new time zone and climate. My head is sure that I'm here, but... my soul is still somewhere in Northern Europe and looking around for the body that flew off. The experience of those snow dunes is still somewhere very near, those immense walls of snow pushed up alongside streets and roads, so high that you can't see over them. Everywhere you look there's snow and your soul knows it. But now you open up your eyes and around you there are mountains covered in reddish-brown pebbles, banana plantations between them, peeking out from underneath the plastic sheets that protect them, and some palm trees planted by the side of the road.

"This is like Tajikistan in the summer, only it's February right now!" Arpo moans with delight. "*Bloody hell*, did he ever find a place to settle down, huh?" I look at his reaction to the place and feel a sense of pride over those palm trees in front of the airport, as if this island was somehow my responsibility. In reality, I know that this island is a place that is created to wither: there's no nutritious topsoil here, no periods of rain to nourish the earth, and even these palm trees wouldn't grow here without proper maintenance. Besides that, there is a lot that is fake here. I'm embarrassed a little while later as we drive by a landscape strewn with nothing but hotels and advertising.

"What's this place here?" Arpo asks. "Some fucking town that has nothing else but hotels, and it never ends!"

"When we get a little more to the west, there's more nature, but here at the southern end... The island's economy is booming, like the tourism brochure says. Places that were banana plantations ten years ago are now covered with hotels. Every week planes full of people are flown in who produce garbage, trample everything and leave a week later."

Arpo shrugs: "Fuck, but people need a place like this!"

I think back to the time when this island pressed itself out of the surface of the Earth in the burst of a volcano and won a place for itself in the world, the power that forced itself out towards the sky and brought with it a river of red, molten lava. Hopefully this island with its radiating power will quietly survive this time of little human ants abusing it. Whatever the future will bring...

We're weaving down the road in the right direction, but time is ticking away, the rapid nightfall of the southern hemisphere is already visible behind the windows. "Do you want to go looking for Harri first thing tonight or should we drop off the bags at the hotel first?" I ask.

"Uh-huh, maybe in the morning," Arpo hesitantly answers.

"Why?"

"I guess because there will be more people around and he won't be able to run away."

Was that a joke? Was it self-deception, trying to avoid of an uncomfortable moment, leaving it for the next day? Or was it something else? I still feel like I'm missing pieces of the full picture. Why would Arpo think that Harri would run away? Are there secrets here I still don't know about? I know from my own experience that a relationship with Harri can mean getting hurt, but I still don't know whether to blame him for what happened eleven years ago or just myself... In my case, I decided long ago that it's better not to hold on to bad feelings.

"You know what, let's go tonight," I suggest after a brief pause. "The last time Justin and I saw him it was an evening, he was packing up his jewellery and he came to have a cup of tea with us."

"Oh!" There was an endearing sensitivity in Arpo's voice. Is he really just now realizing that it's not an enemy he's going to see? It is his own father, after all!

What's it going to be like when Arpo and Harri meet? I've run the different scenarios through my head dozens of times over the past few days and there's one that's become my favourite. This seems to be the appropriate moment to tell Arpo about that scene.

In that vision, the two of us walk on the promenade, Harri is there and he's selling his jewellery.

"Hi!" I call out to him, continuing right away while pointing at Arpo, who's with me. "Listen, Harri, last year you were talking about building that fish store. I brought you a really good worker; he's interested in your project..."

And then I can tell him more about what a good builder he is. While I'm talking, Harri's light blue eyes will turn to the young man. Arpo assumes that his father won't recognize him, because it's been more than 19 years since they last met.

"His name is Arpo," is what I would say next and then stop talking.

His name is Arpo! It's a very unique name. I don't know anyone else in the whole world with the same name.

Then it would be Harri's turn to say something. In my imagination, the essence of what comes out of his mouth should be about like this: "Please forgive me that you haven't seen me these past two decades and that I left you in faraway Central Asia without a mother and a father." But we're not going to coax all this out of him, we'll just say Arpo's name – and the lost father should decide himself as to what to say next.

"Super!" Arpo exclaims after hearing my scenario. "You're not lying. It's the whole truth. Because I do want to build. I'm a construction man – and from then on he's the one who has to say something, do something. That's what we'll do!"

He looks at me for a moment, "Tell me why you agreed to come along? Are you really such a curious person that you flew all the way over here just to see us meet again?" I suddenly realize that Arpo is smart, but at the same time he's also being very self-centred. Not once during this whole long day of travelling have we talked about my life on this island.

We're still winding around the roads in the bus, still heading for the southern end of the island, the same old familiar roads, and I'm talking now about my life, things that happened in this place right here, but at a different time. A little about Djellah and a little about Marco. And a bit about the journals that went missing, and the children that Djellah never had.

"Kids," Arpo latches on to the subject, "are a blessing that some are given and some aren't." I'm starting to understand and appreciate his philosophical sensibility more and more. "And children are a gift that should not be left behind, physically or mentally. Children are sponges, what you pour on them stays in there. Can you imagine the way I live my life: I've had such a fucked up childhood and youth, I know that often times I think like a sadist, a pervert. And I know that I'll raise my child in a way that he won't become like me! If you only knew what a golden child I have at home, he comes up to me and gives me a hug, climbs in my lap – but when I was a little kid, forget about it, me climbing in my dada's lap?" Arpo stares out of the window.

"My kid did get in Harri's lap last year," I remember.

"Well... the man may have changed. But don't start telling me about how he's learned from his mistakes and so on. I'm not a *thing* that you can just use for learning! And children aren't just *roes* that you can spawn and then leave to drift in the waves!"

The bus arrives at Arguineguin.

Arguineguin!

My heart is beating. I cannot follow Arpo's life drama anymore, I have my own to follow here.

If I were to come back to this village in, let's say, thirty years, would I still feel as vulnerable? The future that never happened here, will that always haunt me?

I sigh as I look at the familiar buildings around us, until the bus stops, spits out its passengers and swallows up new ones. The blister on my soul is there not just because of Tom, with whom I had a very painful phone conversation in that booth right over there. It's not just because of Marco, for whom I waited at that cafe over there before running to catch the bus. It's also because of Djellah, who used to hang out of the hotel window, right over there and who never had any children, or because of Javier the traveller, who sat on that same bench over there and told about how he cut off his possibility of ever having kids again. And even because of Harri, with whom we had tea right over there in that cafe and who left his children alone in the world.

We take off again. Pink cirrus clouds have taken over the sky: it's a sunset. I look at the sky and it looks very familiar. Haven't I seen a sky exactly like that in some melancholy moment long ago?

A person's memory is strange. For example, there are dream-like street corners in mine. I don't remember exactly where they are and the context they were in, not even the country in which they are located. They don't have any particular importance for me, but they exist inside of me, surfacing these moments before I fall asleep.

And then again there are things that I know I should remember. But they're just not there, as they've dissipated. Right here on this island is a place where I'm sure I used to call my husband Tom regularly and I remember the fact that I did call, but most of those situations have seemingly been wiped clean – I don't remember them. It often happens that dreams and wishes remain much more vivid than what happens in reality. That's why I remember so well all those children from that colourful alternate reality for whom I waited during my first marriage with no avail. Three little boys, who were just as real in my imagination as my two girls are today. I imagined their faces and saw our future together.

Children. I think that children are important actors in our game of life. Have we all perhaps met behind that curtain that opens on the stage of existence? Harri lost his children and is certainly paying for it in his own way. For a large part of my twenties, I carried around with me those children who were never born. I would like to ask those boys why they didn't come, but in reality there's nobody to ask – they're just fiction.

I miss my family in Estonia intensely right now. "Mummy went to write her book" and "Mummy went to bring uncle Harri and uncle Arpo together," that's the reason I gave them – the girls had met both men several times. Marta accepts it all with a childlike ease. She thinks it's self-evident that her mother writes books. Hopefully one day she'll understand just as easily that her mother was married to someone else before her father and that her mother has done some silly things while travelling around the world.

Do I have something to say?

Eleven years earlier. June 1999
On a bus from Riga to Tallinn, Estonia

Emptiness.

The closer our bus gets to the Estonian border, the more apathetic I feel. Like a person who has just survived an immense shock, I look out wide-eyed at the changing landscape behind the window. It seems hazy. The world around me is in dull colours and faded edges today, but it is possible that the problem is in my eyes.

I'm not afraid of the mess and shame that awaits me in Estonia. "Oh, really?" That's the most thought-like reaction I manage to find inside of myself.

Oh, really? I've just lived in Israel for three weeks, met more people and heard more stories. I left Marco behind, and during these weeks I have been tempted to look up his number somewhere and just call him, but I haven't given in. Why? When the plane left the surface of the Canaries and as I searched the ground below for my familiar landmarks, I felt an immense wave of sadness. My story with Marco, it was left unfinished. We didn't get to say farewell or see-you-later. The plane turned towards the north and after a day of travelling Harri and I were back where we had been before, in Cyprus. Every day I felt the temptation to contact Marco one way or another, but each passing day that temptation got smaller and increasingly hypothetical.

Just the same way, I had never given in to the temptation of finding Harri again. He and I parted in a bizarre way that probably would have astonished me any other time, but on that specific day, all I had to say to myself was, "Oh, really?"

That afternoon I got on a bus in Israel to go from the Tel Aviv airport to the city, Harri was bent over a bag and looking for something – and the bus just left.

I should have run to the driver and yelled, "Stop the bus!" but I just turned around in my seat and looked at the long haired figure in the middle of the road, yelling and waving his hands, until he got smaller and smaller, and then disappeared as the bus turned a corner. That's it, gone.

In Cyprus, before getting back to Israel, Harri and I had discussed our financial situation. I owed him roughly about eight thousand Estonian kroons*, because my income was only ten percent of the sales, but I had been buying food for myself all along with the money I made during the day. Harri was "generous" enough to include all the unused visas in his expenditure, the ones to the US, Japan, Mexico and Korea. "See, the thing is that you can use those visas for some time now," he said, so I suppose he was expecting some gratitude.

Eight thousand kroons. Four months ago that didn't seem like a very big sum, it was just a part of my monthly income as a journalist. At the moment, however, that kind of money was out of reach and freedom was exactly as far as that sum.

Harri didn't threaten me, didn't paint any negative situations for me, just relayed the fact to me in a neutral, interrogatory tone – you owe me this much, so what's going to happen now? I sniffed and said, "All right, I'll pay you!" and we fixed a time to meet the next morning.

Without any plans whatsoever about where to get the money, I walked around the beach and tried to gather my thoughts.

How much had life changed me over these past few months! The same beaches of Cyprus were around us, the ones where I followed my "boss" around, happy and glowing, hoping to find the "promised land"

---

*   8000 Estonian kroons is about 500 UK pounds, or about 700 US dollars.

and make a lot of money. Now my eyes were as faded as my clothes and I didn't believe in miracles anymore, at least not the ones Harri was telling about. I felt a desperate need to just pay that sum of money and get rid of him.

When I think back on the events that followed, a shudder passes through me again, just as if Life has poured a shot of stronger stuff down my throat. What happened that evening? It was something that I really don't know how to explain in a normal way and it was another thing that shoved me into that apathetic "Oh, really?" condition.

I went to spend the night at the youth hostel in Larnaca – Harri was sleeping under a bush near the street lined with palm trees, but I wanted to take a shower and get away from him. At that hostel I met two sisters about my age from the Lebanese Christian community. They had come to Cyprus for a week of vacationing and travelling. One of the sisters had truly unique eyes, the same kind of look-into-you-and-through-you look that first drew me to Harri, but frightened and repelled me as well.

"Are you in trouble?" said that strange girl, almost immediately after we'd said our hellos and exchanged the first cursory phrases. "Don't be afraid. What's happening to you right now is necessary – someday you'll realize that."

"I have money trouble," I said, really thankful that someone was paying me such warm and personal attention. I would've liked to tell her everything, but she probably wasn't really expecting that.

"Don't be scared. An older man will help you tomorrow, maybe even today. You don't have to be afraid of him. Everything will work out just fine."

That calmed me down, actually it made me completely and utterly calm – I was tired of worrying. Who that older man was supposed to be I didn't know, but I was too exhausted to trouble my head with it any further. Is it Harri that will just let the debt go, is it Marco who will find me somehow and give me the money, or is it Tom instead, who's waiting for me in Estonia and is, after all, almost seven years older than I am?

Is Tom waiting for me? I wasn't even sure if he would be, but at that moment I couldn't let that thought go any further. Stop!

Instead, I went for a swim in the sea, just before dusk. I let my body relax, it wasn't until now that I felt how strained it had been the whole day. Floating in the water, without moving, looking at the darkening sky, I was thinking. Water is always comforting, it lets pure thoughts rise to the surface.

I had done some seemingly bad things over the past four months – cheated my husband, cheated the police in Israel, Cyprus and Spain, cheated other people. But if I should somehow get back to square one, if I were sitting in the bar firts time with Harri, or looking at the moon on that mountaintop in Slovakia, I would have chosen the same path all over again.

Did I really not regret anything?

All those faces, stories, events and feelings I had gathered were swirling around in my head. Somewhere among all those images, I saw a pair of accusing eyes. "I'm sorry, but I still don't regret anything," I told those eyes and they disappeared.

Running out of the water towards my beach towel, I felt someone's stare. A woman travelling solo in southern countries soon gets used to these stares, they become an inseparable part of her life, but at the same time she will (or at least I will) usually want to make sure where the stares come from.

A middle-aged man with curly, sandy brown hair and a friendly dimpled smile, wearing a blue dress shirt and khaki pants, was sitting on the edge of the promenade. The smile was for me.

I didn't smile back, but I didn't get defensive either. There are dimpled smiles all over the world, and there are kind girls who tell you that everything will work itself out. I picked up the towel, and wrapped it around myself.

And then it happened.

My throat swelled up and my chest got heavy, the world around me obscured. I crawled between my towel and the sand and felt the earth move. All of those grains of sand around me, each its own small world. I just wanted to get to know this world! God, forgive me for hurting others! After all, I ended up getting hurt myself as well, sometimes while sitting on top of the world with Harri, sometimes while hanging out with Djellah on her window sill, sometimes while waiting something else from Marco. And Tom... I knew that behind all those adventures those eyes looking at me full of hurt were his and there was nothing I could do to get them out of my head.

What happened with Tom was something I couldn't think about before. It wasn't until now, sobs shaking me under the beach towel, that I allowed myself to remember.

It happened in the Canaries, a few weeks back. About five days must have passed since we talked – I didn't have a phone or the money to go on the Internet. I got some money and called. Around the phone booth the sun was shining, the birds were singing and exotic blossoms were spreading their sweet aroma, when from far away, through the static I heard a tired familiar voice.

"I know everything."

"What do you know?" It was the lousiest answer that one could've come up, but it was also the most spontaneous one.

"I know about Marco."

I'm not sure how long the pause was. Maybe it was precisely at that moment when the apathy first hit me, and had grown deeper ever since. Time didn't matter anymore. Did anything?

Through that numbing fog a new sensation came over me. The knowledge that I did not belong anywhere anymore. My husband was becoming my ex-husband and the man who was the cause probably didn't really want me, or maybe I didn't want him, in any case, it didn't seem to be the future that the fortuneteller had predicted. There was no more Tom, and there was no more Marco. There was only Harri with his insane stories, and with the debt.

"Someone sent me an anonymous letter," I heard the voice over the phone speak again. "It was an e-mail that you had sent to Estonia."

Pause.

"Do you have something to say?"

I did not have a single thing to say. There's a big gaping hole in my memory from that moment on: I can't remember how that conversation ended and what happened next. Did I cry? Did I walk along the seaside or the streets? Did I climb up a mountain? One for sure, I didn't lose a single thing during that evening, so my instincts must have still remained intact.

True, I did lose a person.

Or actually more than one.

The next place I remember is a bench, right there at the southern end of Gran Canaria, on a seaside promenade. I was looking down at the sea, listening to the ocean beating against the jetties and trying to gather my thoughts.

Someone sent an anonymous letter?

Yes, I had told people about Marco – exactly three of them, my very best friends. It was one time in an Internet cafe, when I sat there and felt that I couldn't live with all the lies anymore. So I wrote them, each of them, about how I was together with a one-time sea captain who's now a hotel and shop owner here. I wrote about the sand in the mountains, the way it blows in the windows at night, and I wrote about how I didn't know what to do next and how to tell my husband about it all. The story, written down in black and white, seemed so strangely beautiful yet tawdry. I liked the feeling that I had while writing it down.

But one of these three people had betrayed me. Who?

That day in Gran Canaria I lost three of my best friends. It was another reason among the many for which I was crying on the public beach now in Larnaca, curled up in a foetal position under the beach towel, face pressed into the sand.

An incalculable amount of time passed before I calmed down. Maybe I had even fallen asleep. But I felt a pleasant weariness in my soul.

As I crawled out from under the towel and got back up again, I felt the stare on me once more, and it startled me.

The smiling man was still sitting there, about twenty metres away on the promenade, looking at me. I have no idea whether fifteen minutes had passed or whether it was an hour, but there he was and he now started to walk towards me: a curly haired man with kind eyes, big dimples and laugh lines. He looked calmingly bizarre, like a middle-aged Santa. I started to walk past him to leave the beach, when he stopped me.

"Can I help you?" he asked, with a strange accent in English. "Please, let me help you, I don't want anything from you, but I can see that you have worries."

I didn't answer, wiped some sand off my face and gathered myself. So what was my worry? Should I really trust this stranger, while I haven't entrusted anyone with my confusing baggage of concerns, not anyone close to me, nobody in Estonia or Gran Canaria, nor had I tried describing to Harri how difficult things were for me.

"Can I help you out with money? Or do you need to talk to someone, or to have someone talked to?" the man asked on. "Tell me. There's a solution for every worry in the world! Almost every one of them!"

Then I remembered what the Lebanese sister had said. An older man was supposed to help me. And here he was, an ambassador of fate, someone I shouldn't fear.

We walked along the evening promenade, all lit up. Franc had introduced himself by now. He was a Slovenian arms dealer, who had come to Cyprus to make a deal. "My work takes me around the world, everywhere where people need weapons... I just went to strike a new deal in a factory in Belarus, before it I signed a sales contract in Israel, and I'll be flying to Indonesia, to East Timor next week. Wherever you hear news about wars or possible conflicts, you can be sure that we've tried to make deals there to supply people in those areas with arms... I have two passports, one of them I use in the Arab world, the other in the Jewish one..."

Oh, so this kind of money, made by killing other people, is going to help me out of debt, I thought in sheer astonishment. Oh really?

"What's your name? Why were you crying?"

I started answering Franc's questions and told him my whole story, pierced by his short exclamations of surprise, or questions about more details. The story took us around the promenade twice, but I just didn't know how to tell a shorter version. Starting with the angst that drove me to leave Estonia and ending up with, yes, of course, the money that Harri was demanding from me now and that I was so desperate to pay off, in order to go on in peace and without debt, even if I didn't know what the destination would be.

"Come to my hotel," Franc invited me, and I trusted him. It was a five star hotel directly facing the promenade where we'd been walking in circles. The first thing he did in the room was click on the television, probably to bring some normalcy to the awkward situation. It only made things more surreal. A live show from the Eurovision song contest was about to begin: from straight across the sea in Israel, the same place where I'd been so happy three months ago and where I was supposed to return a few days later.

So it was with the background European disco, ballads, and the whole circus that goes with it that Franc told me about his wife, and the daughters who had suddenly become adults, all of them growing distant from each other and about how his life had become somehow dry and brittle ("If you know what I mean?" and I nodded). He talked about money – how there's so much money, how money never makes you happy, but a successful deal does, for a moment.

"Aren't you disgusted by the fact that you're selling tools for killing people?"

Franc looked at me with his great big brown eyes and smiled. "You really are a writer! Why are you asking a thing like that? See, if we didn't do it, someone else would. The history of the world is a history of wars. There are too many people in the world anyway."

Also true, in a sense.

Franc never touched me. He did ask for my e-mail address and the number of the cell phone that was waiting for me in Estonia.

"I'll get to Estonia in a few weeks," I told him, "and I have no idea what will happen then. I just don't know."

"I'll call you," he said. "I'm worried about you. Tomorrow I'm flying away from here and I it's partly my responsibility now that you won't end up somewhere in the world crying in the middle of a public place again!"

When I left around midnight, after another Swedish ABBA clone was declared the winner, after I'd become richer by another life story and another worldview, I felt that God had helped me. My inner balance was restored.

"Here," Franc held out his hand as I was leaving, after rummaging around in his bag. "I happen to have this money here."

"One thousand Deutsche Marks*? I didn't even know a bill this large existed!" I gasped.

"Take it, please take it. You have no idea how little money matters to me. This bill has significance for you and by accepting it you give

---

* The Deutsche Mark was a widely accepted currency in Europe until the introduction of the euro in 2002. 1000 Deutsche Marks was about 8000 Estonian kroons at that time.

significance to it for me as well! I guess I still do feel that I have some sins to atone for. Can you help me in this?"

It seemed that Franc had said something very important to him, even when it was said with a sarcastic smile. I accepted the pink bill – for the past few hours I knew that I'd accept it – hugged Franc goodbye and walked to the hostel. The sister from Lebanon was there and smiling at me, "Are you better now?" I nodded, but we didn't speak about it anymore.

The next morning I handed the pink bill over to Harri, along with all the jewellery that was left in my bag. The employment was over. Harri eyed the bill suspiciously, but didn't ask me where it came from. For the last few days in Cyprus, I got an odd job at the beach fair in Larnaca, where my job was to yell out, "*Mono mia lira!* " and give out darts to men who ran up to try their hands at throwing them. I got enough money from the job to easily pay for food and a place to stay overnight...

When I got back to Tel Aviv and the money ran out, the receptionist of our youth hostel turned right to me and asked, "Do you need a job by any chance? We have this system here where you get free boarding if you want to participate in the clean-up work at the owner's other company, and we need people for tomorrow."

Of course I wanted to. Once again I felt that someone upstairs had grown tired of jerking me around and started taking care of me again.

Next, the apartment in Tel Aviv, where I was sent with a couple of other people, to clean. It was a peculiar place. The owner of the building was set to start renovations at the apartment. The previous tenant had faxed a letter to end her contract and in it she wrote, "Do whatever you like with my things." Apparently she had worked as a flight attendant on international flights, met the love of her life and moved to the US, quitting and leaving everything on the spot.

Our job was to prepare the space for renovations and put all the things left by the previous tenant in large trash bags. No, not just trash and wallpaper. We had to remove all the layers that make up a person's life: the clothes, sheets, pillows, books, dishes, CDs. Like vultures, the

---

* "Only one pound!" in Greek.

neighbours were rummaging through the big bags that we put outside of the apartment in the courtyard. In the meantime, random men marched in and hauled out the shelves that had been emptied. That small world was falling apart from every angle.

I looked at the destruction and suddenly understood that young woman.

She made a choice, she chose to leave, or rather stay where she was, and not ever come back. At the same time, she wanted to take along her home, and she did just that: in her memories. Coming back here to the apartment, she would have had to see and organize this whole destruction herself. Perhaps this home was so important to her that the only way to take it along as a whole was to give it up completely.

While gathering things off the shelf, I noticed a passport. That moment I felt a pit in my stomach. Could it be possible that the girl has been killed instead? How can someone move to another country without taking her passport with her?

But one of the neighbours who was passing through to get another load of things to carry out, helped calm my suspicions. "She had two citizenships, I guess she just took the US one with her when she was working and that was enough for her."

Why am I going back home? That's what I was thinking as I thumbed through that stranger's passport. So I don't have a fancy US passport, but if I really wanted to, I could give up the idea of returning as well. There's a keen knife out there just waiting for me to take it and cut through everything that's already passed, cut out a slice of it and just let it fly out of the window. A sharp and clean blade, a quick and final solution.

I tried to bring myself out of the metaphoric world onto a more realistic ground. Would it be possible? If I were to post a letter of resignation to the publishers who are waiting for me to return to work in three weeks, and another one to Tom saying, "Do whatever you like with my things." Would it be possible to then retain untarnished images of my former life: the dog, the house, the sea, the books, the music collection, to hold on to them as they were, without having to witness their destruction with my own eyes?

That night I walked along the streets of Tel Aviv for a long time and lined up all the facts. Fact one – I have a return ticket from Tel

Aviv to Riga in two weeks. Fact two – I left the phonebook with Marco's number in the bag that I left at his house, so in order to get in touch with him I'd really have to make an effort. Fact three – even if I had the number, I wouldn't be ready to open up my mouth and convey the following request from Israel to the Canaries via telephone lines: "Marco, please buy me a plane ticket and I'll come back to you, maybe even as soon as tomorrow." It doesn't matter whether I want to go there or not, I just don't have the guts to ask that. Fact four – I couldn't give up all my things in Estonia the way that flight attendant did. Call it responsibility or call it greed, but I want to know what happens to my earthly possessions if I should leave.

I put on the old automatic pilot and did several interviews in Israel over the next two weeks, asked questions, recorded stories, took photos, smiled, but all the while a strange freeze had taken hold of my soul, pressing itself out through tears.

So I poured out a whole river of tears at the Holocaust Museum in Jerusalem: sitting there in the large, dark room full of music and numbers, I let the sorrow completely engulf me. Behind every number there's a person whose life ended in a concentration camp, a pulsating being of the universe, with his suffering, his pain, the end of his life that was so full of humiliation. I would like to understand the world better, I'd like to have a better grasp on all these lives, that's why I came on this trip, but now I don't even understand myself – the single number that hangs above my soul in the heavenly cards somewhere, I couldn't even be responsible enough for that one...

Walking on, I noticed that something inside of me had changed for the better. I'm crying, but it's making me happy in a way, because it shows that there's life left in me yet. I'm breathing and I can see and feel.

A little slipper? A little foot that will never take another step. It doesn't matter whether it belongs to the child I never had or the one who was executed, the one whose slipper was found in a concentration camp and put here under the glass.

When the next great wave of tears subsides, I remain standing in front of a photo of an SS soldier, who's looking straight into the camera. The withered body of a dead man was on the ground at his feet, perhaps still warm, maybe not even a corpse at all. At first glance it looks like the soldier is smiling... But, no, that's not a smile. The eyes are squinted too much and the teeth are too bare. A kind of expression you get when you step out of the dark and into the light.

That expression replays itself on my face the next morning, or actually the next afternoon, as I step out of the dark hostel common room onto the rooftop terrace to look at the world and the sun in the eye. "What's going to happen today?" I tried to gather my thoughts, letting my gaze wander over the midday heat on the sandy-coloured stone walls and flat roofs of the old town.

I'm in the cradle of world religions, a historic part of the town where it's almost obligatory to stroll through all the museums and churches. But I'm afraid to go out and walk in those narrow, winding streets, where I felt like screaming out of sheer, ecstatic happiness just three months ago – I have a feeling that if went back there, my frail balance would be totally lost. One step at a time, at least I've made it out of bed, for now I'm just sitting in the sun on the terrace and quivering on the inside. Well then, what now? In addition to all the other culpability, there's the sense of guilt over not being able to go anywhere or not taking in a part of the enchantment of this country.

I climbed back between the cool sheets of my bed. It was the exact same room and bed that I had three and a half months ago, when we arrived in Jerusalem. My spirit was full of expectation back then. Faith. All the pain was still ahead of me. The optimist in me imagined us immediately exchanging all the goods we had for cash and embarking on an adventurous and enriching trip around the world. When I sold my first whistle, I was happy as a little child. Life was three months younger, three months more innocent and beautiful then.

With these thoughts, I pulled the covers over my head. This hostel had a good tradition. Whatever the time of day, the bedroom was filled with a humid, dark silence. Bunk beds, heavy curtains, the quiet hum of the air conditioner, the invisible cohabitants whispering as they pass through the room. Just what I needed to do some thinking in a peaceful setting.

There were things that even in that state sparked surprise in me. How did it happen after all that I went on a trip with someone whom absolutely none of my acquaintances had met before?

Or why didn't I leave him earlier? I remember that Djellah suggested it, Marco suggested it, but for some reason I couldn't do it. Why?

And which one of my friends was it who sent the letter to Tom? What was her motivation? Would I be able to forgive her once I understood why she did it? I trusted her and believed that she cared about me, but... actually, yes, I had lied to her myself, when I said that I was going travelling with a "group of people selling jewellery", while in reality there was just one crazy Harri. Why did I even think that I would come out of all this unscathed?

These were the questions that made the time pass by on that damp day that was more like a hole in time and space. The clock ticked away in the hallway, the loudspeaker of the minaret announced the midday and afternoon prayers, five days were left until I had to leave. Maybe I could pull myself together enough tomorrow to do all the interviews that were left?

In the evening, I finally got on my feet and walked to the Internet cafe. One more time, a few new letters that I didn't even feel like opening: more colleagues asking about my plans, about what I had done in the meantime, and what I was doing now.

I sighed, looking at the glowing screen, and composed letters filled with something. About how I met a television crew from Moscow and how they offered me a job in Russia, so now I was wondering whether to accept it or not.

There was no news from Tom. None of my acquaintances asked about him either. Something was in the air, of course, and they must have sensed it as well. They were probably just waiting, tactful on the surface, hungry for gossip below.

But Tom?

I was free from Harri. I didn't owe anyone a thing. Now what?

My Slovenian guardian angel Franc had also sent me a letter, but I didn't know how to reply. I didn't want to lie to him, or tell him the truth for that matter, as I was having a hard time defining the latter for myself.

I set one foot in front of the other and got myself back to the hostel. This was the lowest point of the whole trip, the deepest hole that I had dug and now I had to fill it up with something. But with what? At nightfall, I pulled out my eyelashes, every twinge of pain briefly providing some satisfaction for me and my faith. I blew on the lashes, sending them scattering, and said, "Dear God, I want to become a writer!" Maybe it will come true, as the old saying goes, 'send the lashes you find into the wind and your wish will come true'!

But maybe it won't? Maybe this well will remain dry? I keep trying to experience something, collect something, I'm skidding along the globe with nothing to hold on to, until I'm finally so exhausted that I what – throw myself in front of a train? Like Anna Karenina did?

Looking at the dark ceiling, I caught a thought that turned out to be the most cheerful surprise of the day.

All of a sudden I had a moment of recognition: I know that Anna Karenina existed. I've seen her! She's more real than Lev Tolstoy himself – I know nothing much of the latter as I lay here in bed, staring up at the ceiling tonight. Anna Karenina, in any case, is more real than hundreds of millions of human ants, who have lived here with their concerns and who I know nothing about!

And then people say: fantasies, make-believe? How do they know that the fantasy never really existed? Maybe *they* are living right here next to us and everyone just doesn't notice them? But then there are some who do take notice and pull them out among us. And that's how I know that the two-man television crew from Moscow does exist and that they're filming a show about the holy city of Jerusalem here. I see their eyes and smiles, I see how they argue amongst themselves and how one of them is jealous of the other's girlfriend, the other is jealous of the first one's innate talent, and how they really did come and invite me to work with them in Russia yesterday!

And somewhere next to this trip with a sad ending is that other one: the one where everything turned out great.

The next morning I was walking in the Arab quarter, in old Jerusalem. Dodging the lewd stares of the men sitting in front of the teahouses, I covered my eyes and the now thin lashes with sunglasses and acted like a regular journalist. A meeting that had been arranged three months ago was about to happen today. I was supposed to visit an Arab family of four sisters and to interview them for a magazine. That gave me some comfort. Be that as it may with everything else, once I get back to Estonia I have some great articles to turn in.

Walking back to the hostel that night, I let my thoughts run free again. Who am I?

I stopped and looked up at the sky over the holy city. What form will my thoughts take?

Maybe it was because of the looks those men sitting in front of the teahouse sent me in the morning, but I saw myself as a piece of meat hanging in the night air. Meat. When I started the trip, I was tender and pink, but now I'm a well-done, brown slab that won't be cut as easily. If a war broke out, I'd run for those hills, see, right over there. I'd find a stream. I'd run against the current, find the spring that is its source, dig a cave there and maybe even survive. That's what Harri taught me and even though I'd gotten rid of him, his teachings had taken a foothold in me.

What about the real world? What about returning home? Could managing my life there actually be tougher than surviving a nuclear winter? Well-done meat is not suitable for an ordinary life.

There was another thing I realized while looking at the lights of the holy city at night.

I had with me now old seamen, world travellers, boat-dwellers, tourists and hippies from countries all over the world. Through them I had become richer, but somehow lost my own self, and became invisible. Nobody in the world knows the truth about me. Everyone has only a warped piece of the puzzle from here or there. Some have heard about my "uncle Harri", others about the "group of travellers selling jewellery", others yet about the "television crew from Moscow"... And the same way I can chop my seamen and world travellers into little pieces one day and nobody will understand where the truth ends and fantasy begins.

Strangely enough that thought provides me with a kind of relief. This time I managed to even talk to people at the hostel before falling asleep.

The next morning, I went into a bookstore and read about the Holocaust, preparing to meet an old woman who had survived the horrors of the concentration camps. Sitting there on the floor of the bookstore and reading, I felt another wave of tears coming. All the humiliation and hideousness these people had to endure!

I bought the book, walked away and tried to calm down. The Jewish quarter. The young, confident people with shiny hair, dressed according to the latest fashion, the reality around us. Just as it was in the Germany of the 1930s, before everything went out of hand... Confident youths strolled around just the same way, believing in the future. But everything can change by tomorrow. The line between reality and incredible events is sometimes so fragile.

For a long time, I looked for a peaceful spot to continue reading and taking it in. With tears of sweat and humidity running down my back, I finally circled back to the old town. A church! I quickened my step and headed for the silver sparkling domes and the golden cross.

And here I was. It didn't matter what denomination the church was. Here, in the damp coolness was a place where I could be sheltered. I let the clamorous flow of people carry me along for a while, then broke out at the right moment and squeezed myself into a spot somewhere underneath a set of stairs, away from the buzz of conversation generated by so many different languages, away from the crowds. The grey stone floor of the old church emanated pure peace.

These are the kinds of moments I live for.

After turning the last page of my book, I got on my knees, pressed my head against the damp, cold stone wall and cried out of loneliness and shame for myself and the whole world. Besides the Holocaust Museum, this is another place where you don't have to pretend to be normal and happy! People are passing by behind me, but here it's all right. I'm in the holy land and in a holy temple. Rivers of tears must have been cried along this wall before me and through these tears, I actually do belong somewhere. I'm joined with someone.

The tears took me back to the other side of Europe, to the village of Arguineguin, to Djellah. Is that what my future will be like? The way she laughed in her smoky voice, narrowing her eyes and saying, "Life is a collection of illusions. How is it possible to believe in one single truth, when truth has so many facets?" And she gave me a conspiratorial smile, as if she'd just revealed her biggest secret to me.

Little by little I have learned to understand more of what those words really mean. Here I am, crying in a Christian church over what happened to the Jews, there's no difference whatsoever where I'm crying and for whom. Goodness and peace are the same everywhere.

Right there in Arguineguin, there were a number of people who all believed in me and smiled at me. Like Terje, the old Norwegian with a white beard who always smelled of beer. He bought a whistle from me at the market and started carrying it around in his pocket, pulled it out every time he saw me, whistled and called out, "You're a smart little girl!"

Yes, so many people have told me along this trip that I'm "smart". Actually, I've deceived them all. I'm just a little girl, nothing smart here!

The peaceful calm and melancholy that comes after crying was broken by a tour group that stopped nearby. I wiped my tears, stuffed the book on the Holocaust into my bag and inadvertently remained there listening to what the guide next to me was saying, pointing a little farther off.

"It's been estimated that right over there is where Jesus was nailed to the cross. And the stairs to Calvary Road start right there!"

What? I had been reading and crying under the stairs that led to the Calvary Road?

The flow of the masses and the desire for peace had taken me to the Church of the Holy Sepulchre, one of the most important pilgrimage sites for Christians.

"Oh, really," I thought while reading the signs on the walls of the courtyard leading to the church, and then headed back to the hostel. What was this all about?

Whatever. I still have some money, I can eat and I have a place to sleep. Maybe tomorrow I'll have strength enough to call that concentration camp survivor and set up a time for the interview.

So here I am, on the bus, saying to myself "Oh, really," and looking out the window as we cross the border. Tallinn is getting closer and closer, I'm back at the point where my journey started. My trip around the world in four months turned into a "trip from Latvia to the Middle East, through Southern Europe to the coast of Africa and then back." How should I present this trip to my acquaintances and colleagues? I hadn't sent an honest bit of correspondence for weeks, since the anonymous letter incident had shaken me to the core. From time to time, I'd send fun letters about my new adventures, but for the most part I just kept quiet, because what else did I have to say?

However, next week I'll have to return to work. Where am I supposed to live? Tom hasn't responded to my letter. Is he all right, will he be meeting me?

The rocking motion of the bus calms me. A certain understanding – melancholic and peaceful – has risen to the surface over these past few hours. Come what may, another period of my life is about to be over. A girl with loads of baggage is returning from her travels.

Tom is at the bus station. When he embraces me, I catch the sour scent of a sad man. I squeeze my eyes shut, hoping that one long strange dream has now ended.

Battling the terracotta soldiers

Two and a half months later. September 1999
Xian, China

Strangely enough we didn't talk much about what had taken place. Tom just decided to forgive me and give me another chance. All the guilt and blame stayed on my side, I continued my life as a journalist and a housewife, without being able to talk to anyone about exactly what had happened. To all who asked, I just mentioned with a cheerful nonchalance that our "plans changed," we didn't get very far from Europe with our "team of jewellery sellers" and others heard about how "I won't be going to work in Moscow, even though I was invited..."

Not a single bit of truth.

And there was no public humiliation, no change of life, even though at times I longed for both.

The same kind of longing washed over me sometimes when I thought about life on Gran Canaria. What was it that Djellah had said? That how over the course of her travels, she had found a few places that she missed so much that it hurts when she's not there. But you have to learn to control these longings, and suppress them, she said, "Otherwise you couldn't live at all, because you can't be in two different places at once!"

Sometimes Franc the Slovenian called me, "How's it going, hope you're not going around crying in public places anymore!"

"Everything is fine," I'd tell him and end the call quickly. Marco and Harri had disappeared from my life too. I had it all back, the sunshine, the neighbour's meadow, the reeds swaying in the wind behind our fence, the flowerbeds that needed weeding, the neighbour's horse trotting by. Everything was exactly the same as a year ago, in late spring of last year, when Tom and I had taken out the loan and bought the place. Now it seemed to me more and more that the angst and urge to get away had just been a passing nightmare created by the winter gloom.

But the sandals I'd worn on the trip had left white lines on my tan feet. These well travelled sandals were now cast in the corner by the door and we saw them every day. Maybe that's why Tom and I ended up here in China.

"You know what, I've decided to do some self-improvement," he said in a joking tone one day. "If it's really that important to you to travel and see the world – why don't we go to China together this fall?"

Everything had been thought through; everything was great, almost perfect. The Helsinki-Beijing tickets were available with a "pilgrim's discount". Tom's old friend was welcoming us in his home in Beijing and was willing to show us around the town, Tom's boss had given him three weeks off...

And that's how we came and spent the past week here in Beijing, sleeping on the floor in the home office of Tom's friend, a young Estonian man who married a Korean girl. They have found their happiness, I'm sure of that after seeing the aura of their marriage from the inside for a week. I look at their life and wonder what is wrong with us, why can't we be like them?

But last night we left the happy family alone for some time and headed for the train station to start an overnight trip to Xian, to see the biggest and most sensational archaeological find of the twentieth century: the immense terracotta army that guarded the tomb of Emperor Qin. But more than the hordes of legendary life-sized terracotta soldiers, what I wanted to experience again was simply the act of moving. A week in Beijing had loaded me with tension. I had decided to be happy, smile at people, smile at the flash of the camera and at my husband, who really deserved it. Can fake smiles and laughter generate real joyful energy? I didn't know what to call this tension that had built up.

Something did happen on the train. It felt like the tension was pressing itself out of me in quite an odd way... I knew that I should keep some semblance of control, be happy in a quiet and balanced way, a way that would be suitable for the reception capabilities of a northern man. But I couldn't help it. I wanted to scream in ecstasy when our train barrelled through a mountain range. It felt as if the energy of the mountains was passing through the train walls and mingling with my own, but maybe what was reaching us was just a white noise and acoustic effects, explainable by physics.

"It's the best feeling in the world, to be in a moving object between points A and B," I called down to Tom from my bunk near the ceiling, where a pillow made of rice was crunching in agreement under my head. "You know, it's almost an orgasmic feeling that I sometimes get while I'm travelling!"

A shadow passed over his face. Of course, I was sorry; I shouldn't have put it quite like that. The spontaneous exclamation probably reminded him of Marco.

He didn't say anything, but the elephant in the room had moved itself again a bit and stepped on someone's foot.

I looked out of the window, happy about the changing scenery beyond, yet holding back the tears.

I had asked all my three girlfriends: please, be honest with me, were you the one who told Tom about what happened to me in Gran Canaria?

"No, I swear, I didn't tell him. I haven't sent any anonymous letters." That's what they claimed.

One of them had to be lying, I suspected each of them in turn, but since I didn't know who did it, I couldn't trust anyone anymore. So I was left with just one old and trustworthy friend – Tom – but I couldn't exactly talk with him about what happened. We did try to touch on the subject at times, at least the beginning of my trip, "when Epp was a bad girl and ran off with some crazy old man".

"When you left me..." Tom began.

"No, you left me!" was my take of the situation and I couldn't keep it to myself. "You should have been with me on that trip. Or you should've told me not to go. But instead you told me, 'Go ahead, do whatever you want!'"

"And had I told you not to go, would you have listened to me?"

"I don't know. That's a life that never happened..."

"You're so self-righteous!"

We never mentioned Marco's name in conversation since I got back from the island. Once I was thumbing through my little Spanish-English dictionary at home and discovered a handwritten note inside in Spanish: "Pleasant learning, for my crazy girl! M." I burned it right away in the fireplace – just to think what would happen if Tom found it, how hurt he would be again!

Looking down from the bunk in our car, I see two heavy-set American women who have just come to occupy the seats and are looking through some photos. Some of those photos are strangely familiar...

"Excuse me," I call down. "Where were those pictures taken?"

Two heads turn up. "It's a really beautiful city in Northern Europe – Tallinn," one of them answers. "I just went on a trip there before coming here. I really recommend going, it's a fantastic place!"

Oh, really? We're travelling here in the middle of China and we get a message that our home is a place that a stranger recommends us to go visit. The world is small indeed and full of weird hints.

We're here, in Xian now. Sometime before the Common Era, thousands of life-sized terracotta soldiers were buried here along with the emperor. We're walking around looking at the dozens of unearthed mass graves, the empty stares of the reddish clay figures, but I can't concentrate.

I was happy to leave Beijing, but for what? Definitely not for visiting this wonder of the world.

These soldiers come alive and turn against me in the little hotel we reach in the late afternoon where I toss and turn in a semi-sleep between hot sheets. I feel my skin burning, like right after staying in the sun. These are my sins, my husband's bitterness and all the words left unsaid between us that are behind the unending torment of this dream-like state. A broken air conditioner on the window is dripping water into my bed. The drops are falling in a torturous cadence, like the way prisoners in this country have been tortured for thousands of years. Drop by drop.

"You're not happy, are you? What's wrong in your life?" My husband asks in a whisper in the slowly darkening room, feeling that I'm not sleeping. "What would you like to change?"

"I don't know!"

If I talked about the dripping water and how it's always better somewhere else, it would be petty. If I talked about the fact that, see, we haven't had any children and that's why I'm so crazy, it would be trivial. Besides, it would mean accusing us of something we can't change. If I said that I'm in love with someone else and I want a divorce, it would just be a lie – the thing just waiting to be set free in me is something else. But what is it?

I hear muffled Chinese spoken on the other side of the wall and for a moment, I'm astonished about how we came all the way to the other side of the world to talk. And why we're even wasting time here? We don't know how to speak to each other anyway. We could rent bicycles instead and go riding somewhere between the cornfields, out of the city, far away. On some country road, we could ride like the wind and forget about our unspoken stories. Like two parallel rails, never really meeting, but still useful to each other in a way.

We couldn't find our hotel at first, despite having a map of the city in our travel guide.

"Hotel?" Tom would ask in English on the street, close to where the hotel should have been. People just passed by and gave us awkward smiles. Some would say something in Chinese.

"Hotel?" we continued our search, intermittently fighting with each other, swallowing down the bitter truth that without each other we couldn't manage here. What a disturbing inevitability. We had fought just the same way while taking pictures around town earlier. The intensity of travelling is not suitable for those who have unfinished business between them, even if they decided to wear "happily ever after" expressions on their faces.

Then I found a piece of paper in my pocket where our friend from Beijing had written some key phrases in characters. I jumped up to a girl passing us by on the street and stuck the piece of paper right under her nose, with my finger on the row of figures that was supposed to mean "hotel".

The girl gave us an enthusiastic nod and pointed to the door behind us.

Unbelievable! We had been asking people right in front of the main entrance of the place and apparently those two golden lions flanking the doorway were supposed to indicate the location of the hotel. Except they didn't think it was necessary to put up a sign in English. They lived in their own world, one whose language we did not understand.

This common ground of incomprehension brought Tom and I together again for a moment. We laughed together, but my cheeks burned feverishly.

Now tossing around grasping at the beginnings of dreams, I feel that the panic stricken search for the hotel is a situation that replays itself in my life all too often. Yes, there are perhaps a lot of things that many people find to be obvious in this world and they don't need explanations. But I have this weight that I can't shake. It's as if I don't understand what's really going on, as if I've ended up in a nightmare where everyone else finds a path that suits them, but I don't. So here I am with Tom, we aren't officially lost anymore and by all expectations we should now behave either like tourists (going out again to conquer the city) or like a family (by pushing the two single beds together). The tiny hotel room comes with a chasm: when we stepped inside, the two narrow beds were pushed up against the side walls and an air conditioner is dripping on one of them. And that's how it stays.

"Let me just try to sleep a little bit, take a *siesta*. I mean a nap," I said and immediately regretted what I had said. Why did I have to use words that hint at something Spanish again?

I finally wake up after my nightmarish afternoon where I've fought a whole army of annoying terracotta soldiers and searched for the right path. Through the hot and humid room, I see my husband, sitting there straight backed and staring in front of him.

"Do you really not remember what day it is today?" he asks.

I don't remember. And then it dawns on me.

It's the fifth anniversary of our love affair. Five years ago today, there was a music festival in our town, and the evening found us spending time at the newsroom, both young journalists as we were. I ran off and he followed me. Under the light of the full moon, we sat in a courtyard, and talked about everything under the stars: about my mother who was dying in the hospital, and my plan to become a writer, and his dead father and his plan to become a writer. It seemed that we had so much in common.

That evening and night in China, layers peel off. We're trying to learn to speak with each other again: we fight and we throw our wedding bands and then look for them under the bed, kiss and try to make up.

By morning, nothing is more clear than it was the day before.

The next day we're walking in an area with several temples. I look on with curiosity and envy as people here pray. I have never prayed like that: bent over on my knees, forehead against the ground. But my ticket here was bought with a pilgrim's discount, I suddenly remember. Maybe this is meant to be a pilgrimage for me?

As a child, I used to turn to God every night with one big and important plea: please don't let a nuclear war happen tonight, neither in my country nor any other country, please! Then I grew up and started to think about other things before falling asleep. The next time I turned towards that *something* was essentially with no reason at all: I was sixteen years old and participating in the protest walk through Latvia and Lithuania, led by the two devoted Catholics Paulius and Petras. We passed by all the churches big and small along the way and kneeled there, our leaders, the Lithuanian politicians, first, and then my friend and I followed suit, not really knowing if it was for excitement, for fun or for team spirit. Praying was exciting and interesting. It required concentration and gave me a strange sensation in my ears, like the sound you hear when you listen to the inside of a seashell: the sound of blood coursing through your body and something else as well.

It was a time when I was pure and sincere and just adhering to something without the sense of distress. During the years between now and then I had forgotten the experience and only in times of trouble did I remember what I knew then, what I have experienced, the fact that this *something* can be contacted. It helps.

I feel a need with all my being, a physical tension: need to get down on the ground just like that, in a foetal position in front of a tiny, nameless temple, like all these people here are doing. The urge is so great. I don't even have time to read the signs to find out what temple it is.

"Dear God... dear gods, whether you're one or many, or whoever is listening to me," I turn to the universe, looking for a logical beginning and addressee to my story, kneeling on the ground, my forehead against the surface of the planet, somewhere in the middle of China. After that, I just break down and start to wail on the inside. "I promise, I promise... I'll be all right with everything that's to come, just help me get through this!"

I'm afraid of getting more specific: should I ask for children, a new husband, or the old husband, money, a peaceful life, or adventures? I just don't know. I'm lost. Maybe someone out there knows?

Tasting the air of an arms factory

Eight months later. February 2000
Near Minsk, Belarus

I can't believe what I have gotten myself into.

My colleagues in one town think that I'm in the other town in Estonia, and vice versa. I don't have any close friends, because after the anonymous letter blowup I don't trust anyone. Tom and I don't talk about our comings and goings anymore, ever since I packed my things after returning from China and moved into a tiny rental apartment. It is in the Old Town of Tallinn, and in a building I saw in one of the photos the American ladies were holding in the train in the middle of China. Life draws some wondrous patterns, if you only take time to notice them.

When the Slovenian arms dealer Franc called me again, I told him that I'm in a "time out" period with my husband for at least a few months. Upon hearing this, he invited me to take a trip. For some reason, I still believed that a trip might be the solution. This is one of the patterns in my life. I let problems be solved by a change of latitude.

"I'll pay for your ticket," Franc promised me. "And there are no strings attached, when it comes to me, if you know what I mean. I'm just inviting you as a friend and as a journalist! With my help you will be able to see some places where outsiders are never allowed!"

"I don't know," I hesitated, a little out of modesty and a bit because the trip to China showed how hard it is for a person in crisis to take in new experiences.

But before I noticed how I'd made the decision, Franc and I were already discussing his schedule for the coming weeks and months. Do you want to go back to Israel? The thought of it made me shudder. No, that would be too much. Do you want to go to Pakistan? I thought it over for a few days and said yes. How else would I ever get the chance to go to that exciting Muslim land? Yes, they will be buying guns from Franc – it was painful just thinking about it, but exciting in a way as well.

But before Pakistan, as it turned out, Franc invited me to Minsk instead. "One doesn't rule out the other. We'll be in Pakistan for a week, but in Minsk for just three days!"

So here I am. Nobody in Estonia knows that I flew to Belarus for three days. If something happened to me now, I could, of course, theoretically be found using my plane tickets and border crossing records.

We're walking around an arms factory. It's clear that the management and probably Franc's colleagues all think that I'm his lover. My ears are turning red and I'm not even trying to pretend to be interested in their guns.

The air in the factory is damp but glowing hot the closer you get to the production lines. Some of the furnaces are as though from hell, flames as high as a man rising above them. There are streams of red molten metal flowing down. So this is how guns are made? Like fates, these rivulets first flow down freely until they find their mould. From then on, they ride down a conveyor line – the farther they go, the more cleansing fires they pass through. Each time a blue flame laps over it, the steel becomes stronger.

"Come up here, the view is great!" the moustached factory director calls to us.

We walk up to a rickety balcony rail. On the whole floor below us there is a pool of orange-red molten metal where the rivulets originate before they run down into the moulds. Future weapons, future pain. I'm breathing someone's imminent death into my lungs.

If I wanted to, I only have to jump down from here. The bliss – the supposed bliss – that you only find when you jump, fly, drown, boil... What do I have to fear? The soul is immortal. What do I have to hope for? A new choice. But what a strange end it would be for my body and what would they do with a corpse like that? What would happen to a human body at that temperature, in boiling metal?

I force myself out of this line of thinking. Every high place holds this temptation for me, to jump. But usually I don't think about the corpses. Maybe I'm more depressed than I realize.

I smile at the men standing beside me discussing something in the sizzling hot air, and I feel the taste of metal in my mouth.

That taste stays there until we all go out for lunch, where I shovel caviar into my mouth to get rid of the taste of metal, but it's not going anywhere. The factory boss speaks, the interpreter translates, then the Slovenians speak, they raise their glasses for a vodka toast, I shake my head and refuse. I haven't been able to follow the conversation for quite some time now. I've even given up trying. More and more I understand that I've made a mistake by coming here. Why? What was I expecting? This is a factory where guns are melted into their shape, these lunchtime conversations lead to new killings, and did I really think that I would leave here unscathed?

I excuse myself and go out for a walk in front of the restaurant. Some innocently white and slender birches, the sparkling snow and the blue sky, the crisp air I inhale to help me ease out of the experience I just had.

Franc is not my friend.

All of a sudden it is painfully clear. He wants something else, something more.

He has been a gentleman and booked a separate hotel room for me, but he does come in to talk. I'm distracted, the red rivers still running through my mind and the taste of metal in my mouth. Where are those guns going, the ones I saw today? Who's going to get killed with those? Someone is most definitely going to get killed, those guns are not going to remain innocent.

That's the way the world is, yes, Franc is probably right...

"What do you think?" he asks.

"What... oh, sorry, I wasn't listening!"

"Oh you! You weren't listening at all?"

"No... I don't feel very good and I still have the taste of metal in my mouth."

"That's normal. It will go away in about a day or so. Listen, I just proposed something to you! I can see that you like me, otherwise you wouldn't have come here..."

I swallow. Burning metal. Of course, somehow it penetrated my saliva and my blood, when we were standing there over the melting pools and when I almost jumped in there. "She just went for a swim in that red sea and never came back, we don't know whom she met there and where she went to..." is what Franc would have told my father, grandmother and grandfather once he found their contacts somewhere – provided he felt an explanation was necessary... I felt the blood running through my veins. The red blood inside of me. Somewhere in there the answer is circulating around, the knowledge of how to be a happy child, the one that my grandparents and my father remember. Maybe someday I'll find that knowledge again.

"...I could pay your rent in Estonia, I could buy you a car," Franc tells me at the same time.

A car, what car? I swallow again. The situation has become very absurd. I must have been in a very self-centred depression not to have seen this coming. Of course, this had to end in a proposal like this.

"I could take you along on all my travels," Franc continues, smiling smugly, still like that younger version of Santa. A strange man who thinks that money can fix everything. But I guess I have helped him come to that conclusion.

"I think that this could be very good for both of us at our respective stages of life," he continues, still smiling in a chummy way.

Yes, I think through a fog. That kind of life would indeed be comfortable for you. A wife who stays in Slovenia and the life that was dry, but I would be the lover here and there, in arms factories and war zones. A life like that could probably offer a budding writer a bounty of material.

For a second, I seriously consider the offer.

It's the moment right before I lose my balance completely.

I've been bawling my eyes out alone in the hotel room, I've brushed my teeth and gargled, but the taste of metal is still there. I've sat in a hot bath and tried to scrub myself clean. My head hurts.

What have I done, how did I end up here?

Franc is knocking at the door: "Come, have dinner with me!"

"I feel sick, I can't", I respond. "I have metal poisoning!"

"Just let me in for a moment. How are you doing?"

"No, no, I can't."

"I just want to be your friend. Let me in. Let's just talk this over."

"I'm really sorry that I came along on this trip with you."

"You don't have to apologise!"

And so on. Through the door, metal taste in mouth, red pool still swimming before my eyes...

At the end he leaves. Two more days of this hell.

Those two days have passed by somehow. I haven't been to the factory anymore – I'm absolutely positive that being in that place is harmful for my health, mental as well as physical. There are images now that I can't forget. Life is full of a series of cleansing fires, but where does it lead to at the end? Who needs my pain and my experiences? The next thought takes me back to the red, bubbling pool, with the diving board, sorry, viewing platform...

The arms dealers and factory owners meet two more times out on the town for lunch. I decide to go along to these lunches, but I can't bring myself to act politely, like a normal person. I'm just writing, on the corner of the restaurant table, completely isolating myself from the rest of the company: recollecting, analysing, pleading, planning. This notebook will be a letter that I give to Tom once I get back to Estonia.

I can't imagine what the rest of this company thinks of me. Probably that Franc's young lover is a manic, an insane character. I don't care what they think of me.

I don't want to be alone with Franc anymore. I'm disappointed in him, as well as in myself. This situation was, after all, such a cliché. Did I really think that it would not end with a sexual overture?

I've just returned to Estonia.

Never before have I seen anything so hauntingly empty and huge as the one-time international hub, the airport at Minsk. Darkness ruled in the halls with infinitely high ceilings, only a hallway lit up helped me find the right place somewhere at the other end of the gigantic dark maze... The arms dealers had already flown off to Vienna and here I was, all alone. There were four passengers on the flight, and vibrating emptiness filled the space inside of me.

At the airport in Tallinn, as soon as I could, I dialled the familiar number with hands shaking.

"Tom, it's me! Please, please forgive me!" I rattle on and on, a clump in my throat. About how I've suddenly understood everything and I know that I made a mistake by going with "Harri on the crazy trip"...

He is so glad. It seems that now, after a long time spent building them, the walls around me are starting to fall, and I know where I belong.

"We shouldn't ever hide anything from each other again!" I exclaim into the phone. "I need forgiveness, understanding. Do you know how good it feels! I just went on a trip, to Belarus..."

"Wait! I have something I have to confess as well," I hear from the other end of the line.

"...Yes?"

"Don't think that I'm perfect. I lied to you about how someone... well... sent me an anonymous letter about your life in Gran Canaria."

"What?"

"See, I knew the password to your mailbox, you gave it to me a long time ago, when you were sick and I had to print out something for you at the office. I just read all the emails you sent and received while you were away on your trip. And I've looked in there later, too, to see how you're doing. That's been my secret, please, don't be mad at me!"

"What? You..."

"Yes, I read what you were writing, to whom and how... But I couldn't just come out and tell you, so I made up the story about the anonymous letter.

Are you still there?

Hello?"

February 2000

At that moment another trust that I've held on to in this world shatters. The walls around me spring back up, the secrets are all back. I manage to think real fast, slick as a spy: oh, so he read my emails the whole time, but that means he doesn't know about Franc, because we mostly spoke over the phone.

And I won't tell Tom anything about Franc, even though two seconds ago I was ready to do so. I have to move on, now. On my own.

Recollections from "there"

Ten years later. February 2009
Las Palmas airport, Gran Canaria

I wake up startled, but where? Can't remember. Where am I? Sitting, facing a huge dark window, yellow halogen lights buzzing above my head. What am I doing here?

I realize that this reality is not going anywhere. Let me deal with it later. I'm remembering something else right now, much more delicate and precious that can be lost at any moment, unless I go directly into it.

It was a market day, in the afternoon heat, and I met Samil, or was it Basil? Once awake, I couldn't describe his face, but in my dream it was all still there. I helped that dark-eyed, smiling Arab sell his toys and he asked me something, after the gang of loud children had left the sales booth.

"Hey, do you have a mother? What does she think about you going around on these adventures?"

I started to answer him when I woke up. It is still here; the way his question made me feel, the answer that had begun to form, holding something sad and defensive, but also a clear message. I want to catch that answer, but it's floating away already.

A dream is like a river, into which everything important flows together. And maybe all the dreams flow towards the most important: into the great ocean, somewhere where we began our lives and where we end them.

I shut my eyes again. Something in this dream reminded me of a moment of reality from right here on this island in that spring ten years ago. I had made enough money in the market to stay at a hotel, so I was drinking wine with Djellah again in her room. This was something that had turned into our little secret habit. Shared wine. It helped escape whatever was clamped down on my spirit. Ten minutes after swallowing wine, and another moment of happiness arrived, full of laughter and humour, and then that moment of happiness began to open up and reveal multi-coloured worlds that it hid. It seemed like without wine and without Djellah I couldn't touch these worlds.

On that particular night, Djellah talked at length about Michael, her former lover who was still waiting for her in the US, the guy who had nightmares and couldn't fall asleep without sedatives.

She poured some more wine to help her along with the story, looking as if she had another one, she might burst out in tears.

That's no good!

We are not good for each other!

I realized that suddenly in that symbolic, dreamlike moment: Djellah and I feed each other's strangeness and sadness. We don't have mothers who would tell us not to do something, and we lack children who would steady us!

As if startled by my thought, Djellah threw her hand up in a wild gesture a little too carelessly and spilled her wine. The red liquid flowed like blood all over her yellow Indian dress and splattered over to the sheets. She sat with her legs crossed on her bed and jovially yelled out, "What the heck?"

It was a colourful, beautiful and decisive moment. When people talk about moments that change a person's fate, this was one of those moments for me. Painful and unpleasant, but at the same time it revealed a new horizon for me, full of relief and the knowledge that I am not going to be alone in my new choice. It won't be easy, but it will be interesting!

"You know what I just decided," I blurted out enthusiastically. "I decided that as of right now, I'm giving up alcohol. I don't remember when I last ate meat. Giving that up was somehow natural. But this moment, right here, right now – I'll remember it forever! This is the moment when I say NO to alcohol! I gave up smoking the same way once, cold turkey. Catching the right hypnotic moment, you know? I hope you don't mind?"

It seems that Djellah was still a bit offended about my outburst. The more I think back on that evening – and I have, quite a few times during these ten years – the more I'm sure about the fact that yes, she was offended. She probably would have jumped up in her yellow dress covered in red rivulets and danced in front of the window of her hotel room, but instead she got a bit down and just said, "Oh, really?" The same night she also made a remark, something to the effect of, "Epp, you're probably never going to come back to this island, you just want to keep moving forward."

This was an idea that haunted me later. The desire to only keep moving forward... was that a criticism or a compliment?

I'm sorry that I'll never get the chance to talk to Djellah again. I would like to explain that for me giving up wine was in no way a judgement on her life. Everyone makes their own choices and that applies to giving up things as well. I just felt that a new door would open up for me on that magical night if only I closed another one. This is what I'd like to explain to her and maybe talk about *the other door* a little too. And I'd certainly want to reassure her that I didn't consider her lifestyle to be the wrong one. I did not think that she was incapable of loving! Or incapable of moving on!

That night I simply sensed that my path and her path were actually different, not as similar as I had toyed with in my head before.

Djellah's death has haunted me. I've known about it for a week now, but I'm still surprised about it, and in a sense I wasn't surprised about it at all – it was as if the news was just a reminder. Someone once told me once, "Death gives life an artistic depth." As literary as Djellah's life was, so was her death. She went just like she feared that she would: while still young and because of cancer. If that's not the *art* in life, then what is? With her deep and somewhat melancholy nature, she probably started to respect that kind of death and came to terms with it. I just hope that she wasn't too alone during those couple of weeks before her death... I doubt that she thought about me for even a moment in those weeks – although, who knows what others think about?

What could be going on in the thoughts of someone who finds out that their body, their best ally is full of a treacherous growth? I remember what Djellah once told me about the time that she was working in a home for the elderly to earn some money and to get a better grasp on the ways of the world. How it was there that she understood that a person really doesn't change with age, but just develops different ways of being lonely. One of those ways is distancing yourself from your own body, because it doesn't obey you anymore and doesn't look like who you thought you were.

Djellah is not the first important person to die in my life. I think, eyes still shut, almost asleep, weaving through all those people. My mother succumbed to a tumour as well, also in early middle age (if you could say that about forty years of age), the same kind of death that gives life the depth of art... and made me almost believe that anyone can die. Unfortunately that belief is just like believing in God – going through your everyday business, you just forget. That's how over the years after my mother's death, I started to take it for granted again that everyone in my life is immortal and will forever be around here somewhere. It seemed that death is somewhere else, not in my people, not in my stories...

But no.

Death is everywhere. I grow towards death each day, as do my daughters and even the egg cells inside of them. Death is what reunites us with the place from where we came. And when I look back at the people I've met along my travels – here and there, sooner or later – then the possibility of death is the only thing that joins us all. Sometimes reality reminds us of that.

What has become of Javier by now, I wonder?

I remember how I met that vibrant vagabond again, after our first long conversation. We bumped into each other at the hotel foyer in Arguineguin – yes, at Marco's hotel. The greenish-brown eyes, the bright smile, the wavy hair sun-bleached to a light brown shade, the round Paul McCartney-ish face, the handsome tanned body, and the vibe, "I'm the freest person in the world", perfectly symbolized by the vasectomy he talked about at our first meeting. Javier didn't really even have a homeland anymore, just like Djellah. He was originally from Northern Spain, the Basque Country to be more exact, but after that he lived for a long time in England, Australia, drifted around on the world seas, so the English he spoke was a charming British-Aussie mix.

I brought to our chance meeting a rattled voice, a swollen nose and dulled eyes. I was in a crisis, partly because of the "Canary cold" as they called this sneaky island virus, but also because of the whole mess in my life, because I was always procrastinating, saying to myself I'll do it tomorrow. Tomorrow I'll quit working with Harri. Tomorrow I'll call Tom and tell him I've found someone else. Tomorrow I'll earn enough money at the market to get a hotel room. My despondence was exacerbated by the fact that two days before I had left Djellah's room, telling her that I was not drinking wine anymore, creating a discord in our relationship that was easy enough to sense.

"Come on, let's go to my bar. You need a hot tea with a shot of rum to fix that throat," said Javier, full of life, smiling to me at the hotel foyer. He worked nights at a bar nearby, at least for a few weeks before moving on.

"I can't," I rattled back at him. "No more rum! I decided to quit drinking altogether!"

"Oh wow... Why?"

Why? That question has always befuddled me, in years to come. People don't trust those who have given up alcohol. And let it be said right now that my relationship with alcohol, meat and coffee has gone from "completely clean" back to "moderate" and each time I end up coming back full circle to the tempting idea of giving them all up for good.

I want to. I need to desist. Why?

Why do I like restricting myself? Is it punishment for my wrong-doings?

No, I think not. Giving up meat and intoxicants is really no punishment for me. Instead, it's more like a game, trying out new rules and testing new limits.

Is there a sense of belonging in that, like an identity search? Oddly enough, I feel no sense of camaraderie or belonging with vegetarians or abstainers, instead I've tried to go through these renunciations in a quiet and apologetic way. "No, I'm not a vegetarian, I just don't like meat that much..." or "Thanks, but I don't feel like having any wine today..."

I also remember what I told Javier back then and how he burst out laughing when I was done.

"I believe that when you give something up, you can open a new door or window, or at least find a small crack in the wall that shows you a new world! I have had peeks into this other world and I have always thought that it's only with the help of alcohol that you can see it, but maybe by giving up drinking altogether... you open up... that other world?!"

"Well then! I've always been all for freedom, and any kind of restrictions just make me gag. But the way you just worded it makes giving up drinking sound like a new kind of freedom! Where did you read that? Who told you about it?"

I thought for a moment. "I haven't read any books at all during these past three months that I've been travelling. I'm pretty sure that it's just my own feeling," I then answer.

"Strange, strange girl! You're one in a million!"

"I am one in a million. There are only a million Estonians in the world!"

Instead of Javier's suggestion of going to the bar, we end up going for a walk. "Moving your body actually gives you the same kinds of liberating impulses as alcohol does," I tell my companion, making him laugh again. "It also takes you to a *door*, you'll see!"

There's a seaside promenade in Arguineguin that turns after the row of hotels and leads straight to the cobblestone timeshare castle of Anfi del Mar. It's about three kilometres there and three back. Of course, during a sunset this kind of a walk is... pretty romantic. I looked behind as we left the hotel. Is it possible that Marco could see me from a window upstairs? If he was at his mother's? I hadn't seen Marco all day and we didn't have any plans for the evening, especially since I said that I was sick and that I needed a little time to myself. Hopefully he didn't notice me heading for the promenade with another man.

I remember that we talked some more about freedom. Javier's opinion of freedom was somehow full of negativism. For him – I think – freedom meant cutting yourself off. He had a goal, and he was saving up to buy a yacht. Arms flailing in excitement, he explained everything to me about the different types of yachts and in his dreams he was already off sailing somewhere, anchor up, and free!

"I've developed a different understanding of freedom recently," I started to look for ways to verbalize it, between fits of coughing. "It seems to me that freedom as a surrounding environment is overrated. You're just drifting in your freedom, not moving forward. I still think that by setting restrictions for yourself, you can find new directions and propel yourself towards them."

"But maybe me giving up people is like you giving up wine, huh?"

"Ah! That's an interesting idea, I should write that down... Let's stop for a moment at that bench right there, I have a few key words I want to write down – my memory is starting to fill up and I can't think along anymore!"

Javier nodded and then suddenly asked, "Did you say before that you don't read books at all?"

"Right now I'm not doing most of the things I did in my regular life before! I don't cook, I don't sit at the computer, I don't clean, I don't go to the gym, or to the beauty saloon... And I'm not reading right now either. Instead I'm just sitting at the market behind my stand, watching people and writing in my journals." I wasn't going to add that lately I had quite a few problems with the diary format. If you're writing about reality, you have to be brutally honest with yourself, but what I saw in those moments of reality in my life wasn't the most pleasant of images.

That's how "writing in the journal" for me has become an excuse to escape into the future, filling up my pages with dreams.

"I, for one, can never fall asleep without reading," Javier told me with an apologetic smile. "I'm always lugging some books from one place to the other!" That confession suddenly brought him very close to me: the muscle man became a geek, we were both practicing our very own ways of escapism.

And so it went that over the next six kilometres, I entrusted my new kindred spirit Javier with all the problems in my life. "I have problems with men. As a well read person, maybe you can help," I started off jokingly. And then I ended up telling him everything.

By the end, we were standing somewhere near the hotel and I was not worrying whether Marco could see us from his windows or not. During this long conversation I had come to understand that my feelings for Marco were not as strong as they should be. Or, let's just say, as strong as feelings can be in this world.

"What can I tell you?" sighed Javier. "Your main problem is not knowing what you want, isn't it? You have to read some clarity into your head!" Right there, under the blinking light of the streetlamp, he wrote down a long list of books for me to read, into one of my notebooks that stayed behind on the island. "And when you've read some clarity into your life then you can decide what you want! Choose whether you want to work with Harri or not, and whether you want to stay with Marco or Tom – or maybe neither! And when you've made your decision, then you'll know, but the main thing is not to feel guilty about your choice!" he said, stressing each word.

Yes, guilt. I had been carrying quite a lot of that around and it was so good to see another human being, a beautiful and confident one at that, smile brightly and say, "This guilt is so beneath you, remember that! And when you don't feel good, read books!" He stood there, the symbol of a happy and stable person, shining under the streetlights. Even though I suspected that inside of him hid an immense well of sadness for the parts of him that had been cut off, anyway his recommendations for bettering my life were indisputably more than adequate. He was like a courier from higher up, sent to deliver me an important message.

"Right now in your life it's... umm..." he went on and started looking for something in his pockets. "Wait, I have this electronic Spanish-

English dictionary, I type in the word and then I get the exact translation. I want to use all the correct words, as precisely as possible!"

But what was that word he typed in there? *What* was it in my life that he had to word with special precision...? I don't remember. From that point on, my memory is fragmented, the picture jumps ahead to the hotel, to my room, where Marco came to look for me half an hour later. And where smelling that familiar scent I decided, yet again, to postpone all choices and decisions until the next day.

I smile sadly remembering all that. The realization has started to bother me that as much as I wanted to, I'll probably never find Javier again on this planet. I'd probably have to pay tens of thousands to private detectives – hypothetically – but would it be of any use? His last name and contact information was in one of the notebooks I left behind. Long ago, I'm sure I had the shadow of a memory of his last name in my head, but even that is now gone. I remember how we stood there under the streetlights, and how I pulled a notebook out of my bag. Right there under my eyes, he wrote down a list of books, then his name and his email address. I can see the hand moving on the paper. I see the result, and the details, but not the whole. There was an H and an E in that name. Also a Z. But what order they were in? What name did they form together? Well, that's something I can't mine in my memory. I'm sure it's in there somewhere, but where?

Just like we don't apparently remember most of our dreams, we probably don't remember most of the things that are *actually* inside us, and we have to manage with just the things that are reachable in the uppermost layers. That's how Javier has disappeared to the place from whence we once came. He could be alive, or he could be dead. But for me he's back "there" and I for him in the exact same way. Does he remember me? What does he remember? Like our six-year-old Marta says, "Are you me? No, you're not! So you can't say what I know or what I feel!" Each one of us has the right to feel and deal with our memories in our own way.

That's how I have two people who I'll always remember from those travels ten years ago and how they helped me over the difficult end. One of them was Franc with his large pink bill and the other, an even more significant person, was Javier. When I wanted to stop crying, all I had to do was think about him or, maybe it was just the opposite, he came into my thoughts right at those moments to help me stop crying at the right time. "It's all logical: you're not guilty of anything!" he said with a wide grin, like the Beatle with the happiest smile, and I knew it was true.

I stretch and look around. Halogen lights are buzzing above our heads, and I can see my reflection in the window. That's right. We're at the airport, at an ungodly hour in the early morning, waiting for a flight back from Gran Canaria to Estonia. Justin is sitting next to me, deep in thought and reading something on our laptop. The kids are yelling and running around with a little Finnish friend they've made; not at all fazed by the clock that says it's 'five in the morning. Justin notices me looking, smiles in a weary and understanding way. I feel the exhausted and light-headed pleasure of the end of a trip – we did it! –, and a calm sense of expectancy: by tonight we'll be back at home, where the only plan we have for the next twenty-four hours is to recover from jet lag.

What else?

If I write this moment down right now, I'll always "remember" it, but the only thing is that in *reality* the moment was a bit different than the way I affixed it to words right now. It's not going to be the reality I remember later, but its shadow. And when I talk about this moment to someone else, they'll also experience a shadow of this shadow.

It's hard to get into your own memory and understand whether something is reality or whether it's leaning towards fantasy instead. After all, I remember so many things. There have been so many happy and unhappy moments in life – but maybe most of them are dramatized, skewed towards either side of reality? For example, Harri's "life movie" that he shared with me ten years ago, was that perhaps also a form of art instead, not the reality?

Some memories are like miniature pictures: so fine, sharp and clear, so beautiful, as if they had been worked on with much care.

This is what my only memory of rain on Gran Canaria is like from ten years ago.

I had walked around for two months feeling a longing: I wanted rain! Rain. That fresh melancholy, the change it brings to your spirit, the sensual touch of water from the heavens, whether it was a gentle one or a torrent, any kind would do... and the touch of it making me feel pure. In a sense, it seemed that rain would help cleanse from all the madness that made up my life.

But not once did it rain during the whole length of my stay on the island. The Canaries were proud of their lack of precipitation, but I was from the north and my biological clock told me that spring meant contact with some rain!

Then came the early morning, when Harri and I were sleeping outside of the town again and I saw it – a miracle. A humid layer of fog covered the mountains. As far as the eye could see there was a white cover on everything. And there, almost horizontal, was the low-lying rain just above us, tiny, fine drops caressing and tickling my body like down feathers.

These foggy mornings may well have been common in the spring, but when they happened I was maybe between four walls or still deep in my dreams. That morning, however, I woke up at the right time, early dawn, stretched out my hand and felt the gentle touch of water on my body. Harri was still sleeping, behind the bush as usual, and everything was full of the promises of a new day and the rain was kissing my hands.

How beautiful that moment was!

The only thing is... Where does the reality end and my artistic hand take over? Was it really like that? I don't know, but I remember exactly that light, the moment inside of myself, the touch of those foggy tears. A gorgeous memory postcard with the smells, colours and sensations, and with the date and time stamped on the back.

But at the same time there are some strange contours in me, the beginnings of something, as if they were from the time before consciousness, things I've definitely not edited myself... I shut my eyes and try to get back into that state just before I fall asleep, and that's when I get connected with those faint pictures from my pre-memory.

And I see.

It's a river at night and I'm swimming in it, or rather letting myself be carried along in the water. I'm overcome by fear, but also the acceptance of my fate. All around me there's a sad, accepting nightscape that has already seen death. What river could this be? I don't know, but the river is part of me and I've been there repeatedly.

Maybe I once died in that river? In any case, it couldn't be a memory from this life! In my life, as far as I can recall, I've only been swimming in a river once, but this was certainly another river, full of sunshine, and another feeling; not that nightmarish, eerie, dark current from the depths of the water. Where that other river locates is something I'll probably never know and all I can do is check and see that yes, it does exist, it still flows through me.

But the river I have from this reality is with me every day as well, flashing as a symbol here and there sometimes, before actual thoughts form. In this memory, the sun is shining – that's what makes the wave of coming fear more unexpected and cacophonic.

We were on one of our few trips together abroad: Tom, me and his college friends, all in a rented bus heading through Europe to a friend's wedding in Hungary. This was in the early years of our marriage, when we were still unshaken by crises. We stopped that afternoon to make soup in Poland, at a camping site by a river. The water was crisp and cold. Whoa! Quite different from the lakes I was used to! I took a determined step, went in the cold river, shivered for a moment, then got used to it and felt pleasure in letting the water carry me farther from the camping site, until I started to drift around a bend...

And decided to turn around to start swimming back.

It wasn't until then that I realized how little I know about rivers: swimming back is not an option! The rapid current of the river had carried me off and nobody from our group had thought twice about my leaving.

I gathered up all my strength to swim back, against the current, fighting, panting, swallowing water, the heaviness and darkness all around me, my body already belonging to the river...

In all that fighting, all I managed to accomplish was not drifting any further. I just struggled in one spot and didn't disappear around the bend.

"You have to pull off! To the side!" someone inside me screamed. "This is your chance!"

"This is your chance! This is your chance!" the mantra pounded on and I turned my fight towards the shore. Instantly it became clear that even swimming off to the side wasn't that easy, the current was still pulling me towards the bend... But I kept struggling, thrusting my arms ahead, using the last of my strength, and then pulling them back, "one more time, one more time!" until my feet could sink into the muddy bottom. This wasn't the same sandy shore where I started about forty metres off – where Tom and the other campers quietly and calmly were cooking fish soup.

The river flowed on, as if nothing had happened. I dragged myself to the shore and threw myself on the ground, trying to catch my breath.

It was just forty metres, the others were right here! For them, nothing much had happened. Epp just bravely went for a swim and decided to get out by the reeds, probably realizing that swimming upstream was considerably harder.

Why do I remember this scene so often, why do I see it again and again? Is this one of the symbols of my life? My husband doesn't even notice that I'm gone, nobody notices – and struggling with my own body and soul, I find out these simple truths: you can't swim against the current and you can't step in the same river twice.. Two years later I went travelling with Harri and got that same experience, except that lesson took longer to learn...

Half asleep now, I remember and compare these experiences, noticing their similarity. Maybe it was before my birth that I chose this kind of lessons for myself?

This hypothesis fills me with a strange sense of security: something in this life is mine and can't be taken away.

However, there's still one question that bothers me. Why didn't I call for help on that river? The idea did pass through my thrashing body, I was a split second away from doing it, but then for some reason, let's say, I decided not to use that possibility.

I try to imagine the situation. "Heeelp, I can't get baaaack!!!" the scream echoes across the water and completely changes the feeling in the air. People on the beach start running around, Tom perhaps jumps in the water and starts swimming towards me. If he could help me is another matter... In any case it would end up in a tragicomically ridiculous situation.

For some reason, it seemed easier for me to risk my life than to risk being shamed.

"Shame" is the word that floats to the surface here. I was ashamed of being weak. Maybe this was what I was supposed to learn in this life? How to get over my shame, and dare to say what was wrong with me?

I nod off again, my head jerking up every now and then, waiting for morning in the hum of the electric lights. "Where did that river lead?" I manage to think just before falling asleep. It wasn't a question of me drowning, that probably wouldn't have happened. My problem was the river trying to take me along. To where?

All rivers lead to the ocean. Does everything come together in the end? Somewhere in the distance there's Tom, smiling because he has forgiven me and I have forgiven him. There are Marco and Harri, smiling because we have finally gotten to properly say good-bye. Djellah and Javier – I didn't get to say good-bye "properly" to them either, because they both hinted at the fact that they hate goodbyes. And so we did go through the technical procedure of the thing, but we did it very fast and nonchalantly, as if we were to meet again very soon... And Franc, whom I left at that airport at Minsk, almost at mid-sentence, he's also there waving at me and smiling in understanding, like Santa.

And then I sleep.

Life is like an onion

Half an hour later. February 2009
Las Palmas airport, Gran Canaria

"I was reading your manuscript in the laptop... How come you never told me about Franc?" Justin asks me when I open my eyes and look around again.

"What? Who?"

"Franc! The one who invited you to the arms factory?"

"Oh! I just didn't think of him! Not before now, when I was getting this book together, when I started to remember things again and when each little string brought along another memory... Before that I had basically been trying to forget everything for ten years."

"Memory block?"

"Well, yes, like when I left my notebooks at Marco's place and just forgot them. The same way with Franc, I wanted to forget him after that debacle in Minsk!"

"By the way, how old was Franc?"

"You know what..." In this groggy state, I've suddenly discovered something rather strange. "Franc's date of birth was 1953, I remember it because it's the same as my father's. And around the same time, maybe a year earlier or later, Marco was born far away on Gran Canaria, and Harri too, here in Pärnu, in Estonia."

Justin shakes his head, but doesn't get the chance to say anything yet, because I've already discovered the next thing, "Listen, you know what else is strange! All those men have two daughters who are more or less my age! Franc, Harri, Marco – and my father too! What's that all about?"

"A coincidence?!" Justin says in a slightly sarcastic tone. "It's called the synchronicity of life, it happens everywhere, all the time – it's just that some people pick up on these patterns and others don't. It's a matter of how you sense the world around you. I read that somewhere."

"Oh really? I have another theory as well. We all met before coming to this world, somewhere out there, on the other side!"

Justin laughs. "Oh man, you and your old men!" Indeed, in Estonia I also have several male friends, who are decades older than I am and Justin has come up with his own theory about that: it all goes back to my childhood, when my best friend was my grandfather. I did have my father, of course, but according to Justin's analysis, he's never held a particularly important place in my world – he always had so much else to do, and now I have so many things to do myself...

"I mean on all the trips that you and I have taken together," Justin goes on. "Notice how you've always been ready to talk about the ways of the world with old men in completely random situations?"

"And what about yourself, doctor Freud?"

"See, I can't do things like that! I didn't have this pattern in my childhood, because my father didn't talk to me much, one of my grandfathers was dead and the other was a mean, distant old man!"

I nod, it all makes sense...

"But Harri," Justin goes on with his analysis of family patterns. "When he left his girls somewhere in Tajikistan back then, of course, he didn't get the chance to be a good father to them. He couldn't pass on his knowledge to his children, so on a subconscious level he adopted you, used you to fill out the empty spot his daughters left."

"Maybe so," I'm surprised, but I do agree. "I helped him compensate for losing his children..."

"I also think that if you've already lost your children once, you never really get them back again, and you know it."

We look out at the morning blush and the outlines of things outside slowly starting to emerge. I think about my father for a moment. At first, he had a lot of work and when he was done, I was already working a lot. In other words, if you do lose your child once, it's not easy to get them back... I had a much deeper connection with my mother, right up until her death, but that's another story altogether.

"But this scenario was the same with you and Marco too," Justin continues. "You said that his daugther lived in Uruguay, while he was all the way on the other side of the ocean, on Gran Canaria."

"Marco had two daughters, one was in Uruguay, where Marco was once married. He'd go there to visit his wife and daughter, when his work as a capten would allow... His other daughter did live on the island too, but she was... well... born out of wedlock..."

"He must have felt the way Harri did, cut off from his daughters. So maybe you were sort of a surrogate daughter for him too?"

"Yes, that's possible."

"In any case, these stories of yours are completely insane, especially when looking at it from my side, as a man" Justin laughs and tries to keep it light. "These kinds of things can only happen to women! Could you imagine me travelling around, crying somewhere alone on a beach and some old lady coming along and giving me money for watching Eurovision with her, then buying me plane tickets and paying for my hotel?"

"Was that really funny for you?" I start to laugh myself. "I was so afraid that maybe it won't show that life is actually really funny. Tragicomical! A crisis in Slovakia, and a crisis in Gran Canaria, a crisis in Cyprus, and crisis in Israel, a crisis in China, and a crisis in Minsk!"

Justin tousles his hair and laughs. "Life with you is like an onion, I keep peeling and peeling and new layers just keep appearing!"

"Maybe everyone's life is like that?"

"But a good part of those onions have gone bad!"

"You can't peel them? They stink?"

"They're too slippery! They slip out of your hand, and you can't see what's in the layers! But in your case, I see inside of those layers. I see how and why you went on that crazy trip around the world with Harri and how you got into an even bigger crisis when you came back."

"More crises!" I laugh again and look out of the window at the parking lot of the airport where contours are starting to show more and more, as it slowly gets lighter. That's how on that border, right between sleep and wakefulness, many past events start to reveal their meanings and reasons. "Look," I continue, "I made my life very difficult at that time, because I didn't know how to *choose*. There was this guy, Javier. I remember how he taught me..."

"What? Another guy?"

"No, this was different. He was like a godsend, a person who came to tell me that, first of all, make your choices and, secondly, don't feel guilty about it. Maybe it was thanks to him that I didn't go completely insane! He was a handsome man... but I couldn't take him seriously at all, not even hypothetically, because he had gotten a vasectomy."

"So you decided not to choose him?" We laugh again together – delirium in the yellow early morning light at the airport where the whole life course of one little human being suddenly seems so comical.

"Of course, I didn't decide it like that in my head," I try to explain when the laughter subsides. "It wasn't until later that I realized that subconsciously I was disappointed. I think that at that time I felt the pressure to have children and any man with good genes who had cut off his you-know-whats seemed like treason, I took that personally."

"Yes, Epp, but see – it was his choice and he didn't feel guilty!" Justin is serious now.

That's true. Many people float on in the painful currents of indecision or guilt, even though they have enough strength to make a decision and pull themselves out. For a moment in my memories, I touch – and then immediately recoil – the feeling of what agony it was when my first marriage went on and on, because the decision to "divorce" was something neither of us could make. It was just easier to let yourself be carried on.

"You know what, when I met Franc in Minsk and lost it and then I flew back to Estonia, I moved in back to Tom. Our "time out" was over then, because I felt like a beaten dog... and I couldn't choose to be alone. I'm not especially proud of that."

"What?" Justin straightens up – I knew he'd never brought these two ends together in my life. "Why did you go back to him *then*? From what I understood, you had just found out that he'd been secretly reading your emails for a year?"

"Yes, that's what happened... But I was so upset then, I would cry for hours on end. Everything just fell apart."

Justin shrugs. "Why didn't you go cry on your girlfriends' shoulders then? When you found out that none of them had betrayed you? To me, that would have been a much more logical step."

"See, the strange thing is that even though they didn't betray me, I had already begun to believe it and to this day, it's like I would almost believe it of any one of the three: she did it. See, that was a moment when I was afraid for my mental health: what is real and what isn't?"

"And then you decided to trust a person who you knew had lied to you?"

"I didn't tell him everything that was going on in my life, because I didn't really trust him either, but I did need that shoulder to cry on. I remember how he came to visit me in my rental place, a few nights after I got back from Minsk and he tried to calm me down. A magazine editor called me and I had to check one fact really quick. I tried to sound more or less normal and promised to take care of it, put the phone down and bawled on. In fifteen minutes, the editor called again, "Yes, yes, right away," I said, and kept crying. It went on about five or six times like that, it was like a bad dream that just keeps repeating itself, one where you can't wake yourself up. I hate thinking back to that day and that month! When I moved back in with Tom, when he took me back, so to say, life did get more pleasant. But looking back at it now, it was just our fear and sense of comfort that made us keep going, avoiding divorce."

While listening to me, stubbornness has risen in Justin. "Didn't you blame him at all? I still think that he's the one who cut himself off from you. Why did you have to go to Slovakia alone in the first place? A young man chooses his mother instead of his wife on New Year's Eve, what's that all about?"

"He had a very special relationship with his mother. His father died a long time ago. But I do understand what you mean. It did take me years before I started to believe Javier about how actually I didn't have to feel guilty at all."

"Yeah," he smiles, but it's an angry one. "Anyway, I would have come with your crazy hippie, you know that. I probably would've felt pretty stupid, but I would have come!"

"I invited Tom along later too. To Malaysia, to India. That awful separation went on for a long time..."

"And you were still obsessed and guilt-ridden when I met you. You carried a picture of him with you, remember?"

That's true, I did! I'm astonished by how easy it is to forget again. I sigh.

I don't know how to talk to my new husband about my previous one. Somewhere right here there's a line.

I'm sure Justin knows that secret as well, thinking back to his former girlfriends, as do probably all couples that have separated – the best moments of your new life remind you of the best moments from your former life. I appreciate the same jokes with my new husband, and use the same words of endearment. An amazingly big part of the essence of being together actually remains the same, as our ex-spouses most likely feel the same with their new partners. Everything is the same – we come from one love and are all moving back in that direction.

"I'm still thinking about your time on the Canaries... Tell me if it's possible," Justin asks, waking me from my thoughts, "that your main problem was that you developed several realities? You went to the Canaries and it seemed to you that the previous reality didn't count anymore?"

"Yes!" I'm so thankful that he could verbalize something so close to the truth. I would have wrestled for another few years before arriving at that thought. "Look, I have thought that perhaps it was all make believe. I've even almost come to believe it myself! After Tom told me about the anonymous letter, I lied to my girlfriends and told them nothing like that had even happened and I made up the sea captain. Sometimes it seems that I had to enter that so-called alternate Canarian reality to write a book about it one day. Maybe in this life there are stories around us that happen just in order for them to be put down on paper later?"

Justin laughs. I like how he's not afraid of the twists and turns of my mind. It encourages me to continue, "Maybe we were waiting somewhere before we were born, *there*, and we chose our lessons. And I chose this lesson, this book?"

He nods in recognition: he knows, as he's a writer, like me. While my first husband Tom just dreamed of becoming a writer, my second husband is more like me: together we climb up towards our dreams, imagine the stories we encounter in the world between book covers, and sometimes we do put them there. "It's strange," I admit, "that even though the travels with Harri did really happen, when I write I still get the feeling that it's all happening over again on the pages, but in a different way, and that exact story is not the same one that I went through in reality."

"Of course, if you didn't have that feeling, there would be no point in writing!"

I'm so lucky to have met him. After Marco, after Harri, after Tom, after Javier there were a few other "what if" situations in my life, but only one of them has turned into reality, a reality that I have fostered for now. I've made my choice!

Javier would be proud of me, I think, smiling.

The funny thing about predictions

A year later. February 2010
Puerto Rico, Gran Canaria

I'm sitting in Harri's kitchen and slicing up onions. Crying is allowed in this case.

"I understood right away back then that the main goal of your trip was to leave your husband," he has just said and I'm waiting for the pain to subside. I still don't like to recall this particular nuance of my life and whenever someone brings up the subject, it feels like I've been punched in the gut.

"Did I tell you about what a psychic predicted for me back then?" I ask. "About me and Tom separating?"

"What prediction? I had my own two eyes to rely on! As soon as I saw the way you two said your goodbyes at the bus station before we went to Riga – it was all too clear for me. How polite and sad he was when he sent you away, as if you were going on an eternal journey. He had the face as though he was already counting on losing you."

I'm helping cut up tomatoes and onions for our vegetarian dinner. Earlier Harri read me a few of his prophetic and apocalyptic dreams that he had written down in the form of poems, then he introduced me to the new version of the Estonian anthem that revealed itself to him, "I gave the words to a composer; hopefully he'll get a good tune behind this!"

So here he is still the same dangerous, sincere, bizarre and mad genius, as he was back then. The old familiar scent of incense wafting around in his apartment keeps me on this wave of nostalgia, even if this wave hurts from time to time.

"Listen, so why didn't you warn me then, or why didn't you warn Tom, if you saw all that – our separation – happening?" I continue, treading carefully.

"Well, I didn't feel that I had the right to interfere in your life path."

"But why did you take me with you in the first place, especially since it was a risky trip that involved mostly only feeling places out? You did do that much to interfere."

Harri briefly stops cutting tomatoes and falls deep in thought, head tilted, box cutter in hand. "Look, I didn't see any ulterior motives in your eyes, you weren't out to do something bad, you didn't have a clever plan hatched out – you just wanted to come with me!"

"But why didn't you turn me down?"

"Listen... It's the same way in the animal kingdom, the female chooses the male. Women have very good instincts when it comes to their choices and a woman's decisions should be trusted."

"Wait, but... I didn't choose you to be my mate! I chose you for my employer."

"Well, yes. But you had to feel some kind of psychoenergetic match."

I'm cutting onions, wiping away the tears and asking him more things that still bother me. "But why did you offer me only ten percent commission! That was so little! Now you tell me that you paid some of those guys who worked for you in Korea up to thirty percent!"

"Well, yes, but I paid for your visas! And I was supposed to get you a ticket to Hawaii and pay for your room there."

"But I didn't need the visas, we never went to Mexico, or Japan, or Korea! And what are we talking about Hawaii for? That never happened either!"

Harri is silent. The air between us suddenly holds so much tension; it reminds me of the end of our travels together.

"Honestly," I continue, "sometimes I think that I should be mad at you, for all that happened to me!"

"So what exactly was so bad that happened to you? You learned how to sleep outside, you learned how to find a place to stay overnight in any condition and how to survive in the event of a huge catastrophe – what happened to you was good!"

Yes, he may be right, I think. All that sorrow and those crises may have been necessary for me, and who knows, maybe it would have hit me without Harri as well? But I still go on, "Harri, tell me, have you really never felt that you've done wrong in your life for which you should apologise?"

I have the courage to ask this, because eleven years older and wiser I do realize one thing: I actually have a secret power over Harri, even though in those days I thought that he was the one who had me by the reigns. Besides, I've matured and thought about the things he told me.

"No, I haven't felt that at all," Harri answers in an obstinate tone, but it's not an angry tone, more like the one of a professor, who is reluctantly agreeing to explain something to his student all over again. "Look, thanks to you my son is here now, alive and well. I sense the psychic energy. Some things are meant to happen in one way and in no other way than that, even if it's not until much later that we realize why it had to happen quite like that!"

"So I was just supposed to come along back then?"

"I do believe so!"

Our conversation is pierced by a moan and a snore from the balcony as Arpo turns in his bed. "What have you done to him?" Harri turns to me. "What did the two of you do this morning to make him fall asleep so soundly at eight in the evening, huh?"

"We walked around a bit in the morning, and last night nobody slept, what's there to be surprised about," I dodge the insinuation he's made jokingly and choose to attack full on, "But what have *you* done to him? I think it is post-traumatic shock that made him fall asleep in the middle of the day like this. This trauma has been going on for him for the past twenty years!"

Harri laughs as if he doesn't fully grasp what I've just said.

"Do you remember a theory you had?" I bring up another old subject. "You were analyzing people on a scale of rationality, intuition, and self-discipline. I've been thinking about that for years and as you suggested, I've worked hard on improving my self-discipline to get ahead in life. But I've also come to realize that there's a very important part missing in this theory."

"Oh yeah?"

"Kind-heartedness! See, you can have the perfect person, who's rational, who has a strong intuition and who can manage it all very well, but if his sense of kindness is underdeveloped then he's a cripple!"

I'm waiting. Harri's not saying anything, just cutting his tomatoes.

"In other words," I carry on, "in the good old words of wisdom for Immanuel Kant or the Bible, however you like it: do unto others as you would have them do unto you. It's a question of choices, right? Just like I chose to improve my self-discipline, choosing work instead of comfort, or responsibilities instead of pleasures, the same way it's possible to develop kind-heartedness through the right choices."

"I've been thinking about my children this entire time," he stops me. "And I'm really very glad that you brought us together in a... friendly way like this."

I think about what he just said. Arpo and I have spent three intense days here, but Harri hasn't even hinted at feeling other possibilities in the air besides this friendly father-son handshake thing. What would their meeting have been like without me? Would the violence in the air and Arpo's threats have been brought to reality at their first meeting?

How would that meeting have happened at all? Would Harri really have gotten himself together at some point and contacted his children himself? Arpo's theory is that he would never have done that, because as time goes by, a year becomes shorter and shorter, when compared to the sum of the ones that have already passed. This is how Harri had let the current of time carry him farther and farther from the moment when reconciliation would have still been somewhat between normal bounds.

We will never know what the parallel versions would have been like, because it happened the way it happened: I brought Arpo here, and they extended their hands. At first glance it looked as if the bared teeth were forming into smiles, even though I'm still not entirely sure about the complete meaning of their grimaces.

"Why do I feel such responsibility when it comes to bringing the two of you together?" I now ask, almost to myself. "Tell me, Harri, why should I bear the responsibility of righting the wrongs of your past, huh? In no way should it be my responsibility to bring Arpo back here to you! Do you believe in previous lives? Maybe we have a connection from previous lives that we consciously don't remember? Something that you call 'psychoenergetics'?"

Harri listens and slowly answers, "In theory, it is possible that reincarnation exists, but does it in reality? This case of ours doesn't prove anything."

"Everything can't be proven. Sometimes it's easier to ask: do you believe it or not? Look at your life. Why has it been so strange? You caused it all yourself because you didn't fit into the system. Nobody else wrote statements refusing to serve military duty, no one else decided to start selling fish in Siberia to make money. But why? – Why? – Because you didn't fit into the system? But why did not you? For example, the Dalai Lama says that in addition to genetics and psychology reincarnation also plays into this..."

Harri listens, his head tilted, and nods, "You know what, from the evolutionary standpoint it is beneficial for us not to remember our past lives. That way when you're born, you start to struggle all over again, not just continue your last life. Because the struggle is good! It develops your psychoenergy, your soul and your spirit. It's not well-being that helps you develop, struggling does! When you've reached to the point of the uppermost strata, the areas close to nirvana, you might remember, but until then it's better for you if you don't."

I'm not surprised that Harri latches on to the talk about Buddhism so easily. He's just as prepared to discuss the Koran, the Bible, the Vedas or the Talmud, and we did do that back in the day, as I recall in another momentary wave of nostalgia.

Nostalgia is a prism that significantly bends how we see the past. I'm afraid, but there's nothing I can do about that. This is the prism through which I see the past today.

The tomato-onion-rice dish is bubbling under the covered pot, while Harri and I are travelling in a world of which we haven't been given a full understanding. I'm trying to pick his brain on a topic that relates to the previous one. Memory! It's something I think about daily. For example, I think about why I have several flashes of my childhood where I see myself from the outside.

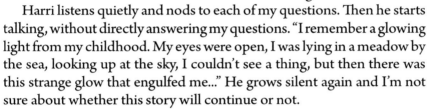

"I'm looking down from up near the ceiling and I see a small girl, sitting in the corner of a room, reading," I describe it for him. "An image like that! I get closer to the girl, I look at which book she's reading and then I distance myself again. What is that? I can't really be remembering an image of myself from outside of my body! Is this a memory trick? Or do spirits travel out of bodies and are they able to remember it later? Or do our guardian angels come into our bodies and we remember the feeling later?"

Harri listens quietly and nods to each of my questions. Then he starts talking, without directly answering my questions. "I remember a glowing light from my childhood. My eyes were open, I was lying in a meadow by the sea, looking up at the sky, I couldn't see a thing, but then there was this strange glow that engulfed me..." He grows silent again and I'm not sure about whether this story will continue or not.

"What kind of a child were you?"

"I lived by the sea in a little village, I was the only kid there; everyone else was sixty or seventy years old. I communicated with nature, watched birds, ants and all the old people around me. But at the age of four I got this question in my head: why the hell have I been born? What for? I've been born, but there's nothing I can do to change that. Why do I have to accept this fact without knowing full well why? I did have a good life, a beautiful one, but for some reason it didn't fit me – because I didn't see any sense in my existence!"

"But why... why did you see it as a problem?"

"Maybe because I was so alone. When it's quiet and you're not distracted by communicating with others, especially with peers... then you start to think. There were no other problems to worry about, no life experience and no reading experience. So that's how I started to wonder about the only problem I could really grasp: why am I here? In the end, I'll grow old, but what is this for? Why do I have to live? And I have to be here for years! I have to struggle here for a long time!" Harri has almost started screaming by now, so Arpo snorts loudly on the other side of the wall and turns over again.

"What a depressing approach!" I laugh, but my hairs are standing on end. In a way, what Harri is saying has touched things I sensed in my own childhood, but what exactly that is I can't tell. I still have to catch the shadows of those memories.

"Nearby, there was a very deep well," Harri continues, "so I thought about jumping in that well and ending all the nonsense. I went to peek into that well repeatedly, but then turned back. In the end, an answer came from somewhere – I don't have to kill myself. Instead, I have to change this whole world during my existence. That's when I ended that discussion within myself. And the rest of my life has been a logical progression of trying to better the world and this way find a reason for my existence!"

"And how have you changed the world?"

"Well, did I tell you, for example, that I was most likely the reason why *perestroika** started in the Soviet Union? Through a person I knew from the fish market in Moscow, I arranged for a long letter to be delivered to the desk of the General Secretary of the Communist Party's Central Committee. It contained the economic prognosis of the Soviet Union for the following twenty years. I called for the state to act quickly and build a new, more efficient economic system. I said that if that isn't done, in ten years it will be too late: the Chinese will pull ahead and our state will be near a collapse. The word I used back then was *perestroivat*** – and interestingly enough, a month later Gorbachev used the same word *perestroika* in his speech!"

"Really?"

"And just a little while later, Gorby said the word *glasnost**** for the first time: say what you want, you won't be stuck in prisons and

---

*   "Rebuilding, restructuring" in Russian, a time of great changes that in 1985 started a process of innovations in the Soviet Union, which in turn led to the collapse of the state in 1991. This process was spearheaded by the General Secretary of the Communist Party's Central Commitee Mikhail Gorbachev.

**   "To rebuild" in Russian.

*** "Openness" in Russian. The policy of maximal publicity and transparency in the activities of all government institutions in the Soviet Union, together with freedom of information.

nuthouses anymore. So I thought, aha, this is my chance! I flew directly from Siberia to Estonia. I had a list of my KGB snitches, so I thought about which one of them was the most efficient. No harm in doubling my chances. If one won't go rat on me, another will. I looked them up in Tallinn, invited them one by one to a cafe and told them both the same story. Listen, right now is the right time! If Estonia wants to get out of all this in one piece, you have to start a people's front to support *perestroika*. I also gave them this plan, to get together a bunch of creative unions and people at universities. My plan was that these snitches will go to the security forces and tell on me, but at the same time the bosses there will be smart enough to pick up on the plan, realize how they can use this to earn some brownie points..."

Harri chuckles a little and continues, "And that's when it was called together, the Estonian Popular Front. The initiative came from the security forces and I'm the one who planted the seed there! I didn't come up with the idea for Estonian independence, but because I understood that this is how the Communist Party could be fractured on all levels. And Estonia would be an example to other soviet republics, so it would spread over all the countries, split up all the parties and create these little cells. And that's exactly what happened!"

I'm thinking about whether to believe Harri's role in the most important events in the last thirty years that had to do with the former Soviet Union... I don't know, and it doesn't matter. What does matter to me is the power of an interesting story.

Harri continues, "Oh, and there are so many ways in which I've changed the world, through people, always through the people... In Israel, I talk so much to the people, because I know that this is the country where many ideas get a chance to be propelled out into the world. And, of course, you yourself are also one of the countless people who have spread my words!"

I linger on what he's saying for a moment and I do recognize myself in it. For example, are my books about environmentally friendly living fruits of Harri's words? His "change-the-world" seeds? What if...? We'll never know and even speculation on that subject is useless. But this particular thing that Harri said has made me believe a bit more that he very well may be some strange... missionary, or whatever you could call it.

"But who infected you then?" I ask him in a joking tone. "Maybe that clairvoyant grandmother who took care of you as a child?"

"Yes, maybe so..." Harri nods pensively and continues in a distracted voice, as if he was just talking to himself, "It seems that life has been an endless series of tests – either you fall or you get up. And every time you get back up on your feet, you're tested all over again..."

"Have you ever been in a situation as good as the one you're in now?" I ask.

"This good? Sales spots, a fishery, the whole network planned out, a good amount of money saved up to take it to the next level and open the fish stores? No, it's never been this good!"

"You have a very important year ahead of you!" I say almost ceremoniously. "I hope that you avoid falling this time!" It may have sounded ominous, but the logic of falling came from Harri's own words. I really hope that everything will turn out well for him.

One more reason to wish for it: I understand now his obsession why he wants so badly to get rich. Ever since he graduated high school at the age of sixteen, he has wanted to be a geneticist. But life interrupted: the trouble with KGB, the insane asylum, the fugitive life, the ban on universities that prohibited them from accepting him. "And now my goal is to create scholarships one day that I can use to help young geneticists, so that someone else will get to do what I couldn't!"

Upon hearing that, I'm ready to forgive him for all his sins.

A strange thought starts to bother me as I try to fall asleep in my bed in the next room, between heaps of bottles, drums and bamboo whistles. Arpo has been sleeping ever since afternoon, our dinnertime conversation didn't manage to rouse him, and not even the divine aromas the stew was sending into the air. In the end, we decided that the day was over. Harri's routine "six hours of sleep" had to start by one o'clock, so here I am.

With a very strange idea that I caught by the tail at the end of that nostalgic dinner.

Maybe the psychic in 1999 was talking about Harri instead? "A man connected to water will share your life and you will see water from your living room..." is what she said. Connected to water? Not a day went by that Harri didn't talk about fish! And he had two daughters my age, just like the psychic said.

Well, all right, I think. Who knows which moment in time that old soothesayer saw: Harri and I walking somewhere, discussing something, sitting on a mountain overlooking the sea? In his own way, Harri was my life partner at that time and most of our life together was indeed with a water view!

And our life together ended in a kind of divorce, even though in the end I couldn't understand why it was emotionally so difficult for me to leave him.

It's funny how I didn't realize it back then that there wasn't supposed to be any other prince. Just like in old Greek myths, a prediction had come true, although nobody knew it at the time.

I have a last thought before falling asleep. Didn't I decide at some point that my lesson was not to believe in predictions ever again, and to keep my head clear?

An endlessly long night

Three days earlier. February 2010
Puerto Rico, Gran Canaria

"His name is Arpo!"

I've said it now exactly the way I practised in my head and the way Arpo approved, but it turned out altogether differently than I imagined. Harri was exactly where I thought he would be, next to his sales stand, nodding back at my greeting with no sign of surprise. He stood in front of us, mumbled an "oh really!" every now and then. But it was obvious that he hadn't been listening to me for quite a while. He was looking directly at Arpo and smirking.

Arpo was smirking right back.

All three of us know that Harri knew from the start the identity of the young man beside me.

Harri is silent.

"*Nu, davno ne videlis**," Arpo is the first of them to say something and for some reason it's in Russian.

"Yes, so this is what you're like!" With these words, Harri extends his hand and Arpo accepts it. On a darkening beachfront promenade,

---

*   "Well, long time no see," in Russian.

lit up by streetlights and the light from the shops, one family is having a historic reunion. When Harri left on that day, nineteen years ago, was there a hint of how long he would be gone? Was their present meeting already in the air back then?

We talk awkwardly about this and that, in the Estonian language now, but about unbelievably mundane things. What airline we took and how was our flight here from Estonia? Yes, indeed, the weather is really nice here, but a week ago it was pouring rain and that's very rare! Etc...

The sun is setting, it's time to fold up the shop, Harri announces. I watch him gather up the jewellery and start to fold up the shelves. "I designed this stand myself," he boasts, noticing me looking. "I made it wind resistant and easy to roll around. Every morning before the big store is opened, I get my stand from their warehouse and at night I roll it back there, seven o'clock on the dot, seven days a week!" He gets his giant, wheeled stand in motion and starts pushing it off the street towards the warehouse inside the store. Arpo and I make a move to help, but Harri snaps at us, "No, don't touch that! This is a one person job. I need to get a good sense of balance here!"

A moment later the whole open air market has collapsed in on itself. An empty courtyard yawns in front of us with just a locked warehouse door in the middle, instead of the beach towels, swimwear, newspapers and other resort town goods that occupied the space just a brief while ago.

I adjust my bag and look at Arpo, "I guess it's time for us to go today, it's getting late and we have to go find our hotel..."

"What? You booked rooms here?" Harri's sharp voice sounds like a reproach. "No need, you're coming to my place! I have an apartment here with two bedrooms and a huge balcony! You'll at least come for dinner!"

Arpo and I look at each other. Yes, we did discuss it in Estonia, whether there was any point in wasting money on booking rooms at a hotel... But we did do it in the end, mostly on Arpo's insistence, because "you don't want to depend on a person like my father!"

We're off, following Harri through the dark seaside parking lot and across the street, then over the grass, under the palm trees, in the dark, warm night.

Suddenly Harri breaks out in a run, his colourful robe and curls trailing in the wind behind him, disappearing up the mountain in fast leaps into the darkness.

Was Arpo really right?

Was his father really running away from us?

I'm ready to run after Harri and track him down, but Arpo, who's walking beside me, just motions for me to pay no mind, "Let him go, *nahhui!*"* I can tell that he's disappointed too, or maybe he understands something I don't?

Then I notice that Harri has stopped right there at the top of the hill, he's waiting for us and panting just slightly. "That's the distance I run every night," he announces. "I have my own routine here, to keep order in my life: in the morning, I always make some oatmeal and eat a pear, for lunch I always drink a bottle soymilk and for dinner I always boil some vegetables! At night I always lift heavy water bottles to maintain my muscles. And, see, this part right here, this is where I always run!" Harri puts special emphasis on the word *always* each time. Strange! Is he really finally tired of all his adventuroes drifting?

We reach the foot of the mountain. The whole town of Puerto Rico is built like an amphitheatre: the town centre is the main stage, surrounded by a little harbour on one side and mountains on the three other sides. I remember hearing already eleven years ago about how the climate of the island is the best right here: even when it's overcast and chilly elsewhere on the island, then in this "bowl" the air is always at least a few degrees warmer than elsewhere, because the warm air rises and helps disperse the clouds. So it's no surprise that the holiday-makers have completely taken over the town from the fishermen and their offspring. All sides of the bowl are full of white hotels and vacation rentals. It's at one of these complexes that Harri starts working on the lock of a gate. The tiled courtyard ("*Mama rodnaya***, what a shitty tile job!" Arpo exclaims), the row of palm trees, the pool glistening in the night...

We step inside the apartment.

"*Mama rodnaya!*" Arpo shouts again. "How do you fit in here yourself?"

---

* Russian curse word.

** "Holy mother" in Russian.

"Well, I didn't know you were coming, so I didn't get the chance to make room here, but it's only a matter of rearranging things a bit!"

Yes, it's an apartment with two bedrooms, but Harri's own bed with worn sheets takes up most of the floor space in the kitchen, right next to the dining table covered with jewellery. Sliding alongside of it, you get to the glass wall on the other side of the bed and the table. From there, a door leads to the balcony that's like an entire room in itself, with a sofa and all, even though the sofa is covered with woven backpacks at the moment. Harri hunches over to get through the linen bags hanging between the balcony and the kitchen, squeezes by some African drums, and throws off the tarp covering everything with ease.

The warm night air flows into the room, but Harri's already pressed himself back inside and is now continuing the tour of his place.

"So, this here is one bedroom, I could make enough room here for one person to sleep..." Yes, that's right, there is the corner of a bed hiding in the back of the room, under the heaps of boxes and bags, but it's covered with ten-litre water bottles. "I understand the frogs and the butterflies and the Indian dream catchers, the handmade chessboards, but why the empty bottles?" I can't help saying.

"I'm keeping them because soon, maybe even as soon as in six months, I'll start my own fish store here!" Harri sounds so solemn saying this, like someone who's gotten to the point in their life where they dare speak of their hearts greatest desire out loud.

"But what are the bottles for?"

"You need little containers like these in a fish store. Sometimes you have to quarantine sick fish to get them well again and so on. Why should I go out and buy these containers later, when I can just keep the ones I've got right now?"

I nod. It's understandable. But looking around this room, it's just so awkward. At some point, this had been just a regular, furnished apartment for vacationers, but now the closet and the chest and everything in between is full of bags and bags of "stuff". Long bamboo sticks, little whistles, turtles with wobbling heads, exotic and huge musical instruments that make a hollow sound when you blow in them, immense bunches of Indian incense emitting intense aromas, hats that fold up like fans, and, of course, bags and bags of bracelets woven by Tibetan refugees...

"*Mama rodnaya!*" Arpo calls out at the same time again. He's gone ahead to peek inside the next door. Another room. This contains nothing else except things, stuffed from floor to ceiling, no furniture. Large cardboard boxes labelled "To Harri Hommik", drums stacked high on top of the boxes and in front of them on the floor heaps of smaller and larger plastic bags filled with rings, necklaces and all kinds of colourful things. Man, if my daughters only saw this, I stop to think, what a wonderful childhood memory it would be. I'm sure it would be impossible to tear them away from this room!

"Dada, how come you don't sell all these drums?" Arpo stands there, hands in his pocket, in the path that intersects the middle of the room and looks up at the towers of drums reaching up to the ceiling.

"No point in it, it's not the right time yet! You have to feel it..."

Arpo snorts at that. Then he notices something. "Fuck, are these really natural seashells?" He holds up a fine mother of pearl shell between his workman's fingers. Large transparent bags of the same kinds of shells can be seen on the floor, several of them.

"No... This is from the Philippines, the work of the local people. The dull layer of the seashell has been polished off."

"Dada, how much stuff do you have here all together? How much is it all worth?"

"I don't really know at the moment," Harri answers in a sharp tone, standing with hands on his hips in the middle of his belongings. "I do business all on my own, I don't have to report to anyone, so why should I waste my time on doing inventory, what would that change? There's a lot here, it's all here and all mine – that's good enough for me!"

"Do you have storage spaces like this anywhere else in the world?" I think to ask.

"Yes, I have a storage room in Korea, also a rental space. The way I've arranged my life right now is that I spend summers in Korea – a very good country for sales! – and winters here. I do stop in other places on the way in the meantime, especially in Indonesia." Harri smiles proudly.

"Because you do want to do some travelling after all!" I admit, but it seems to irritate Harri. "I don't want to travel!" he shouts expressively, emphasizing each word. "I have to! I have to go to the villages in different places around the world, where my contacts, the craftsmen live and work – I have to gather up everything. Nobody besides me would find them there, they trust me, they work for me... And, well, they're really good partners for me, sometimes making me a profit of up to a thousand percent! For example, I spend ten cents on an item, but then I sell it for ten euros!"

This makes Arpo's eyes pop in surprise. Dada and his wonder apartment have left quite the impression on him.

A platter with a stew made of sweet potato rests on a large African djembe drum. We're sitting on Harri's balcony and enjoying the meal. "This drum skin has been destroyed by moths, all the hairs have to be scraped off, I'll get to it soon enough," Harri says in between mouthfuls. I keep expecting him to start asking his son about his life, but to no avail.

"Do you know what the best place to live in the world is?" he asks instead and carries on just as he did when we were travelling together, when he'd make conversation by spinning the planet and characterizing the different places he'd been. "As far as I've seen, the best place to live is indisputably Hawaii! Costa Rica in Central America and the island of Bali in Indonesia share the second and third spots. On that Bali island... there's a mountain lake there, it's a really good spot! I built a house there!"

"But the Canaries? Is this a good place here?" I cut in.

"It's not that good here! It is possible to earn money here, true, but in the list of top twenty places to live, it is in the teens!" declares Harri with obvious pleasure. "It's pretty cold here at night!"

So we go on encircling the globe, but still not talking about Arpo, who's sitting right here in the same room with us.

"Wait! Let me show you guys pictures of my house in Indonesia", Harri jumps up and gets his camera. In one picture he's squatting underneath palm trees on a construction site with dark-skinned locals. In a second one vertical beams have been erected for a building, and in a third one there are long hallways with aquariums. "There are two big fish tanks behind the house. These beams are where another building for fish is going to be," Harri describes. "That's where my fishery is, in the middle of the island of Bali."

"But who's raising your fish over there?" I ask.

"Two very trustworthy men who love fish with all their hearts and whom I have trained; I have them on a salary, they breed and raise fish... There are almost three hundred species there! The whole fishery is there for the second year already, just waiting for me to start opening fish stores all over the world."

"Dada," Arpo interrupts. "Can I go smoke a cigarette on the balcony?"

"What, you smoke?" Harri eyes his son long and hard, but then pulls back. "You don't... do you drink alcohol too?"

"No, I don't drink. It doesn't interest me!"

"See, that's good, that's very good! Well... go ahead then, I can't keep you from it! Where was I?" Harri stands in the middle of the room, looks worriedly on as his son smokes his cigarette, and starts talking again, "See, when I officially register my business in Indonesia, they'll give me and my whole family a residence permit. Then you can all – all my children – come move there. A big house is almost ready and you can stay as long as you want!"

"You should ask your grandchildren to visit too!" I just can't help saying. How is it possible that two hours have passed since we met again and he's still going on about himself and not asking a thing about his children and grandchildren? I'm disappointed and I'd like to help, in the back of my mind I'm feeling nervous for him, as if he were failing some important life test right now...

"Ah, yes, grandchildren. How many children do you all have now?" Harri now thinks to ask.

"*Nu chitai**,*" Arpo seems flustered and it's no surprise, because it is only once in your life that you get to hear your father ask that question. There's no way to practice or prepare for that.

Harri, on the other hand, is still acting very happy and natural, as though it were completely normal not to know how many grandchildren you have. Or is he really that good of an actor? He laughs briefly and starts discussing the matter in a calm manner, "Well, I have thought every now and then about how many of them you might have by now. You were four... So I bet there are about ten grandkids by now, or twelve?"

"You have five grandchildren." Arpo counts them off on his fingers, and Harri nods in approval upon hearing the name and age of each child, but then announces, "But still, only five? That's not a lot!"

---

*   "Well, count them," in Russian.

"*Ty chevo**, you try providing for them! I have two kids and I'm planning on raising them myself, like I should, not like..." Arpo stops mid-sentence, but the hint found its mark; you can feel it in the air.

The family night continues with photos of children and grandchildren. "Aah... Rita's Rita, like always!" nods Harri. "Looks as smart as she did when she was just a baby."

"Our Rita's got three degrees!" Arpo beams with pride over his older sister and then continues, at ease, "And Rita was the only one of us who remembered the Estonian language. We got to Estonia and she was all bla-bla-bla, *vabandage, kuidas sinna***...? We all stared at her with our mouths hanging open: Rita, how the hell do you know Estonian? We were away for ten years! She remembered, the fucking brains on that girl!"

"Wait, what? You didn't remember Estonian? But you could speak it amongst yourselves, how did you forget? Or did you start speaking Russian to each other?"

Arpo looks at his dad, about to say something, but then just lets it go.

"Your sons recalled the language later, when they came back, learned it all again. But Eva, by the way, still doesn't speak Estonian," I break the silence, sharing my knowledge about the family Hommik. I want Harri to feel uncomfortable.

"Can't speak Estonian? How can that be! Eva was a big girl when I left!"

"Can't," says Arpo just like that and stares at his father and seems to also purposely be making him uncomfortable, "we all still speak Russian amongst ourselves. But when we came back to Estonia, Eva didn't. Who would she practice her Estonian with then?"

"Why didn't Eva come back?"

"She ran away from us a long time ago in Tajikistan, when she fell madly in love... Disappeared without a trace, we filed a missing persons report and years went by before we found her again. Now she's living in Uzbekistan and raising pigs."

---

*   "Come on now" in Russian.
** "Excuse me, how do you get to..." in Estonian.

"Oh, really?" Harri picks at the drum in front of him. "Eva had the strongest intuition of all four of you and she told me a long time ago that we should find a home for ourselves somewhere in a well-developed country in the south, where we could all get together as a family. I remembered what she said, and it was always in the back of my mind as one of the goals in my life. I was looking for this place for a long time and now I've got it, in Indonesia. It's the ideal place, no industry anywhere around, just a clean mountain lake, in the middle of an island, eight hundred metres from the surface of the sea, which is the ideal height for a person to live at – this is precisely the right place on earth to live through whatever catastrophes may come and where you're all welcome! But our Eva herself, she lives in Uzbekistan instead now..."

"Yes, that's where she lives! But she's alive, Dada! We were afraid that she had died."

"What happened to Tanya, where did she go?" Harri suddenly asks, smoothing his beard, about his former partner, the stepmother of his children.

"Her! She sold all your stuff, took her sons and moved away! We came home one afternoon and discovered that the apartment was just completely empty. Later on she got in touch with us and let us know what happened..."

"Huh? So I did lose all that timber. Well, then again, if I had built that house on that island there, I wouldn't have this life here right now, no house in Indonesia either..." Harri wags his head with a musing expression, but then seems to connect some loose ends, "But wait, I had an agreement with Tanya that if anything were to happen to me, she would sell the timber and use the money to send you back to Estonia! What happened there?"

Upon hearing that, Arpo chuckles. "Well it really is a shame, Dada, that you didn't tell us about this agreement! Tanya dearest did take care of that first part really well, sold all your things double quick, but then forgot about the other half!"

"You were so young back then, that's why I didn't tell you!"

"Young? Bullshit! We had to figure out how to get by really fast! We have an old saying in Tajikistan: the best defence is a good offence. When people tried to tease and hurt us at first, then... Then soon enough they learned that messing with us is dangerous!" Arpo laughs.

"Let's just say that I've been in the so-called army for a long time in my life."

Harri is silent and nods. I can't read anything from his expression.

We're walking along the streets at night. Harri has urged us to go out in his own impatient way. The initial idea, to find our hotel somewhere on the mountainside, has already been abandoned and we're just running after Harri, trying to keep up with his tempo, going around to see the town at night.

Speed walking through the dark, Harri is telling us again about his theory on how the ancestors of the Estonians lived up in the highest mountains and how they descended to come live amongst men and improve their species. "It's been written that until you haven't raised the level of happiness in the world, you have to live the quietest and humblest life of an ordinary person. And when you have improved human kind, you'll be back in the status of a god!"

Harri's hair is flying around in the wind, his eyes are glowing unnaturally, and quite frankly, his appearance suits his preacher style really well!

"How do you know, Dada," Arpo asks mockingly. "Where is that written?"

"See, it's an old, mythological Estonian folk song. I researched all the old myths that had been recorded from the oral tradition at the Estonian Literary Museum back when I was working next door at the museum of zoology. And you know what? I've researched this on the Canaries as well, and started to tie new ends together. The Guanches, the old inhabitants of the Canaries, have believed in a female god ever since ancient times. You know what her name is? It's Taara!"

"Taara? Like the old Estonian head of gods?" I'm surprised.

"And you know who Taara also was? Her history is recorded in Hindu mythology – Taara was the daughter of Shiva, the god of war, and they came down the mountain together. I have a clear picture of how it all worked. Once, probably about ten thousand years ago, they came down from the Himalayas, from a mythological land called Shambala that is still spoken of in Hindu myths. Shiva went to India, but her daughter went over the Ural Mountains to Estonia. From there, her descendants sailed on some time later. They were also known as

Vikings and they arrived here, on the Canaries! Guanches are tall, light-haired and have blue and green eyes, get it!"

"So you think that the indigenous inhabitants of the Canaries were really Estonians?" I'm astonished and amused by the heights to which Harri's imagination can reach, but I'm still trying to approach it with some logic. "Have they retained some of the language then as well?"

"When the Spanish conquistadors got to the island, they cut out the Guanches' tongues so that they couldn't speak their own language anymore – nobody knows what their language sounded like and the new generation started to speak Spanish. There are no words that have remained! But it is known that their houses were very much like the ones built in Northern Norway around the same time. You did know that Northern Norwegians are genetically very similar to us, right? Southern Norwegians on the other hand are of Germanic descent. When the Germanic people came from the south two and a half thousand years ago, they weeded out the locals. Some integrated, but another part tried to save their genealogy and moved up north..."

"Hey, Dada!" Arpo interrupts loudly. "Can you hold on for a second?"

Yes, Harri holds on and waits for us to catch up.

Our tour of the town has taken us to the sea, near the place where Harri sells. We're standing underneath the warehouse yard awning and trying to see the images Harri is conjuring up before our eyes. See, here in this warehouse yard is where the aquarium shop of his dreams is going to be located. "The first year I brought it up, the owner of this space just laughed when I told him that I want to rent this whole space and build an aquarium here. The second year he was listening more attentively and by now we've already agreed on the rental price and all we need are the permits from the town government to fill up this space with a building! I've been watching the Chinese do business all over the world and I learned how to gradually melt into the local scene. What you do is first get a small, humble sales stand in the best place and then wait there until a bigger spot opens up, and then – grab it!"

Harri is showing us physically how that may happen, and then continues.

"Oh, I've been brainwashing the good people of this town for years: the police, the officials... They've started to believe that an aquarium like this would be good for the town, it would bring in more visitors."

"How are the fish going to get here from Indonesia?" I try to imagine it. The whole "flying fish" concept just seems so incredibly far-fetched, but considering that flying fish around is how Harri made a fortune in Siberia back in the day, I understand that the possibility of pulling this off is just one of those things you have to believe in.

"First you put the fish in plastic bags," Harri explains in response. "A little bit of water and a lot of oxygen. I've got it all figured out, how much they need to survive. The plastic bag with the fish is put in a box lined with styrofoam, which keeps them warm, and that's how they fly!"

"But isn't it quite stressful for the fish?" I ask, suppressing the memory that Harri is a man prone to accidents.

"It is quite stressful, yes! In the dark box, all bunched together, there's enough oxygen, they won't die, but really it's not quite living either!" That sentence, for me, seems to carry some hidden meaning and for a moment I remember the air-conditioned office in the large beehive where I once worked. But I stay on the topic of fish, for now.

"So what's going to happen if those boxes don't make the flight, as baggage sometimes tends to do..."

"See, that would mean death for them!" Harri's voice is full of eerie pathos. "The fish can't get stuck anywhere, I've figured that to get from the aquarium in Bali to the ones here they have a maximum of thirty-five hours... But I know everything will go just fine, my intuition tells me so! And I can see that they will rent it out to me, I can see it in their eyes: they all want to see how fast I can do it!" Harri's standing there beaming, and then adds, "I'm a local legend here!"

"Dada, how exactly are you going to build this?" Arpo has either had enough of his father's boasting or is just trying to get a clearer picture of it being a construction man himself.

"Look, right here on the sides is where the rows of aquariums are going to be and the middle area will be used for selling crafts. All the local restaurants will soon be infected with the aquarium craze, I just know it, and they'll come here to buy their fish," Harri explains without any hesitation, with a strange light reflecting the future in his eyes. "And the tourists, they'll just come to look. They'll appreciate getting to visit this aquarium paradise at no charge and to remember this place they'll buy something from the stands in the middle, some little trinket... Look, guys, here is where a new stand for jewellery is going to be. I've already had it made in Indonesia, and it's just waiting for its time to come. It has a couple of dragons in the middle, one of them is shielding its eyes with a paw – and that paw will be holding a little Estonian flag! But here is where the entrance is going to be with a large sign right above it..."

Harri stops, takes a deep breath, filling his air with lungs, and throws up his hands, "Taaramaa*! I don't care how they pronounce it and what they think of it, but this will be the name of my shop! In pure Estonian language! I even have the logo: a hexagram in the Estonian flag colours, blue, black and white, and the image of a dancing Taara right in the middle! I didn't have to come up with that, it already exists: the Mongols have an image of Taara that has remained to this day!"

"The Mongols had a Taara too?"

"Well, of course, the same Shiva's daughter!"

The three of us are leaning on a railing and staring at the white foam of the waves glistening in the dark and beating against the rocks under us. We've walked along the beach to the beginning of the promenade cut into the cliffs.

"Dada, I studied to be a captain! I haven't even told you that yet," Arpo says, looking out on the water.

"Oh, really?"

"Yes, I worked at a port for a few years, until my back... we lifted heavy propane tanks at the port and my spine gave out. I had an operation. After that I changed my specialization, started learning everything about construction and started my own construction company!"

Harri nods, but doesn't ask anything, just points at something behind us. It's a massive, bare cliff. Somewhere above you can just faintly hear a highway that leads south from Puerto Rico and see lush, fleshy cactus colonies a few metres high, pointing their conic bodies up towards the sky.

"By the way, I lived here for a few winters!" Harri says.

"Where?"

---

*   "Land of Taara" in Estonian.

"See, when I came back in the winter following our trip, I was still an illegal here. I was selling right here where the promenade bends. And lived there, see, right under the cacti!"

I look in the direction Harri is indicating, above the promenade, trying to imagine it. This really is a good place, because not one tourist would bother hauling themselves up an uncomfortable cliff during their walk, and while looking down from the highway it's also too steep for anyone to have access. At the same time, it looks like there is a place altogether suitable for sleeping in the middle of the slope, between the cacti. It's completely possible to live here like that: on the one hand you're doing business right on the island's main pedestrian walk that's even mentioned in the tourist guides, and on the other hand you have complete isolation right next to that main road.

"I had bags of goods hidden between the cacti," Harri continues. "In the morning, I climbed down, arranged everything I'd brought for sale and just worked comfortably until the evening."

"But how did you get food?"

"See, yeah! I couldn't really go downtown from here. I sneaked down during sunset once a week and bought enough food for another week. I lived a healthy life: only slept out in the fresh air, and calculated exactly how much I can eat or drink in one day so as not to get in trouble."

"But why did you have to sneak around town?"

"Well, some cop drives by and sees me walking around town and he's going to think immediately, "Now, now, where's that guy selling again?" So I had to stay put and keep a low profile in one spot for days and nights on end. But I did get enough tourists here! My sales were at least two hundred euros a day and not a cent of it went to rent or social taxes!"

Harri's memoirs go on for quite a while. When the police acquired motorcycles a few years later and started to check the promenade, he moved to the famous seven-hundred-step stairs in Puerto Rico, where many tourists climb each day. And he settled in right in the middle of the stairs, so the police didn't feel like coming to chase him off, neither from above nor below. A few times during these illegal winters he did get fined and when a new law came that allowed him to apply for an official residence and work permit, he turned to those same cops: he had to prove somehow that he had been in the area for years already.

"Man, did the police laugh and pat me on the back. And then they gave me a document that helped me get my work permit!"

It's still the same night. Tonight we're not sleeping, even though we all know the principle Harri has adhered to for ages already: you have to sleep exactly six hours every night, not a moment more or less. We're back in the room, and Arpo is proudly showing us his construction company's portfolio on his laptop, and already he's arguing with Harri over how to best do business with Russia. It's not until now that I really can see that they're father and son: both men trying to out talk each other and neither of them giving an inch. As an added bonus, Arpo has his mp3 files of Russian music playing at maximum volume. "*Ty brosila menja!**..." someone is crying and moaning at the moment. Poor neighbours!

"But how did you manage when Tanya moved away?" Harri continues the heavy topic that was abandoned before.

Yes, Harri, I egg him on in my thoughts. It is a logical question. Four growing kids living without a single source of income! What could that be like?

Arpo clears his thoughts and starts gathering the right words. "Well, let's just say that, frankly, we stole to survive. Brother Asko and I broke  into a warehouse, and we got sixteen huge bags of cream of wheat and eight bags of starch. We ate that for three years! A teacher at our school stood up for us and arranged for us to have a free lunch. And we'd go fishing with Asko, usually at five in the morning. Then we made this Korean salad and sold that at the market in the mornings. To this day, I can cook so well I could open my own restaurant right now! *Plov, tchurpaa***; all that stuff!"

"Well then, it wasn't so difficult after all!" Harri cheerfully interjects, but then quickly gets a sideways look from his son.

---

*   "You left me!" in Russian.

**   Traditional Tajik dishes.

"Of course, we were teased a lot, we were called all kinds of names, we were famous all over the city. And we did let our fists fly on quite a few occasions..." Arpo bursts out in laughter. "So that's how we lived!"

"So who decided that you'd all move back to Estonia?" I ask. I haven't heard the detailed story about them coming back to Estonia. Seems like everyone who comes in contact with Harri gets an incredible fate? Even I did, not to mention his children. The experience they must have had when they were left alone – it's something I'm having a hard time imagining. I can see how Harri was probably a weirdo known all over the city of Nurak and how his teenage children had to live with the fame of being "that lunatic's kids", besides having to deal with the practical concerns of where to get food and how to find money to pay the electric bill.

But there are choices in life. There are currents you can break out of and that's how they chose to break out of a difficult situation, swimming back against the current over thousands of miles to reach the land where they were born.

"I decided!" Arpo beams.

"You were the youngest, yet you decided something like this?"

"There's nothing strange about that," Harri announces with a solemn emphasis, looking at Arpo. "Let me explain it to you. Every one of my children is different. Arpo is the most active, Rita works the hardest and is the smartest, Eva is the most romantic and intuitive, and Asko is the most balanced and productive. Each of them strongly represents a part of me. In any case, Arpo is the one of whom you can expect just about anything!"

Arpo laughs and peeks at his father, unable to conceal his pride. I'm getting overwhelmed and exhausted from all the emotions and maybe also because of the early morning hour that's upon us...

"But why did I decide that? It's very simple," Arpo continues. "I was seventeen by then, Asko was eighteen. We had these passports made up, just in case, they said that we were the same age, twins, so if anyone drafted us, we could still stay together and have each other's backs!" We're listening to Arpo's memoirs now. He was fifteen years old when he made friends with a Tajik army commander, "You ever heard of Shamil Bassayev? He was that kind of guy: had his own squad of twenty men, one day almost all of them were shot, a few survived and he said he'd had enough! He got out of the war. But he still had the weapons and he was willing to teach others, just to pass the time. Thanks to him, I'm a sniper, I know all about explosives, I can take apart and put together all that stuff. In Dushanbe, people still sleep with an automatic rifle right by their pillow!"

"That's like in Lima, Peru," Harri adds excitedly. "They also have these parts of the city, where people sleep on the street and use automatic guns instead of pillows. I walked through there and saw it! That's where I..."

But Arpo is riding the memory wave and talks over his father, "Wait, wait, I have a really good story! A friend of mine was working in a cafe in Dushanbe one year. That was the year that they finally dared to open up a cafe or two, when everyone wasn't getting killed all the time. Some *avtomatchik** didn't pay his bill and started getting in his face – my friend really just took a steel bar from the fence and stuck it through his neck!"

Pause. "And did he survive?" I ask.

"Survive?" Arpo laughs. "After that everyone paid their bill nice and fast at that restaurant!"

Hearing this story makes me understand even more why they left Tajikistan for Estonia.

But Arpo continues with his description of the Tajik daily life, "And then all these things started to happen. We were walking home from our lectures at the university, some locals start hitting on Rita, pulling her into a car – people disappeared very fast around there. Asko and I started beating them off, got the best of them... The next day more strange things: the cops take me right in the middle of the market, asking me: Come here! Who are you? Let's see some papers! Everyone knew that they'd just take your passport and you can't get a new one in that country, they won't give you back your old one until you bring them, let's say, three hundred dollars. I told them that I didn't have it with me, but in reality it was in my pocket."

"They didn't search you?" I find it hard to believe.

"I wouldn't have let them! They were intimidated by my personality! They sat me down at the station for three hours to play with my nerves.

---

*   "Militant with the gun" in Russian.

Then they had enough of me, they wanted to take away my sugar and my bouillon cubes I had bought in the market. So I was like, all right, let's split this stuff! I want something to eat at home too! Done deal, they agreed, we split my food and I was out of there. Two days went by, a car pulls up to us on the street and they start pulling Rita into the car again, we jump in again, punching, fighting... And that was the day that we decided we'd had enough! The ones we beat and cut, they were bound to come get their revenge on us. We may have been able to win nine times, but what about the tenth time? We stuffed our things in bags and took off for the train station. We just left that apartment, to hell with it!"

"And your oldest sister Eva was missing without a trace at that time?" I asked just to make sure.

"Yes, we really had no way of finding her. People really do tend to stay lost around there. If those types had been able to pull Rita into the car, we would have never seen her again either! The fact that we even found Eva a few years later was a miracle. It was through this Russian organization called *Istchu tebja**..."

"It was much harder for you to find me!" Harri snickers. "You know why? It was that Soviet era training, when I constantly had to hide from the security forces!"

This startles me: why is he comparing his children to the KGB?

"How did you get across the border anyway?" It's five in the morning and our conversation goes on in the year 1999. It's funny how that same exact spring, when Harri and I were battling it out on this same island, his three children were on their journey back home. However, the moment they tried to buy a ticket to Tallinn at the central train station in Moscow, it turned out that their problem was much deeper than whether they had enough rubles in their pocket ("We had scraped together exactly enough to get the tickets, we were flat broke after that!").

"Do you have a visa to Estonia?" the Muscovite at the ticket counter asked them.

---

*   "I'm looking for you" in Russian.

"What the fuck, we don't need one!" Arpo recalls his reaction. "But he was still all *vizu nada, eta zhe Evropa*[*]! They told us to go to the Estonian embassy and apply for one there... There was a long, long line in front of the embassy that stretched across the street. Everyone wanted a visa, just to get to Estonia!" Arpo laughs, sitting cross-legged on the floor of his father's balcony, wildly gesticulating as he talks. "Fuck! The whole street was full of people We saw that at this rate it would take us three months to get to Estonia! So we marched straight up to the door, knocked, told them we were Estonians returning from Tajikistan and on our way back home to start a life there!

They looked kind of confused, but still gave us some piece of paper. It wasn't a visa, just some strange letter. So we get to the border, right? The Russians look at it, flip it over, look at it again, "Yeah, okay!" They took a ruler, put it on the paper, tore off half of the letter and said, "This half stays with us." All right, so we're crossing the border with the other half!"

Harri laughs wholeheartedly with his son.

"So a few kilometres on it's the Estonian border station," Arpo continues, picking the words in between new bursts of laughter. "'How did you get here? How did you even get over the Russian border? Oh, so the Russians took half of this here paper? So you're leaving this half to us then!' In the end we got to Estonia, but without any visas!"

"But what was that paper then?" I still don't understand.

"That's something we'll never know! It was just all these letters typed this way and that. We didn't care. We just wanted to get to Estonia!" Arpo laughs and continues, "Boy, did we leave the cops scratching their heads! And Maarika, she called the cops on us!"

"What?" Harri shudders. "Your mother called the police on you? Why?"

"She told the cops that some Tajiks showed up, take them away."

"I don't get it!?"

Arpo laughs again. "It took us two hours to explain to the cops how we are this person's flesh and blood. We told them our whole life's story right there! So then they ask us, "How did you get here? Do you have passports? So we show them: look, here are our Tajik passports. But

---

[*] "You need a visa, that's Europe, after all!" in Russian.

the names really are Estonian indeed. The cops ask us, "But where are your visas? How did you get across the border!" Hahaa!"

Harri is laughing along again, "And then you told them that there was this paper, but the Russians took half and the Estonians took the other half, hahaa!?"

"*Nu vot*, and then the cops called the border station! What did they discover? A paper like that never officially existed and we had never actually crossed the border, hahaa!"

I've been listening quietly for quite some time, but now I can't resist asking, "But still, why did your mother call the police on you?"

"Well, we started to ask her some uncomfortable questions and I guess she just cracked!"

At dawn, I can still hear the muffled conversation on the other side of the wall. "We all still remembered mom's address by heart," I hear Arpo say. "We went there, but she was gone, she had been evicted because she didn't pay rent. So we started looking for her and finally found the hole where she had ended up because of all her debt..."

"What happened after she called the cops on you?"

"Oh, we just left her alone – let her live without us if she really wants to then!"

"How's her health? How does she look? I feel really sorry for her, God damn it, too bad that things went like that for her. And for you too, of course. You were left in a bad situation. But you managed to struggle out of it. After all, genes do count for something!"

My last thought before falling asleep is whether all this really is happening.

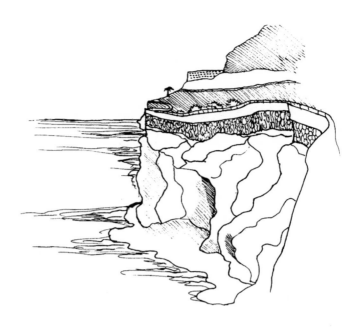

To remember or to forget?

Two days later. February 2010
Puerto Rico, Gran Canaria

It's midmorning. Harri's already left to get to the market on time. It's been two days now that we've been here visiting the Canaries, Arpo has moved in full-time with his father, but I'm splitting my time between the tranquil hotel and our colourful apartment life. There's always something going on there. New and unbelievable pages of Harri's past are revealed ("I was invited to play a role in a movie in Moscow, the director stepped up to me and told me that he needs someone interesting-looking, like me!"), the same goes for Arpo ("You can't imagine how many sins I've committed! If I hadn't met my wife, I'd probably be in jail!"), I get to see Harri's reactions to his son's lifestyle choices ("Who bought these *meat* patties and put them in my fridge? And what's that in the bathroom there? *Paper*? What did you get that for? It's much better to use water, don't you remember!"), and so on, and so on...

Arpo and I are sitting on the balcony and watching people walking below, all going in one direction. The tanned masses, with beach towels hung over their shoulders, heading towards the sea. This view is framed by palm trees on one side and a pool on the other. So it's no surprise when Arpo sighs again, "Bloody hell, did Dada find a good place to live or what?"

"It's actually not that simple to live here," I can't resist adding. "Eleven years ago, I was so confused on this island, I can't even tell you if I was happy here, or seriously depressed."

"Well, sure, but there's good and bad in everything." Arpo takes a long drag from his cigarette, leans on the edge of the balcony and suddenly says, "You know what, Dada is so lucky that we didn't meet earlier. Thanks to that he's still alive."

"Really?"

"That anger we held against him, it has started to dissolve over these past few years. Now we all have our own kids. I'd never do to them what he did to us, but at the same time I'm also not going to kill my kids' grandfather for all that either!"

A few hours later Arpo and I are walking along the promenade in the cliffs. We are at the same place where Harri and I tested the waters years ago and where Harri later settled down to sell, sleeping somewhere between the cacti nearby. During the daytime the promenade is filled with tourists, half-naked men and women, with beach totes and flip flops, walking in both directions, their eyes always on the sea. Small planes circle the air above the water, advertising banners trailing behind them. The Beatles records are playing in downtown restaurants and in front of them youngsters stand hollering, "This way! Step this way! The coffee is on the house!" A lot of things in this resort atmosphere are exactly the way they were back then. "Eleven years ago," is the phrase I've repeated so often when talking to Arpo.

The waves are beating against the cliffs. Sitting here on a rock above the sea has its little risks and that, in turn, is an added pleasure. I'm taking notes in my notebook, but Arpo seems unsatisfied with just the risk of sitting there.

He takes his camera and climbs along the rocks in his shorts and sleeveless athletic shirt, laughing like a child and jumping around, chasing crabs. I see him slip for a moment, but he doesn't lose his footing. I should think about him less, it suddenly occurs to me. One of the missions of my trip has been fulfilled. The father and the son have been reunited and from here on it should be up to just the two of them to sort out everything between them. But what was that second mission I had again?

I've told Arpo a little about my life here on the Canaries, but I don't know how much he's read into the hidden meanings in the phrases I've dropped about the secret of the missing bag, and an old friend. Arpo has listened to my stories and has either tactfully left the questions unasked, or is just not interested, because he's busy putting his own world back together.

Marco.

Should I get in touch with him again, and tear open that chapter of my past? I stare down into the waves, as if expecting an answer to surface.

I do have his phone number. Fishing my phone out of my pocket, type in, "I'm on the island again." The letters shine back from the screen. How quickly would he call back? Maybe in a minute. But then what? We'd meet, and talk about all that old stuff again. Would I ask him once again about my bag? How likely do I think it will be that he will hand over the journals after that? The thought makes me snort.

But maybe he wouldn't call back at all, and how would I feel then?

I erase the message and slide the phone back into my pocket. The man on whom I cheated with Marco back then is gone, and Marco should also disappear from my life. I've come to understand that not a single chapter of life really completely ever ends. It's our choice whether to open these chapters up again, now or some time later... The latter, of course, might very well mean that we'll never do it. But the chapters themselves, they'll never end.

However, it seems that I'm not ready for that new opening today.

It's the afternoon of the same day. Arpo has gone to explore downtown alone. I've climbed the mountain to reach my hotel room, or rather the shared rooftop terrace of that complex. This hotel has been constructed on the slanted mountainside and the six rooms on our floor have access to a huge terrace or a small park, depending on how you look at it.

I hear the quiet, relaxed conversation of the German ladies in the room next to mine. It makes me feel secure, perhaps because I can't understand it very much. Life is flowing on right here next to me without any disruption and I can focus on my memories.

A grey cat is walking around with a satisfied and arrogant air. Multi-coloured exotic flowers and trees have been planted all around the terrace that is covered with a layer of small rocks. Right here, sitting on the white walls under the palm trees you can watch cars make their way up the twisting mountain roads and then disappear behind a curve. Or look at people the size of ants walking around down below between the white houses, the light blue pools shining on the rooftops of the hotels, the mushroom-like umbrellas sprouting in an orderly fashion along the beach, the blue and white rows of yachts at the harbour, and all this on the backdrop of the ocean that extends as far as the eye can see. The weather today is just slightly overcast, the sky is blue-grey, and so is the sea. I can't even tell where exactly the horizon is. You can just stare at something like this endlessly, until you completely forget yourself...

The idyllic afternoon is abruptly ended by someone beating at my door.

"Fuck, Epp, can you imagine having a father who's really fucked you over, so that your whole childhood and youth is one *yobannoi huinya** ..." Arpo marches in, heads straight for the terrace, pulls out a cigarette and starts flicking his lighter, hands slightly trembling.

"Did something happen?"

"*Shit!* Doesn't that guy understand where I'm from – I come from Tajikistan, because that is where he left me! Have you ever seen real arrogance in your life? Some fucking *avtomatchiks* come along, waving their guns, guns that are loaded with bullets that really will kill you, laughing and kicking you in the face. See, that's what an education means in Tajikistan! That's what I had to grow up with!"

Looking at Arpo, I can see that he's telling the truth: the way the raw power is spilling out of him right now and the way the muscular man in front of me physically is expressing the phrase "I could kill him" right now...

"Come on, let's go look at the sea," I invite him and we walk through the small rooftop garden, straight to the concrete wall and sit down.

---

*   Russian curse words.

Arpo looks down on the town. "I only got into the army back then for one reason – not to be helpless and to settle the score with that man who's hustling around on that square down there"

"I think he realizes that he was wrong in leaving you all there..."

"Yes, of course, he feels guilty now. He knows exactly what he did and what he didn't do, fuck! He's hoping that all that has expired, that everything has been forgotten. Like hell, I've forgotten! Another thing he's hoping is that if he can be useful to all of us, we'll all shut our eyes to the past. And that's how it is. For me it's comfortable to know that he believes we've put it all in the past. I want to work with him. But if there should be some problems here later on, then fuck, Dada, get yourself to a cliff fast and jump off as quickly as you can, because that will be the fucking easiest way you'll go!"

"What's getting you so upset right now? I don't understand, you were having such a good conversation last night and you told me yourself this morning that the most powerful force is forgiveness..." Just like his father, Arpo loves to philosophise and he had just told me earlier about how he has "no reason to squash him, because it won't prove a thing".

"I don't understand if he's a complete *tolpayob**. I mean fuck, why does he come and tell me – can you imagine, tell *me* – how his new son Johan has travelled in sixteen countries in the world at his expense! Did you know that?"

"Yes, I knew. Harri was boasting about this last year." I remember how proud Harri was talking about how his new spouse Ann and their son Johan manage quite well with their life in Estonia, so Harri only has to call them every few months and send money. How he takes them along on trips every now and then, combining his inventory replenishing trips with their entertainment. From what I've gathered, Harri has a good relationship with his sixteen-year-old son Johan. I've deliberately chosen not to relate all that to the man representing Harri's older brood.

"*Nu vot*, you would have thought that he wouldn't tell me all that, that he'd have a little more tact than that! So the three of them went to see some elephants and giraffes recently, two weeks in Kenya... Can you imagine! I haven't gotten any help whatsoever from him in twenty whole years, ever since I was eight years old! When he left us, can you

---

*   "Idiot" in Russian.

imagine, we had times when we went into fields and scraped together seeds, because we didn't have enough to eat! And he's off on safari and whatnot with his new son!"

"That is a little out of proportion," I note sarcastically, sending Arpo into a laughing fit, "Very well said, a *little* out of proportion, indeed! I'm buying clothes for my family from second-hand shops or even going to churches where they give away clothes. But in the meantime his new son is going around to safaris and hanging out with fucking elephants!"

"Well, when you were little, didn't you get to travel around with your father? You told me about how you sold fish and flew all over Russia?"

That comment only fuels the fire. "Bullshit! Imagine this six-year-old boy, who day in and day out, literally in any kind of weather, has to be on his legs the whole day and pump out aquarium compressors?" Arpo looks like he's about to punch holes in the concrete terrace wall. For now he's just holding out his two hands, opening and closing his fists. "That's how it was, compressor pumps, from morning to night! And I have a very simple question: what does Johan do? Why isn't he working? How come he's just spending money? And don't tell me that Harri has learned from his mistakes and is a better person now, fucker! I'm not some *thing* you can just learn from!"

"When did he tell you this?" I ask with a sigh.

"*Nu vot*, right now, when I went for a walk down there. If that man wants to live, he better learn how to get along with me. He has two choices... Either he's our friend or dives off these cliffs. Asko and I don't play around!"

I listen to him swearing and feel so incredibly sorry for him. How the conflict inside is just tearing him in two. Love and hate.

He tells me new stories about his childhood, peppered with swear words in Russian... "The worst was having a power outage in our apartment, where he had a whole room just full of aquariums – and there were plenty of them! The compressors didn't work then, but the fish needed oxygen, they suck the air out of an aquarium in ten minutes, if there are lots of them in there. Once they turn their bellies up, there's no getting them back! Compressors in both hands, all four of us were pumping, with our legs too." Arpo winces. "And when the lights came back on, we'd count the dead."

"What about Tanya, that Korean woman, your so-called step-mother? Did she help?"

"She was sitting in the other room, she didn't care! And her dear sonnies never fucking touched those compressors either! Tanya basically enslaved us, especially after Harri disappeared!"

"From what I understood, Harri took Tanya in mostly so that she would help him take care of the fish?"

"*Oy blyat*, that Tanya never did a damn thing with the fish! We were her slaves, and we never had anything besides work! Her dog bit off my toe and I got a beating because I let the dog out of the other room. Look!" Arpo pulls off his sandal and extends his foot out. There's a big scar encircling his big toe. "It was sewn back on at the hospital! And look, see this scar right here?" He shows me his knee. "Can you imagine beating a child with a belt, with a belt buckle? He did it!"

I try to imagine it, but I can't. I just can't. The Harri I know, aside from his choleric manner of speaking, is more like a Buddhist, who doesn't eat meat and wouldn't hurt a fly. That's what I also tell Arpo, at a very low voice.

"He doesn't eat meat? What does that have to do with anything?" he's irritated. "That's just his whole genetics bullshit, the pure food bullshit! You want me to tell you what we could eat as kids at *all*? We were only allowed clean vegetarian food brought down from the mountains, these grey, tasteless purees! We'd risk a beating if we asked for anything else!"

All this is too much. My head is spinning. "Have you seen that scar on his shoulder?" Arpo continues. "We were left alone for three days. I climbed out of the window and went to the neighbours to ask for food. That exact moment he happened to come back and it was against his principles – our family doesn't beg. He attacked me, I ducked and swung – he fell on the sharp edge of a shelf with his whole body! Man, how the rest of us came and congratulated me, "Well done, Arpo, we'll have some peace and quiet around here for some time now! When he got better, the same old shit just went right on!"

"Unbelievable," I sigh again. "Whenever we talked about you guys, he was so proud of his children and his genes, he was always praising you all."

"Bullshit! He loved his genes, not his children. *Nu*, for example... I wanted to know too what candy tastes like. One time I went to a friend's house, his father gave me candy and I was busted with it at home!"

"So maybe you were even happy that your father disappeared?" I ask.

"Of course! It was the best thing that could've happened to us! And well, it was good for him too – his life was more in danger with each passing day. Get it?"

I do. But there is only one paradoxical-logical conclusion that can be made from all this: "When you put it like that, things actually went well – considering the situation? That he left and never came back?"

Arpo understands exactly what I mean. "I know exactly what I hold against him the most! He shouldn't have taken us away from our mother in the first place! We had a good life in Estonia until then. Mother played Beethoven on the piano, the rooms were messy and sometimes we didn't have a thing to eat, but we liked our life!"

Yes, Arpo, I would like to tell him, you can't turn back time, you can't relive the same situation. Even if Harri regrets the choices he once made, it changes nothing of the way things are today. Or does it?

But it's a long while before it's my turn to talk again. In the bright sun in the middle of a terrace with flowerbeds planted full of cacti, a muscular army man squats, puffing one cigarette after another, looking at the town, the sea and the mountains with squinted eyes, and he's talking and talking and talking, calming down all the while. Childhood pain gets peeled back layer by layer down to details I'd rather not hear about.

I want to run down into the town and warn Harri. Be good and useful to your sons for the rest of your life, if you want to live! I would like to hug Arpo very hard and tell him to talk about all this with his father, because he needs forgiveness, but that is possible only when things are talked about honestly. I know. I've learned straight talk in my life the hard way!

But I just sigh and keep listening.

At dusk, I walk downtown to where Harri's wrapping things up for the night and surprisingly enough that's where I also find Arpo. He left the hotel a few hours ago, a strange and pensive expression on his face, and I've been worrying about if and what exactly will happen to him on this island today.

But it seems that Arpo doesn't have any problems anymore? He's laughing, looking at his father and talking about something.

"Epp, you know what," Harri calls out when he sees me. "I just discovered that there's one more word that the Spanish have taken over from the Estonians when our language was the lingua franca."

"Oh yeah?"

"*Carretera!*" Harri looks at me.

"So...? That means 'road' in Spanish, right?"

"*Käru-tee-rada**! Get it?"

Arpo laughs and pats Harri on the back, "All right, world explorer, pack your things, it's my time to cook tonight. In honour of both of you, I'll work on my vegetarian *plov* recipe!"

"With dates?" Harri asks.

"Dates? *Nu davai***!"

They're both laughing and I can't understand if it's the same "decidedly happy" mask they're wearing that I had on during my first marriage, or are they truly happy about each other's company. Because, like it or not – there are genes at play.

---

*   "Path for a cart" in Estonian.
**   "Let's go" in Russian.

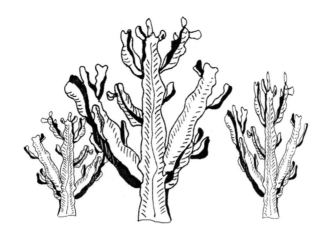

A hike back into a dream

The next day. February 2010
Between Puerto Rico and Arguineguin, Gran Canaria

The next night Harri has decided to take us on a hike in the mountains. We are going to leave in the dark, since that's when his day of sales work ends. "We'll walk straight over the mountains to Arguineguin, and stop in this beautiful valley filled with cacti. That will take about three hours and then we'll walk back over the mountains!" After hearing the plan, I decide to go along for half of the trek, the first three hours in the mountains, and then come back from Arguineguin in ten minutes, in a taxi. This is the where my tolerance of risk and my energy will reach their limits.

At first, Arpo laughs incredulously when hearing the whole plan, "I mean, only complete idiots go into the mountains at night to climb around on loose rocks, but... all right, I'm in!"

The three of us are bound by a love of risks.

I'm panting. We've just turned off the highway and I've already scraped the skin of my palms during our first descent and "controlled sliding". I didn't remember the gravel covering the ground to be this fine and loose! That obscure angst is back that the mountains at night invoke in me – maybe it's because almost all of my nights in the mountains were passed listening to Harri's strange apocalyptic predictions or his bizarre life's story. It's enticing and frightening all at once: the dark mountains that appear to be so far at first, but it is possible to get right near them, to touch them, to join them, even at night. It's like being on top of the world with your unusual choice, looking back down into the valley and the lights of the city or the villages. I experienced this eleven years ago right here on the Canaries. Sometimes we'd spend the night on the outskirts of the city, at the foot of the mountain under a cactus somewhere out of the way ("If you don't smell piss, then nobody's pissed here," Harri taught me). But sometimes he wanted to go higher and farther so, of course, I climbed along with him. That's why these mysterious mountains and smell of the dry sand turned up in my dreams time and time again.

We're climbing up, Harri's in the dark ahead of us, I'm climbing in parallel with him and Arpo is right below me. "Please, don't climb right under me, ok?" I've called down several times. I have to concentrate extra hard to make sure that I don't send any loose rocks down to hurt Arpo.

"I have to be right below you," he calls back. "If you start to slide, I can catch you!"

"But what if a rock hits you on the head?"

"It won't! I grew up in the mountains!" Just slightly out of breath, he tells us about how he and his brother went to the mountains for three days, "Real mountains! I mean, these here are just little hills compared to the mountains in Tajikistan!"

"Why did you go?"

"We were picking *fistashki*, you know, pistachios. Usually we got about twenty kilos between the two of us. We'd roast them at home, sell them at the market and get a little more money. At the other side of the mountains there was also this Uzbek water reserve, we used to call it the sea, and there were really good fish in there. But the jackpot was killing a porcupine, because that meant twenty kilos of meat! We hunted sparrows and doves too, of course!"

I'm startled by the sight of Harri, who's standing right here near us in the dark, waiting for us and listening. His expression is an especially proud one. Come to think of it, his warped choices in life have made

his sons grow up to reach his ideals. The two boys left alone in Tajikistan without a cent have gained the kind of experiences that really
would make them the kinds of people who would survive when civilizations collapse and there's real trouble.

"Did you have guns?" I ask Arpo.

"No, not at that point. We shot birds with slingshots,
but they were some really good, strong ones!"

We go on climbing, all together. It's obvious that for
Harri it's difficult to go as slow as we are going.

We get to another pass, "What in the hell did they do
here!" shouts Harri, who's climbing ahead of us. He's arrived
at the top of the mountain and is now taking in the sights on
the other side.

A short while later Arpo and I get there as well.

A road is being built in the valley that will apparently connect to the
main highway of the island that goes north and south from here. The
asphalt road turns the whole valley into a big cul-de-sac, lined with streetlights. These lights aren't turned on yet, but at one end of the circle there's
a trailer that's lit up by a speck of light casting a shadow over the entire
valley. All together, the dark valley looks like a landing strip for UFOs.

"They're probably going to build a new hotel complex here," says
Harri and breaks the silence that we've all fallen into looking down at this
strange sight. "It is a bit far from the sea, but they could probably build
a walkway to the beach from here... and tourists mostly swim in pools
anyway! Maybe it would have been ready if the recession hadn't hit."

"I feel so sorry for this island!" I burst out. "Maybe for some this is
a sign of great success, filling up another ancient valley with hotels, but
I'm just so sorry for this valley!"

Arpo snorts, "What the heck?" Harri sighs and gestures in resignation.
"You know what, it's all just temporary anyway, let's keep going!"

Three different mountains loom around the valley, like oblong
loaves of bread with their ends put together. Are we going to go around,
along that gentle slope, or are we going straight along this steep drop?
Straight, of course!

"Somewhere behind there is a magnificently beautiful valley full of
cacti, I've been here," Harri yells us and starts scaling the mountain at
a maniacal speed.

"Dada, we didn't come here to sprint up the mountain, we came to enjoy it!" Arpo calls out and tells me, "Well, get going, I've got your back!"

Harri has run off again, somewhere far and high. I can't catch my breath, my heart is going crazy, but I want to keep up with the tempo.

"Epp, there's a rule in the mountains!" Arpo's also breathing heavier. "Remember: don't ever let anyone else set the tempo. Quickly climbing the slope with little caution, at the ends of your limits – do you know how dangerous that is! Your hands and legs are shaking, the rocks can start sliding and you can lose your balance. And if you don't have anyone directly below you to help out, there's nothing you can really do – once you gather up the momentum, you'll just tumble down!"

"But Harri's going ahead so fast!" I'm gasping for air.

"Let him run! I grew up having to run after him, you've been there too, but now? Let him, *blyat*, run ahead! We're sitting down for a bit and resting now, going at our own pace!"

I sit back down and look at the city lights glowing behind another mountain and the UFO landing strip in this valley, with apprehension and the energy of the mountains pulsating inside of me. What a strange feeling: I didn't run after Harri. This reminds me of a strong feeling from my dreams. What was it again? He was running in the mountains, ahead of me. A war had either broken out or just ended. I was trying to catch up with him until I gave up. And I was left alone. Or maybe, on the other hand, this meant becoming independent.

"Dada!" Arpo roars beside me, looking up. "Have you seen this mountain before? Do you even know where we're going?"

There's no answer. Either he's gotten somewhere very high up or just doesn't think the question needs to be answered.

"A lot of loose gravel, a totally unknown path and in the dark too. We're complete *tolpayobs*!" Arpo hisses through his teeth. I understand. For us it doesn't matter at the moment, if Harri has been through these parts before or not. We're all alone here now. In this darkness, it does seem especially absurd: why doesn't Harri have any friends or acquaintances here after all these years who could step in for him at the sales stand for a few hours? Or why couldn't he just tell the store managers that his stand will be in their warehouse for a few hours more than it usually is? Really, why did we have to come hiking here in the pitch-black night?

"Why is he so strange?" I sigh audibly.

"He'll drag you to hell with him, but you'll have to climb out yourself!" Arpo answers. "You want some water? You can drink now, if you've caught your breath." He takes the water bottle I took with me for the hike out of his bag. "By the way, another rule for the mountains for you: in the future, it's better to take tea along, either green or black tea, because it quenches your thirst better than water!"

"He probably thinks he's like a scout troop leader, that's why he's running ahead so far," I sigh after taking a sip.

"A scout leader has to be *below* a beginner hiker, not above! Even if he was just a few feet ahead, he couldn't do anything if something happened! If you start to slide, someone has to jump on you and push you down, but in order to do that, this person must be below you, because otherwise it's just physically impossible to catch you – you'll pick up speed really fast and... A person rolling down a mountain is not a pretty sight, not a pretty sight at all!"

I'm itching to get going, but Arpo is still sitting down, "No, let's wait another moment!" Seems that there's a power struggle going on here. Let Dada wait! Instead of running after him and trying to keep up, Arpo starts recalling a time when he was six years old and when they had just moved to Siberia. Dad took his sons on a forty-kilometre hiking trip by Lake Baikal.

"You wanted to go?"

"Are you joking? Of course I didn't want to. Three days on the heels of that maniac! He went ahead, going as fast as he could, and the four of us ran after him. I didn't know how to tie my shoes very well yet, Rita wanted to help me, but Dada wouldn't let her. He told her I'd have to learn it myself! Can you imagine a little kid with his shoelaces untied trying to keep up with that lunatic?"

The second story gives me the shivers even more. It's from a few years later, when they had already moved from Siberia to Tajikistan. "Dada took us to an island on the Uzbek water reservoir, told the boatman, 'Let us off on the island, the kids and I are going on a little extreme hike now.' So the motorboat takes off and leaves us there. We're trapped, steep mountains all around, cliffs that were impossible to climb. Can you imagine: being with that moron on a small piece of land and he's angry as hell... In the end, we had a family crisis meeting and since Eva was the best swimmer, she was the one to go. A teenage girl, nine kilometres over a deep, deep lake, went to get the motorboat from the village to come pick us up! She made it! That's an extreme hike for you!"

"Well, I guess he was trying to toughen you up," I'm still trying to find justification for Harri's bizarre behaviour. "His brand of logic can give a reason for all kinds of idiotic things: if there's a catastrophe, you'll survive just fine."

"What? If a person falls down a mountain, he'll be a properly toughened handicap! A person can drown while he's toughening them up!" Arpo starts swearing in Russian. At the same time, I hear a call from higher up somewhere: Harri is waiting for us.

"Dada, remember, I have a bad back, I had an operation, I can't keep up with this crazy tempo!" Arpo is still calm on the outside, but I can sense the angry tension rising in him.

Harri is sitting on top of the mountain, intensely looking at the two of us crawling up the mountain on all fours and yelling back, "See, I had huge problems with my knee caps! One time in Siberia, when it was winter and really slippery outside, I was walking with an aquarium suitcase in each hand and suddenly I slipped! I knew that I had to keep the fish from getting hurt, so I fell straight on my knees!" He's already acting it all out for us. We've just reached the crest and now we get to see his performance: two hands held out at the sides, he throws himself down on his knees. "Like this! And then I discovered that I can't get up anymore, I've dislocated my knee caps! I knew that there should be a hotel nearby, I came straight from the train station, all alone in the evening... And then I crawled. Pushed the suitcases ahead in front of me and crawled. Boy, did their eyes get wide at the hotel when they saw their client crawling in through the door!"

"And then... they called the ambulance?" I ask.

"To what ambulance are you going to call in the middle of Siberia? I somehow made it to the hotel bed, my knees still hurt the following morning, but then I did get up on my feet again and just kept going.

But why am I telling you all this? For years and years, I had pain in my knees whenever I walked. And you know what helped?"

"No. What?"

"Exercise! I just walked and walked and ignored the pain until it went away!"

I can see Arpo turning his head and gesturing for me to let it go.

"Afghan custom: women first!" Arpo calls out and lets me pass ahead to start climbing up again.

"How do you know about this Afghan custom?" I shout down to him, laughing.

"I basically lived there! From our city it was just forty kilometres to the Afghan border! This Afghan custom really caught on in Tajikistan too when the war began – let the women go first, then we'll see if there are any land mines around or not!" I hear him laugh behind me.

"Tajikistan is an Islamic state, right?" I call down. "Do women cover their body, hair or even their faces there?"

"If your father was a commie, you could even wear a miniskirt if you wanted to! But there were these completely covered women who looked like haystacks around town as well!... What is it?"

I notice we've reached a path. I stop and wait for Arpo to catch up. The clearly visible path leads down the gentle slope of a mountain pass. But where's Harri? Has he taken the path or did he choose the harder option: off the path and straight up?

"Daaadaaa!" Arpo roars.

From above we hear, "Here!"

I see, Harri's gone up. I take a long hard look at my skinned palms and then at the mountainside covered with more of the same fine gravel.

"God damn it, we're not getting up from here! If there's a path beaten in right here, I'm sure there's a reason for it! Daadaa!" Arpo yells. "Come down, let's take the path!"

"You can get up from here!" the answer comes from above. "Come on!"

We wait. Arpo's pacing back and forth and trying to figure out where the path leads, cussing the whole time, "Who the hell comes hiking in an unknown place in the middle of the night!" and then staring up at the slope where his father's voice came from. "I'm completely sure there's nowhere to go from there, definitely no way of getting down to the other side! Man, stubbornness is what's going to kill this man one day!" he curses and then tells me, "Listen, you sit down right here on the path, wait here and don't go anywhere else!" With that he starts climbing up the steep mountainside.

All right. So I'm all alone now, soaked through and through, squatting and trying to catch my breath on a mountainside that smells of dry sand, looking out over the world. It's the same moment I've seen in my dreams. All alone. I look down at my skinned palms and try to beat some of the dust off my black shorts. A dog is barking far down in the valley, pigs are squealing – somewhere down there might be another "zoo". Are they sacrificial animals or just meat? The thought of it is sad and eerie. Is it inevitable? It's exactly the same feeling as in my dream, where the world around me seems to have ended.

I'm sitting here trying to look inside of myself: what is this feeling that's overcoming me? Is it fear? No. I don't have anything against being alone here in the mountains. Not a living soul within site or hearing range and who knows, maybe the sounds of dogs and pigs came from inside the mountain, from far back in ancient times? Or was it a sound from within me reflecting back? The rest of the world seems somewhere very far away. I'm having a hard time believing that somewhere out there is my very own home, my husband and my children. In this reality, in this moment they simply don't exist.

It's no surprise that many yogis choose the mountains for their place of meditation. The silence of the mountains is strange. It wraps itself tighter and tighter around me. I sense more and more that I can hear the blood coursing through my veins, a sound like the ocean in my ears, and in that sound my emotions are starting to settle.

The feeling that's come over me is melancholy. The world is imperfect. Arpo and Harri are not meeting each other's expectations. Arpo has to forgive Harri for his past actions for which Harri has never apologised. From Harri's perspective, Arpo is probably too stubborn and wilful, and vice versa. In some twisted way, this behavioural pattern is reminding me of something, but what exactly?

Suddenly I remember: right here in these mountains eleven years ago I thought about how somewhere, far away at home in Estonia, Tom has to forgive me, but I don't know how to ask for forgiveness, because as far as I see it, I haven't done anything wrong – it's just the way things went! The same way that Harri left his children, because circumstances forced him onto this path.

I hear the rumbling of little rocks and the murmurs of a conversation. Yes, it's real. They're coming down the mountain: Arpo's white shirt is visible in the dark, right behind him Harri is descending in his brown robe, melting into the grey night, rushing past Arpo and stopping once he reaches me. "I don't understand. Did they change something here? I'm pretty sure that I've come up this mountain before! In any case, there is this magnificent valley with cacti right behind all this!"

"It's all right, Dada," Arpo says. "Let's go to your valley, but let's take this easy slope right here. Paths in the mountains are not bad things!"

And so we walk down the path on which Arpo told me to sit tight a short while before.

"Dada, come on now, wait! We have a young lady with us!"

My hands and legs are shaking, I'm afraid of faltering and losing my balance, even if we are going up a mountain on all fours. So I'm infinitely grateful for Arpo's outburst.

"No complaining!" I hear Harri panting from above. "The world will be hit by a catastrophe soon and we need to train the kinds of young ladies who will survive!"

"You don't need physical conditioning for that, just brains!" I shout back. "I already know that if something goes terribly wrong, you have to get away from civilization and head for the mountains!"

"Who taught you that bullshit?" Arpo starts to laugh. "The mountains are where you're most visible! Every soldier in Tajikistan knows: the enemy has a clear shot at you while you're moving around in the mountains!"

"No, I mean go hide in the caves!" Yes, of course. It's another one of Harri's old stories. I haven't thought about it for years, but I've never forgotten his strange teachings. Who knows, maybe Harri's advice could turn out to be sound? Better to know and to remember: what you need is fresh water and caves!

"What you need is fresh water and caves!" Harri interrupts our discussion, "You need to keep a level head. Of course, you don't have to go running around the clearings on the mountains, but you just have to quietly hide out in a place near water. Pure drinking water is the greatest treasure in the world and drinking water crises are coming in a big way! I told her to go to the mountains also because, you see, sea levels are going to start rising. Some idiotic catastrophe like a nuclear one could make it rise that much faster, if they cause the polar caps to melt quicker than they already are... In any case, heading for the mountains is fool proof!"

"Sea levels..." I'm thinking out loud now, we're all taking a brief break, I'm resting my palms on my knees, standing there and looking down on civilization. Downtown lights are glowing in the valleys by the sea right in front of us. Pools are lit up and shining blue in the night, I recognize the ones in the Amfi del Mar hotel complex.

The night pulsates at a different rhythm down there than it does up in the mountains. Sitting here, it seems that we have a better overview of the ways of the world. "That's one thing I'll never understand," I continue. "Why do people buy expensive real estate right on the water? Why is the price of their houses and their land so high, despite the fact that it's a well-known secret for quite a long time now that the ice caps, for example in Greenland, are melting and the sea levels are rising?"

"Hah! Humanity is suicidal, after all!" Arpo calls out and laughs.

"So where in the world is it safe? Where should you go if something happens?" I bring the conversation back to an old topic. Somewhere nearby – I can even point exactly to the spot where it was on a mountainside right near Amfi del Mar – Harri and I once spoke on a night much like this one about which countries in the world would be good places to go if another world war should break out.

"Indonesia, for example!" he shouts. "Or go to Kyrgyzstan! On the border with China, behind Lake Issyk-Kul there's a place where nobody in the world will ever go! That's a good place to survive." And he adds, with exactly the same kind of emphasis as he once did, "These places in the world do exist, but there aren't many!"

"Or Amur, *blyat*," Arpo adds. "Hundreds of thousands of square kilometres and not one living soul! That's where you'll survive!"

"In Siberia, there's the northern part called Buryatia," his father adds in turn. "There's nothing to do there, the place isn't of interest to anyone! Again, another good place to hide out."

"But in Europe?" I ask.

"There isn't a single place in Europe where it would be safe!" Arpo livens up again. "You've flown over Europe in a plane! When you look down – it's all been divided up into little squares. You can't find a place to drop even a little rock without it hitting someone in the head!" True, Arpo knows, after all he has built houses in many places around Europe and he probably felt it there, the claustrophobic feeling of having people absolutely everywhere around you.

"But how about the Alps?" I'm not giving up on Europe. "Those are huge mountains. It should be quieter there..."

"No, it's not," Harri responds quickly and certainly. "Ski resorts and more ski resorts – there are roads up and down and around all those mountains. It's all full of people! Of course, it is better than a big city – but you should go there only if you can't make it anywhere else! Find yourself a quiet place with drinking water and stay safe until the commotion is over."

"But being armed to the teeth and knowing how to use weapons is still the safest way to be!" Arpo adds in his best case scenario. "If anyone comes near, you waste him. See that's safe!"

"In any case, I'm planning on surviving and without a gun!" I yell. "Do you hear meeeee!"

The sound reverberates in the valley below.

Harri adjusts his position and starts telling us another apocalyptic tale. "But do you know that according to scientists things are especially delicate right here on our neighbouring island, in Tenerife. Should there be even the slightest earthquake the island will be split in half! A huge piece will fall off the island! And this is going to cause a huge tsunami that's going to roll over the Atlantic Ocean and wipe clean the whole East Coast of the US, right up to the Great Lakes!" He's silent, eyes shining expectantly in the dark night.

"But then it's dangerous to live here, isn't it?"

"No, it's not! I've thought it all through. Gran Canaria is east of Tenerife, but that wave is going to go west!"

We're sitting down again on another mountaintop after almost an hour of sweating while coming down one mountain and climbing up another one. The mysterious valley of cacti is still nowhere to be found! The three of us are sitting together – Harri has even given up on running ahead of everyone. Maybe he's already proved something to himself as well as us and he's now taking things easy. We're resting our eyes on the dark view from the mountaintop and listening to Arpo's recollections of the war in Tajikistan.

"There's a very simple rule to communication between people in that land: you hurt my family, I'll hurt yours!" he tells us. "At the beginning of the war, this arrogance took on some unnatural proportions. If you did anything even the slightest bit suspicious, by morning your whole family would no longer be living – all three of your wives and your ten children, grandmothers, grandfathers!" He laughs.

"Did a lot of men have three wives?"

"No, not a lot of them. But if they didn't, the neighbour's wives would get it just in case! Let's say there's a little village, three brothers in houses right next to each other, everyone with one wife. And then an *avtomatchik* comes along: I'll clean it up!" Arpo demonstrates how the rain of bullets from the automatic weapon hits the women, three adjacent houses, and I can really see it.

"Aa-haa-haa! And later on it maybe turns out that it was the wrong village, but that's *pohhui**! Everyone is like *pohhui*!"

Is this really the same man who told me yesterday about how his son kisses him good night every night and how he's all for affectionate and gentle love...? When he talks about the war and violence, it's as if something is completely askew in him, or should I say that he's toughened up?

"*Nu vot,*" Arpo continues, laughing in this demonic way. "The guy gets home and sees what happened to his house and his family. In his case, the solution is very simple. He ties a black scarf around his head and becomes "black". Those types weren't tolerated anywhere, because since they usually didn't know who killed their family, they just killed anyone, indiscriminately! The only person who wouldn't get it from them was the civilian – a person who didn't have a gun. Everyone else did! For this man, the world is separated into two parts: those who could have killed his family and those who couldn't, because they don't have a gun."

---

* A Russian curse word, meaning "whatever".

"Wait, so how many sides were there in the civil war? Or *are* there, to be more exact?"

"Right now it's a little calmer, because the bigger battle is going on across the border in Afghanistan," Arpo says and then gives an overview of the colours of the Tajik civil war: the Pamirs who want autonomy are white; the state forces are red, the opposition is green. "In any given city, you'd have the colours changing every few days: red, green, red, green. A little bit of white in between and a few crazy blacks in the mix too!" Arpo describes and talks about his friend, with whom they lived in the same apartment building, "This regular fifteen-year-old guy, went to school with us – he and his family, they were Pamirs. The life of Pamirs was definitely far from simple. The state forces were constantly on their backs, raiding their houses. They'd knock on the door and take their television sets, take away half of the family... The way the Germans took Jews during World War II. And then one day this family in our building also gets a knock on the door. Our friend was taken and they said he'd be killed if the family didn't pay up. Everyone is screaming and shouting, his mother is crying, his father wants to talk, but ends up getting beaten down. In one hour, we got quite a lot of money together from all over the building and we bailed him out! They were waiting with the kid in front of the house in the meantime, beating him every now and then. Three of them holding and beating him... But he was lucky, he survived!"

So where is this mysterious and enticing valley of cacti? It has disappeared. This must be already the fifth mountaintop we've scaled. Atop this mountain, we found a little mound or *stupa* built out of rocks. (Harri tells us that this is an ancient Guanche custom and then, of course, gets on this wave of explaining his theories again: the same kinds of *stupas* are built in Nepal and India, it must be a custom that has reached the Canaries through Shiva's daughter Taara!) We've also found another path and are now following it along the ridge of a loaf-shaped mountain, forward towards the sea. Where will this path lead?

I'm short of breath, aching inside. I'm exhausted! Tired of the company of these two men and tired of the search for this damn cactus valley. The mountain seems to be whispering something to me, but to hear it I should be alone again, not struggling to keep up with them.

I'd like to just throw myself down on the ground and listen, heart beating against the surface of the mountain.

"What's this now?" Harri suddenly yells in his high-pitched voice ahead of us. Something has genuinely surprised him and that's not something that happens often. "Come here, look at this!"

Arpo quickens his steps and so do I: yeah, there is something there!

At the peak of the summit, a huge metal cross as high as a two-storey building has been dug into the ground. It overlooks the sea, the highway and two valleys below. Right underneath of us it's not just a highway, but there's also a little village with restaurants and hotels. Patalavaca! I recognize the village when I look down, leaning against the cold metal and catching my breath. Nostalgic dance music is wafting out of the restaurant and nightclub nearest to us. It's around about one o'clock in the morning, it's just a regular day of the week, but on this island there's a party every night. Listening to it from the mountain above, the music sounds especially apocalyptic.

"I've never been on top of this mountain!" Harri's voice is full of excitement. "And I've never thought to look up here. I've never seen this cross before!"

"See, Dada, sometimes it pays to walk down paths too!" Arpo comments. True, he is the one who suggested that we take this path to its end. He's also looking around like he was newly reborn: hands on his hips, breathing heavily.

This is a very special moment.

"I just remembered a weird dream I had," Harri starts to talk. "I was on top of a mountain, just like this one, looking down on the sea and that's when I saw it: a huge wave coming from far away, a tsunami. I started shouting really loudly, some of the people down in the village heard me and started to climb up. Then the wave came and swept over everything! But me, one other guy and five women survived. After the wave passed through, it was *total* peace, beautiful and clean." Harri turns, sweeping his hand through the air, his hair blowing in the wind. "This man and I, we looked at each other and said, all righty then, we'll just go on living."

"I wonder if you and that man then shared those five women?" I ask laughing.

"See, that's something I don't know, because then the dream was over!"

Arpo starts laughing too: "Let me explain to you how two men share five women. It depends on the culture! For example, Estonians would each take one wife and then, let's just say, go fishing a lot! But Tajiks? One of those guys would off the other and keep all five wives for himself!"

We all chuckle together, but it is so beautiful here that the chuckles soon subside. The three of us are standing there, hands on our hips, as if we were on the edge of infinity, under a huge cross.

"Those stars we see can be dead already a long time," I point into the darkness above us. "When you start really thinking of that even a little... it's enough to drive you insane! Those are all suns with their own systems, they're born and they die, but we find out about them too late: a hundred, a thousand, sometimes even a million years later! If there is life out there, we are not able to find it out!"

"I think that one day we'll be able to transfer people to other planets through telekinesis," Harri starts talking. "Another question, of course, is whether there's any use in contacting other civilizations? I think not! It's better that we don't look..."

On this dark mountain peak, it actually sounds like he *knows* something. I shudder.

"I mean, take a look at the history of the world yourselves," Harri continues his train of thought. "Has the meeting of civilizations ever brought anything good? What follows is just..." He takes a pregnant pause before continuing with zeal, "A huge conflict! Do we need that? Huh?"

Do we?

I look down and hear the sound of the sea below. Is it that the acoustics are good, or is the sea just especially loud?

The sea. So much water pushed and pulled by the winds and the moon. I believe that if I really wanted to, I could run, gather speed and then fly over the highway, jumping straight into the sea. What would be left is a black circle in the water, but I would already be in another world. Down there in the dark depths is where answers to faraway galaxies and everything else lie.

February 2010

The magical moments are over. We're descending into the village. When I turn up my head, I can see the small cross shining on the peak of the mountain. Interesting, how the music that echoed so loudly all the way to the top of the mountain is actually not that loud right in front of the restaurant. The acoustics of the mountains deceived us.

If we walked from here to the promenade like normal people, we'd arrive in Arguineguin, the midway point of the trek according to Harri's initial plan, in about fifteen minutes. So far the whole hike has taken over four hours.

"Is there a taxi stand around here?" I decide to be the one to quietly give up. "I'm going to take the cab home now."

A moment later we're all sitting in the car.

It was good seeing you!

The next night. February 2010
Puerto Rico, Gran Canaria

I can't do it anymore, it's like a hangover. The whole day I've kept away from Harri and Arpo, after sitting last night for hours in that kitchen full of air so thick you could cut out a slice of it. It's as if the mountains had released something inside of all of us. Or maybe that release came from the knowledge that our departure was right around the corner.

I can still see that scene, the painful interrogation from last night.

"Listen, Harri," I started. "I was just putting two and two together, thinking about dates and such. You said that you flew to Singapore and Thailand in the beginning of the '90s, started doing business with the goods you bought there... But how did you manage to buy the plane tickets to get there and the jewellery to bring back if you didn't have enough money to fly back to your kids in Tajikistan?"

Pause. "Shalalalaa!" Arpo sings as he goes out on the balcony to have a cigarette. The air gets even thicker.

"So you *did* choose not to go back?" I deduce, while Harri just sits there, his head bent forward, with hair hanging over his shoulders, as if he was trying to do some especially difficult math in his head. "Life is a series of choices and you made that one. It may have seemed to be more convenient at the moment. But you could have broken out of that choice. You could have chosen to go back to your children!"

Harri doesn't have an answer. Instead, he lifts up his head and starts talking about how great business is in Korea and that Arpo should go to work in Korea too, even if it's just for one summer. Apparently you can make tens of thousands of euros there in three months. That's how good of a place it is for selling jewellery!

"I'm not leaving my wife and my small sons alone at home for such a long time," Arpo says, putting extra emphasis on each one of the words. "I just won't leave them!"

"Listen, Arpo," Harri decides to finally talk about the elephant that's been hanging around for almost a week now. "I was thinking about looking you guys up in Estonia anyway, I had all your contacts. If this situation hadn't come along now, I would have personally taken the initiative and gotten in contact with you – in about a year!"

"But Dada, tell me: what difference does it make whether it's this year or the next?" This question comes with a sarcastic laugh.

Harri answers, in a serious tone, "And I will answer that question! Because then it couldn't have waited any longer!"

Sparks are flying through the air.

"Well yeah, next year would have been the anniversary – twenty years?" I cut in with my question that makes Arpo howl with laughter. Harri, however, keeps his composure.

"Yes, that too... But I was thinking more along the lines that I've developed everything to a point where I'm finally making it and I have something to offer my children!" With that he starts nonchalantly going through his heaps of things to look for gifts for his children and grand-children that Arpo could take with him on the trip back to Estonia tomorrow.

A short while later, all I can hear is the muffled sound of conversation through the wall, because I retreated to the other room to fall asleep behind the dream catchers and bamboo whistles.

The next morning Arpo gives me a recap of what I missed the night before, "I reminded him of the old Tajik principle: you cut off my family's hand, now I cut off your family's hand. Blood revenge! And I sat down face to face with him and told him: look, Dada, our whole family was raped and you were the one who did it! Now what?"

"Then what happened?"

"He hid his face, he must have thought I was going to hit him. He answered, 'I had a tough childhood myself. I was tortured in school because I was this small kid who was a little too smart.'" He said that he wanted us to become good people, and that's why he beat us – he wanted to beat us into being honest citizens, can you imagine? That's what he said, *blyat*! That there were too many of us, he couldn't manage us all and that we supposedly started stealing..."

"So did you?"

"Well, yeah, we did get in some trouble as kids... But we had such a hard childhood..."

That's the moment when the hangover seized me. A terrible, painful instinct that told me to run away. I've thought about whether I should start untangling this mess any further. Should I go meet Harri's ex-wife in Estonia now, Arpo's mother? Listen to her side of the story? Meet that woman with the so-called aristocratic mind set and good genes, who'd play Beethoven on the piano for the kids instead of cleaning the house? Reconcile her with her ex and her son? Listen to probably yet another story of a difficult childhood?

I'm not God and I'm done being a missionary. Because I have a life of my own too.

Over the course of all these days, I've thought about contacting Marco. Last night while sitting there in the mountains and looking down at the town lights, I realized that I can't leave like this, I can't have this whole week be about Harri and Arpo's relationship. What about my own past? And my journals? That much I've come to believe from Harri's blatant hints and cursing that Harri really didn't take the journals. *If* they still exist Marco has them, right where I left them.

I send him a message: "Do you want to meet? I'm in Puerto Rico."

Two minutes later my phone rings. "Epa, you're back!"

Fifteen minutes later, Marco is on the terrace at my hotel. It's a miracle. He's not even late this time!

"Marco, I have something to confess," I start off. "I lied to you and I didn't admit it last year either. I just couldn't find the right moment and it was uncomfortable too... You know what, Harri isn't really my uncle. Please forgive me for lying!"

He smiles. And says, "Epa, I threw away your bag! Please forgive me!"

All right. I can manage without my journals, but at least I know what happened to them now.

I look him in the eye and tell him, "Marco, you know what? I just want to lie down on the roof here for a little while and look at the clouds. Alone. It was great seeing you and forgiving each other, right?"

Spanish-style kisses on both cheeks briefly bring a little too close that familiar scent from years ago. The scent then leaves along with the man. I raise my hand and wave as the door closes behind him. There's lightness in my heart. It feels good.

I'm sorry. Did you believe all that?

Actually, the scene I just described never happened. Even if I can see it right before my eyes.

But I do remember another different reality, of punching a message into my phone on the third day of my stay on the Canaries, as I sit by the cliff and the promenade while Arpo's chasing crabs nearby.

"Do you want to meet? I'm in Puerto Rico." I press send, knowing full well that without getting in contact with Marco, I'll never get rid of this old haunting feeling or ever get my journals back.

Nothing happens. Not in two minutes, not in twenty.

Two hours later I send a second message, while writing on the rooftop terrace and enjoying the idyllic surroundings.

"Call me when you get a moment."

Right after I send it, Arpo storms into my room with his angst and his troubles, and I manage to even forget for a while that the message hasn't been returned.

The same night I try calling, but there's something wrong with my phone and I can't call Marco's cell phone. But I'm not suspecting anything other than the temporary malfunction of my cell phone.

However, I'm still offended and two days go by before I send another message. "I'm writing a book here, maybe we should meet?"

Little by little, I'm starting to panic. Is he even alive?

I'm worried, so I go to the reception desk of my hotel and the helpful young girl there finds me the number of the right *supermercado* in the phone book.

Ten kilometres away the phone rings at the *supermercado*.

It's Jorge.

"*Hola*, Jorge! Is Marco all right, is he still alive?"

"Yes, of course. Why? Who's asking?"

"Epa. *La periodista del Estonia*! Remember?

"Ah, Epa! Epa-Epa, Marco is right here!"

A moment later Marco is on the other end and starts swearing when he hears that it's already the sixth day I'm in Puerto Rico. "Why didn't you let me know you were on the island?"

"What do you mean? I sent you messages!"

"I haven't gotten any messages! Did you dial the code for Spain before the number?"

"The code? What? No, I didn't!" The world of numbers and technology has tricked me one more time, I realize. On the other hand, you could also call it fate. But I'm not ready to give up.

"Please come to Puerto Rico, we have at least a few things we need to talk about!"

"I'm heading out to Las Palmas right now. There's something wrong with my car, I have to take it into the shop!"

"But come stop by for just a minute... I have something I need to confess to you and I have just one question for you!"

"What? I really can't, the car shop is going to close! I'll come and stop by later tonight!"

All right.

He calls at midnight. "I was late getting to Las Palmas. By the time I got there, the shop was already closed! And now I'm running late, because I was supposed to meet a friend like three hours ago. I'll come tomorrow!"

"Marco, I'm leaving tomorrow, for the airport!"

He's silent. "You're leaving tomorrow? Then I'll come to the airport. Tomorrow morning!"

At that moment, I can already clearly see the future. I see the patterns of life that have already shaped that future. He's not coming. He'll be late. Whether it is three hours or three minutes, it doesn't matter. He's going to be fatally late, Spanish style.

"Please, just tell me one thing. Did you throw away the bag or not?" I squeak into the phone the one thing that I didn't want to talk about over the phone.

"Hello? I can't hear you! Let's talk tomorrow!"

"Harri's not really my uncle!"

"Tomorrow morning then, all right? *Mañana por la mañana!*"

We agree on the exact time to meet at the airport and I already know that I'm going to wait until the last moment, but he'll be somewhere else, because time flows differently for him. His memories are probably completely different from mine. He also has the same supporting characters in his life: the weird hippie Harri, Djellah who loves Indian dresses, and he has that strange Epa, who left her bag in his life and who forgot to dial the country code before the phone number. He sincerely hopes he can make it to the airport tomorrow!

"Marco, you know what? I just want to lie down on the roof here for a little while and look at the clouds. Alone. It was great seeing you and forgiving each other, right?" I say it out loud just for the fun of it – the way I was planning on saying it in my daydreams. I gingerly spread out on the roof of the hotel and fall asleep in the night sky with my eyes wide open. Another trip is about to end. This was a good one – it didn't just move me in space, but in time, memories and dreams as well. Have I figured out the answer now? Have I come to understand anything better?

Tomorrow I'll say goodbye to the island and these people and fly home, to my husband and my children, to the cold winter, the burning wood ovens and the frost flowers on my windows. The planet will continue to circle in its orbit. Twenty eight degrees north of the Earth's equatorial plane, somewhere in a corner of the Atlantic Ocean there's a volcanic island, where one man will remain wondering whether his son has forgiven him and another man will... well, be chronically late. And the monuments of my past memories will remain standing here: all those trees, stairs, mountains, waters, street corners and bends in the road, the men and women drifting above them, the boys and girls, everyone whom I've met.

Maybe I'll come here again one day, for example on "that important step, where I first met Djellah". And I will recall some more.

Post Scriptum

Two months later. April 2010
Tartu, Estonia

I would love to add a surprise chapter here about the incredible and deliriously happy day when I found my journals.

But sadly, I can't. That day never came.

So a big part of this book is the shadow of a shadow, the memory of memories. Not quite make believe, but a distant cousin, from the colourful and confusing landscape of recollection.

The next installation of my recollected travel memoirs will take us to Asia, where I work in Malaysia on an archipelago of manipulating people, and then fly to India to find God.

Thank you for coming along!

CPSIA information can be obtained at www.ICGtesting.com
Printed in the USA
BVOW012232071211

277793BV00002B/131/P